A WEEKEND To PACK

THE FALL OF HONG KONG 1940-45

SABRESTORM

Designed and typeset by Ian Bayley.

British Library Cataloguing in Publication Data
A catalogue record for this book is available from the
British Library

Published by Sabrestorm Publishing, The Olive Branch,
Caen Hill, Devizes, Wiltshire SN10 1RB United Kingdom.

Website: www.sabrestorm.com
Email: books@sabrestorm.com

ISBN 9781781220214

Contents

Pre-war Hong Kong.

Foreword by
Admiral Sir George Zambellas

When we think of the Royal Navy, most people instinctively picture the uniformed sailor. But Britain's maritime power has always relied upon a much wider cast of characters, including skilled dockyard workers and willing reservists, for the administration and support necessary to sustain its global reach.

George Bearman, an electrical engineer in Hong Kong and a member of the Hong Kong Dockyard Defence Corps, is a representative of this rarely appreciated group.

This book, principally of his letters to his family after their evacuation from Hong Kong in 1940, illustrates eighteen months of 'Cold War' with Japan following the Fall of France and until Japan launched its attacks in December 1941.

The global nature of the conflict is demonstrated as George reads in Hong Kong of air raids on Portsmouth and hears of the Royal Navy sinking of the German battleship Bismarck, an important turning point in the crucial Battle of the Atlantic.

But these are interwoven with the kind of everyday occurrences that any of us will recognise, whether arranging the movement of a piano or sorting out a tax return. We can also empathise with his painful separation from his family; those of us regularly separated by Service life will be among those able to appreciate it most keenly.

During the evacuation of George's family, their ship was struck by a typhoon and they had to temporarily disembark in the Philippines, where they were shown great kindness and hospitality. This knowledge adds a new dimension to my appreciation of the outstanding work HMS Daring and HMS Illustrious achieved in delivering humanitarian aid in the Philippines in the wake of another typhoon in 2013.

Ultimately 'A Weekend to Pack' is an evocative human story of a family caught up in an almost unknown dimension of the Second World War. I commend it to you.

Admiral Sir George Zambellas GCB DSC DL
First Sea Lord and Chief of Naval Staff 2013 - 2016

View from the Peak, Hong Kong Island - Kowloon in the distance - February 1939.

George, Hilda, David - taken in 1939, on the steps leading to Central British School playing fields. (Reference to George's 'white' work clothes - letter October 2nd 1941)

Hong Kong and the Evacuation Crisis - July 1940

The week beginning 1 July 1940 saw almost 3,500 British women and children evacuated from the British colony of Hong Kong, following threats of invasion from the Japanese. Few in the colony believed the evacuation to be necessary, virtually all that it would be short-lived. But, these were uncertain times.

"War and the fear of war spreads far and wide over the globe," Movietone News reported, as they captured the anxious, tearful goodbyes of the wives and children preparing to board ship, and those of the husbands and fathers to be left behind on the dockside.

"Families wonder where and when they will meet again"
(Pathé News)
Tension between Britain and Japan had been growing.

Needing to expand to survive economically, Japan made no secret of a growing resentment within the country of the extent of western influence in the Far East. Japan was also at war with China, and Britain supporting the Chinese Nationalist Army[1]. In June 1940, the Japanese deployed troops along the border between China and Hong Kong and issued a formal warning to the British to cease sending supplies to the Nationalists.

It wasn't the first time the Japanese had deployed troops along the border, and the military in Hong Kong had long been demanding the evacuation of British women and children, arguing that their continued presence would hamper a defence of the colony.

---

1. China had been embroiled in civil war since 1927, with Britain supporting Chiang Kai-shek's Nationalist party against the Communists. Japan and China had been fighting on and off for many years, and formally at war since 1937. The two Chinese factions had formed a truce to meet the Japanese attack, but it was a temporary, uneasy alliance, and Britain had continued to send supplies to the Nationalists.

Hong Kong's rural New Territories on the Chinese mainland, while covering 335 square miles, was sparsely populated, leaving the very vast majority of the 1.7 million people in Hong Kong in the summer of 1940 - the number boosted by almost 800,000 Chinese refugees escaping the war with Japan, and including an eclectic mix of nationalities - to live and work within the 32 square miles of Hong Kong Island and the 18 on mainland Kowloon. For the British military, fighting in such close proximity to their women and children would, it was felt, affect the morale of the troops and compromise operations.

The British government had so far resisted the military's demands. The Japanese troops positioned along the China/Hong Kong border on previous occasions had been stood down after a period. Britain was also anxious to keep the relationship with Japan as positive as possible, and an evacuation could be seen only as an aggressive move, while few believed the Japanese likely – or even capable – of waging war against Britain. Japan had been an ally of Britain during the First World War, and there were many beliefs widely held to point to the inferiority of Japanese fighting skills, such as, that poor Japanese eyesight would leave night flying impossible.

But, by the end of June 1940, Britain had been at war with Germany for 10 months, and seen Germany invade Poland, Denmark, Norway, Belgium, Luxembourg, the Netherlands and France. The Russo-Finnish War had seen Finland forced to surrender territory to Germany's ally the Soviet Union, also in occupation in Lithuania, Estonia and Latvia. Italy's Mussolini had declared war on Britain, while Britain herself, having lost 68,000 killed, wounded, missing, or taken prisoner, had been forced to withdraw her troops from mainland Europe at Dunkirk, between 26 May and 4 June 1940.

The British army in Hong Kong had lost many of those with most experience to support focus in Europe, while the navy's China squadron of submarines, cruisers and its aircraft carrier was withdrawn to reinforce the western fleets when Italy entered the war. Aircraft production had been prioritised for the defence of Britain.

And in June 1940, the Japanese troops had been stationed to effectively cut land communication between Hong Kong and the Nationalist government in Chung-king (now Chongqing). Chinese agents reported that the Japanese supported National Peace and Regeneration Army of Wang Ching-wei was considering an attack on the colony – and propaganda from Tokyo boasted of the Japanese being in Hong Kong within the week.

In the colony, road and railway bridges in the New Territories were destroyed among other defence measures taken, and on Friday 28 June, the order for evacuation was given.

"Refugees until the war clouds have cleared"
(British Movietone News)
On Monday 1 July – after a weekend to pack –1,500 women and children boarded the SS *Empress of Japan*, among them the wife and two sons of George Bearman, electrical engineer at the naval dockyard, HMS *Tamar*.

In that summer of 1940, George was half-way through a three-year posting to Hong Kong, on secondment from the Royal Dockyard in Portsmouth. The family – George, Hilda, David (11) and Edward (nine) – lived in an apartment in Kowloon, along with Kim (an adopted terrier), and Amah, to help with housework. Kim and Amah would remain with George in the flat in Kowloon, as the evacuees set sail for the Philippines.

In George's letters – recently discovered in that proverbial chest in the attic – the stories of friends, family and colleagues are interwoven with that of George and Hilda's, and of the colony of Hong Kong as the war clouds continued to gather.

And while the evacuees and husbands and fathers in Hong Kong waited for those storm clouds of war to clear, letters were all they had to bridge the miles of separation.

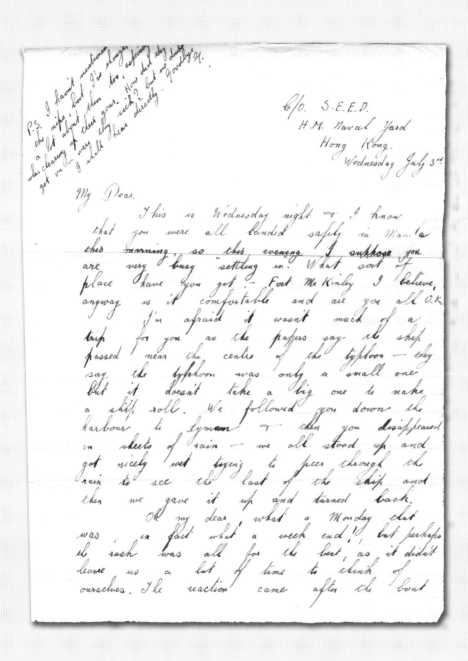

C/o. S.E.E.D.
H.M. Naval Yard
Hong Kong.
Wednesday July 3rd.

My Dear,

This is Wednesday night & I know that you were all landed safely in Manila this morning, so this evening I suppose you are very busy "settling in". What sort of place have you got? - Fort McKinley I believe, anyway is it comfortable and are you all O.K.

I'm afraid it wasn't much of a trip for you as the papers say the ship passed near the centre of the typhoon — they say the typhoon was only a small one but it doesn't take a big one to make a ship roll. We followed you down the harbour to Lyman & then you disappeared in sheets of rain — we all stood up and got nicely wet trying to peer through the rain to see the last of the ship and then we gave it up and turned back.

Oh my dear, what a Monday that was, in fact what a week end!, but perhaps the rush was all for the best, as it didn't leave us a lot of time to think of ourselves. The reaction came after the boat

P.S. I haven't mentioned the wifs but I'm longing to hear about them too, especially when clearing up their gear. How did they get on - were they sick? but no doubt I shall hear directly. Goodbye H.

George Bearman's opening letter to his wife Hilda on July 3rd 1940.

12

July - September 1940

Oh, my dear, what a Monday that was...

Wednesday July 3rd 1940
C/o Superintendent Electrical and Engineering Department,
H.M. Naval Yard, Hong Kong

My Dear,
This is Wednesday night and I know that you were all landed safely in Manila this morning, so this evening I suppose you are busy 'settling in'. What sort of place have you got? It's Fort McKinley[2] I believe. Anyway, is it comfortable and are you all O.K.?

I'm afraid it wasn't much of a trip for you as the papers say the ship passed near the centre of the typhoon – they say the typhoon was only a small one, but it doesn't take a big one to make a ship roll. We followed you down the harbour to Lyemoon and then you disappeared in sheets of rain. We all stood up and got nicely wet trying to peer through the rain to see the last of the ship and then we gave it all up and turned back.

Oh, my dear, what a Monday that was. In fact what a weekend! But perhaps the rush was all for the best as it didn't leave us a lot of time to think of ourselves. The reaction came after the boat had sailed, and for sheer despondency I think the Yard would want some beating this Tuesday and Wednesday. Ah, well – we'll recover and, in any case dear, this is supposed to be an attempt to cheer you up, so forget all the 'ifs' and 'whens' and just think you are out to see the world.

Nothing has altered here since you left, except that it's never left off

---

2. An American military base, with an area set up to welcome the evacuees.

raining, but I don't think that is an alteration, and I am quite O.K. Yesterday we had a Chargemans'[3] meeting and then I cleared up some of the boys' rubbish, and tonight I bathed the dog and went to see a film at the Star.

Now dear, this, as I said, is only a short note to help cheer you up, as we had a notice late tonight giving an address we could write to, and we believe there is a ship mail tomorrow – there's no air mail until next week.

So, Goodbye my dear, remember I love you, and don't worry about me, or about anything for that matter, and Good Luck to you,
from,
Your George

Sunday July 14th 1940
C/o S.E.E.D., H.M. Naval Yard, Hong Kong

My Dear,
I'm writing to you now, but I haven't any address to send it to, only the vague one of C/o the Consul General and I don't know how long a letter will take to reach you that way. I'm hoping that tomorrow will bring one from you with perhaps a more permanent address. I have had the letter you wrote on the ship – and I'm sorry you had such a rotten trip – and judging by some of the other fellows' letters, I'm afraid you have had a rotten time after you landed.[4]

I do hope you all have kept well through it all and then one day you'll be able to laugh at all the discomforts you endured when you were refugees.

---

3. A chargeman was responsible for the work of 10-20 craftsmen, divided into 'gangs' and who had working for them the semi-skilled men of the 'Tickler Branch', in charge of the dockyard's unskilled workers. Upwards, a chargeman reported to an inspector, and at the top of the hierarchy, was the Foreman of the Yard.
4. The typhoon struck not only the *Empress of Japan* but also Manila and destroyed much of the tented city at Fort McKinley prepared by the Americans for the evacuees. The people of Manila responded generously to a radio appeal asking for temporary accommodation for the women and children from Hong Kong, but to begin with there was a great deal of confusion.

Mrs O. mentioned seeing you at Del Monte Sanatorium. She said you (and others) arrived in a lorry but there wasn't room there for you and so off you went again. In view of that, and the fact that no letter has arrived since you landed, I am wondering where they have put you. I wish I were with you and then it wouldn't matter so much where we went. I heard that you are eventually going on to Australia, but don't worry my dear, everything will be all right one of these days.

How are the boys – are they keeping well, especially David with his asthma?

I am quite O.K. – and have taken Davis in as a lodger on a share basis, so that will reduce expenses.

I've written home to your mother and mine to let them know you are all right, but haven't heard from them, only Auntie – but nothing new.

Well dear, I am going to stop now and hope I have a letter from you waiting for me in the morning. Keep a stout heart dear. It won't be very long before we are together again.

Good night then dear,
George

Tuesday July 16th 1940

Dear,
I really did expect a letter yesterday morning, but no, and then I heard a sea mail was due and would be delivered today, so again I waited but still no letter. I am getting a bit anxious now as all the other fellows have received two and three letters written from the billets while I haven't received one. Still, another air mail is due in today, but it won't be delivered until tomorrow and I can't wait for it as I would miss the air mail back to Manila.

The reduction of staff here looks a little nearer, so if I should get a shift I shall soon apply for you to join me – but like every other damn thing it's all in the air at present.

Let me know all your troubles dear and stick it out. I'm lonely too and I hope it won't be for long, so cheer up – that's what I keep saying to myself when I walk in the flat (plus a few cuss words). Anyway, I love you dear and think of the coming back.

Goodbye my dear,
George

Sunday July 21st 1940
C/o S.E.E.D., H.M. Naval Yard, Hong Kong

My Dear,
Yes, it turned out just as I thought. I hung on to the letter I had written you, in the hope of being able to add a bit after receiving yours, and then eventually had to post it to catch the air mail to Manila. However, the next day I received both your letters together, and was I glad – dear, I've been lonely too. This isn't life as we want to live it. It's only half living, coming home from work and then what ever you do is only done to pass the time away until it's time to go to work again and work itself has no interest. On Saturday you think 'another week gone' and then the thought of the weekend!!!!

But dear, in the future we must try to get some good from this; I know I am always the worst offender but believe me, the indifference has only been one of expression and not of feeling. A man can be engrossed in things and appear to be entirely indifferent to a woman who is wanting for him to talk, but let that woman go away and the loneliness is such that he can no longer get engrossed in anything. I know how you feel over this, dear, as I feel – but our love will help us through until it is all over and we are together again.

I expect you know by now, in fact by the time you get this you may already have had your sailing orders. You are going to Australia and we were asked where we wanted our wives to go, Sydney, Melbourne or Brisbane. I said Sydney; actually I don't know anything about any of them except that Brisbane will be much more hot in their summer, so don't go there if you have any choice.

Now, don't worry about Australia dear. I know it's further away but if you are to come back here, it's just as easy to get back from there as from Manila, and life for you and the boys will be less worrying there. The Government will find board and lodgings for which I shall be stopped £1 a week, which is cheap, isn't it? And in addition, I shall make you an allotment. You should have second-class passage to Australia, and I hope you enjoy it better than the Manila trip.

Have you got all your baggage yet? If not, don't leave Manila without kicking up Hell's delight about it, but I rather think you have as Mr Tubbs heard from Mrs T. that your trunks had arrived at Baguio but they were sending them back. Mrs T. wrote that you refused Baguio as it was expensive – now if that's so, remember you won't pay anything for board and keep, and if you have paid anything the cashier is in Manila to refund it. Actually, by the sound of your letters, you are far more comfortable than the people in Baguio, although perhaps lacking in congenial society.

Now dear, a little news about me. I am quite OK and Kim is still with me, complete with fleas. He has only had one bath a week, I'm afraid, since you have been gone and so probably has a few more fleas than usual, but I give him a good dosing occasionally. I am still in the flat and will remain for the present. I told you Davis is here on a share basis, so that cuts expenses considerably. I have no plans for the future but will make them according to circumstances – if I stay here I shall try to keep the flat on (or get one like it) ready for you to come back. If I go, I don't think it will be yet and then it depends where I go, so don't you worry about that either.

I've been twice a week to the Walkers'[5] so far, for chow and a yarn. I read your letters to both Pamela and Vic and they were glad to hear you're comfortable at last – you certainly deserved it after that first

---

5. Women with livelihoods dependant on business in Hong Kong or whose work was deemed essential for defence of the colony were exempt from evacuation. There were also many who evaded the order. Some acquired 'essential' jobs overnight – mostly, it was noted, 'women of position' in the colony – and the continued presence of these women in Hong Kong became a source of bitterness for the evacuees and the husbands abandoned on the harbour dockside.

week. They have been really decent to me and I think Pamela has written to you.

I've been to the beach every Sunday so far and am going today and as we have had no rain this week and the weather is hot, that is as good a way as any to spend the time.

I haven't sold the piano and I am afraid I won't without giving it away – there's a long list in the paper every day and they get no answers. A chap in the Yard managed to sell his – for $60. I'm not going to do that unless I have to, so, for the present it's 'wait and see'.

Tell David, 'Many Happy Returns of the Day'. I did really forget it when I wrote last week and I'm sorry, but I'll make up for it and give him a nice trip to Australia for his present. I do miss them, dear – they could make as much noise as they liked if they were only here now, but I'm glad they are with you. You tell Edward not to cry about me. He is to think of Mummy these days.

Now dear, that's all for now, unless there is a letter awaiting me in the Yard, in which case I'll squeeze a little bit in. Try and look on the Australia trip as a holiday and remember I love you and all will be well sometime soon.

Goodbye, dear, and Good Luck
George

P.S. Nothing fresh has happened and it's Tuesday so I now post what I think is my last letter to Manila.

Well, Goodbye dear and hope you enjoy the trip,[6]

Cheerio
George

---

6. On August 1st Hilda and the boys along with many of the other dockyard families would sail for Australia on the *Indrapoera*.

Sunday July 21ˢᵗ 1940

C/o S.E.E.D., H.M. Naval Yard, Hong Kong

My Dear,
I've just finished one letter to you. It's lying on the table in front of me, but I'm starting another now and will finish it later if there is a sea mail to Manila. I think these will be the last letters you will get from me in Manila and you will have a long wait then until you get to Australia – we can send air mail to there though.

How did you solve the money problem? Have you had any trouble? And I believe things are dear in Australia but when you change an English £1 you get 25 Australian shillings, so that will make it up. I am glad the kids are well and I do want them to enjoy their trip – yes, and you dear, think of it as a cheap holiday in Australia. Why, I'm almost glad you're gone – it's only the selfish part of me that wants you back – my dear.

You certainly went through it that first week in Manila. That night at the hotel sounds especially nice, but I don't think you should have any more experiences as bad.[7]

So David came through it without another attack – yet. Well I hope he is still the same and remains so. You never know, this trip might cure him, and anything is worth that. Mrs Tubbs has written to Mr T. for medicines for the boy, so it sounds as though she is worried about him.

Well dear, I'm going to leave this letter now, until I see the times of the mail and perhaps there will be a letter from you to answer also, so,

Goodbye for now.

---

7. On the first night in Manila, Hilda and the boys found themselves staying at a hotel. Visiting the bathroom in the middle of the night a fellow evacuee discovered a line of naked men in the corridor. The hotel was in fact a brothel. After barricading themselves in for the rest of the night, Hilda arranged for alternative accommodation the following morning. She and the boys were finally re-billeted at a bungalow on a sugar plantation in Pampanga. Notwithstanding the shock she received at the 'hotel', Hilda would remember the kindness shown to them by the female 'staff' for the rest of her life.

Monday

Dear,
This is Monday afternoon (in the office). A mail did arrive, but not for me. I rather think that your living 60 miles from Manila causes considerable delay in both yours and my letters, so this letter I think I had better post today, for sea mail tomorrow. The air mail letter leaves here on Wednesday, so you should get both before leaving for Australia (Damn it).

Enjoy the trip as much as you can and have a good look round. I don't suppose you'll ever visit Australia again so make the most of it. Don't worry about me, and any news from England I'll pass on until they get your address. Give my love to the boys and tell them they are to look after each other and you and we will look forward to the day when we are all together again.

Goodbye my dear,
George

Dear Hilda,
With your letter all stuck down for posting this signal arrives, so I'm sending it on. The Admiralty are going to pay all the board and lodging in Manila and Australia, up to a standard sum, no doubt. I don't know if there is any catch to it, as it seems too good to be true. Also, if you like, you can apparently get digs on your own and they would pay you the standard sum. Anyhow, it seems as though conditions are going to improve.

I have also just received your air mail letter and I am glad you are comfortable. Let me know your address in Australia as soon as you can, although I expect I shall find somewhere to send a letter to.

That's all as this is in haste, so once more Goodbye and a Good Trip, and I hope it's not for <u>too</u> long.
Cheerio,
George

C O P Y

Subject: EVACUATION OF NAVAL, DOCKYARD AND HONG KONG ROYAL NAVAL
VOLUNTEER FORCE FAMILIES TO AUSTRALIA.

From : The Commodore, Hong Kong.

Date : 20th July, 1940.   No. 118. F/40.

To   : SECRETARY, NAVAL BOARD, NAVY OFFICE, MELBOURNE, AUSTRALIA.

- - - - - - - - - - - - - -

      The Admiralty have approved payment from public funds
of cost of Board and Lodging of families of Naval and Dockyard
personnel evacuated from Hong Kong (Vide enclosures No. 12, 2 and 3.)

    2.   I have communicated this decision to all Naval officers,
ratings and their wives and enclose copies of these communications
(Enclosures 4 and 5.) Dockyard personnel and their wives have
also been informed.

    3.   It will be noted that in paragraph 4 of Enclosure 5, I
below. have given naval wives the option, provided the Authorities in
Australia concur, of leaving the accommodation arranged for them,
subject to certain conditions as regards payment of their bills.
I hope that there is no objection to this, as, if the stay in
Australia is lengthy, many ladies, especially those with children,
may prefer to set up house on their own. This is also intended
to apply to Dockyard wives.

    4.   The families of Hong Kong, Royal Naval Volunteer Force
personnel are a liability of the Hong Kong Government and do not
come under the Naval Scheme quoted above.

    5.   Nominal lists of Naval, Dockyard and Hong Kong Royal
Naval Volunteer Force evacuees are attached. The term "Dockyard"
is intended to include all Admiralty Civil Staff, i.e. Dockyard,
Naval Armament Depot, Victualling Yard, Torpedo Depot, Boom
Defence Depot and Royal Naval Hospital Hong Kong.

              (sd.) A. R. Peters

                  Rear-Admiral.

    4.   It is the intention to place evacuees at private
boarding establishments in Australia, the accounts of which
will be paid by the Government.

       Grade of accommodation is dependent on rank of husband.
Provided that the authorities in Australia have no objection,
bills in respect of rent and food, not exceeding the cost
of such accommodation, can be paid by the Australian authorities
in lieu.

Evacuation details - July 1940.

Saturday July 27th 1940
C/o S.E.E.D., H.M. Naval Yard, Hong Kong

Dear,
I thought when I wrote early in the week that it was my last letter to Manila, but we have just had a signal down to say that a mail leaves at 1.30 today that might catch you before you leave. Of course, as usual, it's all a last minute job as it's 10.30 when we get the signal and being Saturday morning I've got a lot of work to do, so my letter will only be a short one. I've been working till 10 o'clock in the evening since Wednesday – we're supposed to finish today, but now the No1[8] has just gone up so we certainly won't finish.

No doubt, by now you know most of the arrangements for Australia. You will be given digs, for which I will be stopped £1 a week. In addition I will make you an allotment of 30/- per week (English) and then I also have to pay off the £20 you borrowed. I suggest that you open a banking account in Australia with whatever English money you have and then you can add to or draw from it according to how you get on. The American money I think I should keep if you have anywhere safe and if it's not too much worry.

I have the opportunity of sending more things to you from here direct to Australia, but it would have to be at once and the things would arrive the same time as you. Well, I looked around and decided there was nothing important that would warrant you being tucked up with more than you have, until you are settled in. However, let me know if there is anything you want me to send in case there is another opportunity.

I'm glad you have enjoyed your stay at Pampanga – at least it apparently hasn't been too bad and judging by some of the letters reaching here some of the women have had a rough time. Of course, "rough times" vary according to the individual and I think the absence of "help" is the big thing missed. There has also been a lot of sickness I believe, most of the "dog" variety, but very bad in some cases.

---

8. The stand-by signal indicating that a typhoon or tropical cyclone is within 800 km of Hong Kong and could affect the colony.

No dear, I did not put in to speak on the wireless and hearing them last Tuesday I was glad I didn't. I would have liked my name read out at the end but as for talking, I thought it was a lot of tripe and not half as good as the women's broadcast from Manila. I want to talk to you dear, but not like that.

Well, I'm afraid that is all I have time for, so Cheerio dear, and Good Luck on the Voyage. Last year you were getting nearer to me[9] and I know you are going further away but I still love you dear, no matter how far you are away.
Goodbye
George

P.S. Moan like H--L if you aren't comfortable in Australia as it always seems that those who shout get on the best.

Dear Edward and David,

I'm glad your swimming and diving is improving – how about arithmetic and English? No, I am really glad you have had a good time and I hope you enjoy the trip to Australia. Don't trip over the "Line" on the way and David, don't you cut a bit off for fishing with. Goodbye and Good Luck to you both.
Dad.

Monday August 12th 1940
C/o S.E.E.D., H.M. Naval Yard, Hong Kong

Dear,
First of all I hope you had a decent trip from Manila, decent for you I mean and, dear, I do hope you have as good luck in Sydney as regard your lodging as you did at Pampanga – but then I expect our letters will cross and I'll have all my questions answered before you get this.

---

9. George sailed to Hong Kong six months before Hilda and the boys joined him.

Well Hilda, I didn't write to you last week so I suppose before you get this there will have been a delivery of mail and all the other women will have had letters but you. I am sorry, dear, but believe me, I couldn't and didn't want to write – and so listen to my tale of woe.

A fortnight ago, July 30th to be precise, a bad place came up on the middle finger of my right hand, so I went to the surgery and they poulticed it for a week, and did it come up? But it wouldn't come to a head. I worked overtime all the week and it poured with rain every day, so I expect I would have been nice to live with that week.

Anyway, the next Monday, August 5th, I went to the surgery at 9 o'clock and the Doc had one look and says, "Hospital". I arrived at the Naval Hospital at 10.15 and was in bed with my finger opened by 10.30. They gave me gas so I didn't know anything about it – a slit about an inch right in to the bone – but I knew all about it during the week. Perhaps I'm making a fuss about a bad finger, a Whitlow by the way, but believe me I'm afraid I shall always make a fuss of anything that hurts as that did. Well, I was discharged from Hospital today, August12th with my finger getting better. I shall start work on Wednesday August 14th, and so by the time you get this all will be well again.

I'm sitting on the verandah writing this and dear I am "Homesick"; yes, I know I am supposed to be Home, but it's you I want here – no place will be Home when we are not together.

How are you, my dear – and the children? And don't you worry over me for I am all right now and the Hospital wasn't so bad as I made it sound. The finger only hurt when they dressed it – three times a day and the rest of the day was a good rest. Reading, draughts, (I never lost a game) and jolly good food, including a pint of milk a day and a bottle of beer, so the rest probably did me good.

Eve and Stanley Smith (twice) and Vic Walker came to see me, and Davis once, and that all in one week, and tonight (my first night out) Vic is calling with the car and I'm going to their place for chow.

My dear, I do love you so and you seem so far away now, but my dear there will be a homecoming for all of us one of these days.

Goodbye Dear, don't worry and remember you are on Holiday. George.

P.S. I have had a letter from your mother that arrived August 10th – air mail and it took 8 weeks coming out. I think the air mail is a swindle now.
George

Thursday August 15th 1940
C/o S.E.E.D., H.M. Naval Yard, Hong Kong

My Dear,
Your cable arrived just too late for me to send your letter direct to your address at Sydney, so I suppose it will now go to Brisbane first and then on to Sydney. This letter I'll send direct but will mark it "Evacuee" in case your first address is not permanent and if it's anything like Manila it won't be, will it?

Are you comfortable? That's the main thing, and how are you all? But no doubt I shall hear in good time.

My finger is getting better, but I haven't started work yet. I've been attending the hospital to get it dressed this week and will start work again next Monday. The sooner the better for me as the flat is so empty now.

By the way, I called in on Lang's yesterday about the piano – they were very elusive, hinted that they might offer $200 and I stuck out for $300 and eventually said I might consider $280. What do you think of that? Are we dropping too much? If there was any more free freight I'd like to ship it to you for you to sell, but I'm not certain if a piano is allowed to be imported.

Well Hilda, so Pompey[10] have had their first air raid. But we had a signal here to say that there were few casualties and damage was confined to Old Portsmouth and Gosport, so we will hope that Randolph Road[11] is still OK. And now I'm going to leave your letter for a bit as it's teatime. I wrote to Auntie Hillie[12] this afternoon and as the air mail to Australia doesn't go before next Tuesday I might hear from you – so Cheerio.

Well Hilda, this is Tuesday afternoon (20/8) now and I post tonight. Yes, I got your letter from Brisbane, and was I glad to hear from you?! So you, like me, had to do a bit of poulticing – I was sorry about that, dear, as I had been hoping that you would enjoy one sea trip. But as you say, it seems as though you were never meant to be a sailor.

Your wanderings are over for a little while and you can settle down for a bit and find a school (groans from the boys). By the way, while I'm thinking of school fees, you must let me know how the money goes; you have by this time started to pick up the allotment of 30/- and I am not trying to cut you down to that and if necessary I can increase it. We are not hard up, so you must tell me how you get on – but don't forget you must not pay for any board and lodgings unless you break away from the scheme and arrange to collect £1, which as you know I am being stopped.

I returned to work yesterday, but am still an outpatient at the Hospital; every three days I go and get it dressed, but I don't think that will be much longer as it is healing up all right. Peter Caplow from the Yard is now in the same ward as I was in and is very bad. They have operated again for another abscess in his side – he is on the danger list. He's had three blood transfusions and then two days ago he had some sort of attack and they had to give him a heart stimulant and oxygen. I spoke to him this morning and he can only whisper and to me seems very bad – but there, I suppose there is still hope and perhaps things aren't so bad as they appear. (Use this news discreetly.)

---

10. Portsmouth – the first raid took place July 11th 1940.
11. George and Hilda's home, 37, Randolph Road in Portsmouth. Before sailing for Hong Kong Hilda put their furniture into storage and the house was let to tenants.
12. Auntie Hillie looked after No. 37 in George and Hilda's absence.

Hong Kong is just the same, so that is about all my news now, but I'll write again later this week as I believe there are two air mails a week now. Goodbye then dear, all my love to you,
George

Thursday August 22ⁿᵈ 1940
C/o S.E.E.D., H.M. Naval Yard, Hong Kong

Dear,
I'm writing again this week not because I have news for you – I haven't, what news I did have was in the letter I posted last Tuesday. I'm writing this for the reason that I just wanted to talk to you. My dear, every time I write I think that I mustn't let you know just how lonely it is here now – that it will only make you feel worse. And so I ask how you are and scrape together a bit of news and say, "I love you and good luck, George," – oh, my dear.

Yes, I know I had six months on my own before but then I did have a date to look forward to and things out here hadn't been associated with you all then as they have been now. Even now as I write the wireless is on very low and I'm listening to a piece from Cavalleria Rusticana. Why is it that I accept things so and am so placid when you are with me and then feel like this when you are gone? Every single thing I do now is only done to pass a few more hours away and every hour I think of you and wonder what you are doing now.

Ah me! I got as far as that and then in walked our Mr. Davis, who had been working overtime and my particular mood wouldn't let me continue writing while he was there, and so now we have had supper and he has gone to the 9.20 pictures.

Well, I read through what I had written and wondered whether to send it or not – it certainly won't make you any more cheerful, but it's all true my dear. I am dreadfully lonely, and I didn't mean just tonight. Now don't go sleepless over me because I told you that. I shall pull though all right and when in the future you think I want shaking up a bit, you just say the one word, "Evacuation," and I'm sure that after cussing a bit I shall think of you and less of my book or such. Yes, my dear, I do indeed love you and I only hope our parting isn't going to last too long.

We've just had two days of terrible weather. A typhoon only just missed Hong Kong yesterday and today it rained hard all day, and no doubt we shall get a few more days yet.

My finger is getting better. I go again tomorrow morning for another dressing, but it was only last Saturday that they put the dry dressing on and pulled the cut together – previously they had plugged the cut to keep it open. Anyway, it's healing up rapidly now. Have you had any more trouble with your face? I hope not, as I know how that sort of thing can make you miserable. And the boys? What is the latest about them? How cold is it in Sydney after summering, or should it be simmering, in Hong Kong and Manila? Oh, how I wish I were with you, exploring all the new places together.

Sometimes I'm sorry we came East, but I only have to listen to the news and then I still think we are best off, if only for the boys' sake.

Well my dear, I didn't intend to write tonight, hence the pencil, my pen being in the Yard. I'm afraid it won't be very entertaining, but I just had to write to you. I'm off to bed now dear, so Goodnight to all of you,
George

Sunday August 28th 1940
C/o S.E.E.D., H.M. Naval Yard, Hong Kong

My Dear,
I hope that this letter will be a bit more cheerful than the last, not that I feel any more happy over this business. I never shall for that matter, but having blown off steam one week I'll try and go a few weeks before the pressure is high enough for the next explosion.

I got your eagerly awaited letter from Sydney yesterday (27/8/40), and even then over the mails there was more bungling. I was very lucky to be one of the few that got a letter from Sydney – there were plenty from

Melbourne but not Sydney. Mr. Samson hasn't heard since Manila and since I was at the Smiths' last night with him you can guess he was very pleased to hear your references to his wife. If he doesn't hear from her next mail, he is going to write to her care of you as otherwise he has no address to write to.

Well dear, I had been hoping that at last you would have once decent sea trip but this one seems to have been your worst. What can I say? I know how you must have felt, and it makes me want to cuss again – it's the fact that it all seems to have been so unnecessary that gets your goat. However, try and forget that trip dear and hope that the next one will be better. Does that make your head bad, to think of the next one? But at least you'll be coming to me, whether it's to England or Hong Kong.

Now, first of all about the money. Your news re the 30/- per adult and 15/- per child was the first we had heard about that. As you say, that gives you 25/- for grub in your new place. That's not too bad I suppose but as you said in your letter still stick (as far as you can) to the fact that Admiralty say they will find you board and lodging for which I pay £1 (sterling). Of course, in addition to your 25/- they give, you have my 30/- (sterling) per week allotment. You didn't mention having heard about that, but have you got it now?

Did you hear about having to change your £1 notes into Australian currency before September 5th? And also, how is the money – what have been your expenses through all this? I should hang on to the American notes if they're not too much worry, but I'll leave that to you.

How is David now, dear? You said in the postscript that he was queer – do you mean just a cold or one of his attacks, and if the latter, is it very bad? I suppose, as you say, the changes of temperatures that he has had, have done nothing to help him. You mention tablets from here. Do you mean Cinnamon Tablets? Anyway, I'm hoping that he is better by now. How about yourself? How are you keeping now and how about your face? If there is anything to be done to your teeth you had better get it done in Sydney as you don't want that to occur again.

I was glad to hear the boys had started school again. They have certainly had enough holidays this year, and I hope they do all right. But I know it will be hard for them to settle down.

Everybody is all right at home, up to July 1st. That is the latest letter I received (from Auntie Hillie) and she mentions that your mother and brother John had been down in the car from Southampton and called on her. They had had a couple of air raids, but not bombs, although by the wireless news Pompey has had two bad air raids. In the first the damage was all in Old Portsmouth (including the brewery) and in the second a cinema was hit and the gallery collapsed, and so was Drayton Road School. Anyway, we hope "37" is all right, and if it isn't well – we weren't in it. I will forward on letters by ship mail.

I've got one bit of news that will annoy you. The Smiths have moved to Hong Kong side at last, only they didn't decide to move until last week. I discreetly enquired of Wing On my position if I moved without giving the month's notice, and they said they would want a month's rent in lieu of notice. I saw Eve's landlord and tried to get the rent down to $80 but $90 was the lowest he would come and since by moving we would only save $2.50 a week each and then would have to pay the month's rent of this place and moving expenses, I decided not to move. If I only knew when you were coming back I would have jumped at it if it had cost $200, so if you should come back soon, let me down lightly, won't you.

My finger is getting better – actually I suppose it will be a couple of weeks before I can finally leave it entirely uncovered. It is healing all right but every now and again a little place will discharge and of course it won't finally heal until it's all out. That is quite normal and I am not now attending the hospital. I use my hand quite all right, and in fact the bandage is only a ruddy nuisance now.

Well dear, I've written this in bits and pieces and it is now Sunday morning, and the post goes Tuesday. You remember they made us work the Holiday at King's Birthday? Well, they are now giving us tomorrow, Monday September 2nd in lieu (damn). Six of us are going to Foster's matshed[13] in his car, including Mr. Tubbs. So, once more we pass the time away.

Well now, I'll finish for this week and tell you more about my doings (not that there's much) in my next letter.

That's all then dear, so once more I must say goodbye. Keep as cheerful as you can and remember I love and am always thinking of my Queen and Two Bits.

Goodbye dear,
George

Wednesday September 4th 1940
C/o S.E.E.D., H.M. Naval Yard, Hong Kong

My Dear,
No mail from you this week, so I am only starting my letter now and will finish later on, as there is another mail in from Australia on Friday. I am still OK and I hope you and the boys are likewise. David, how is he? Has he got over his attack?

I told you in my last letter that they gave us a holiday last Monday, so we had a long weekend. On Sunday I went to 11 ½ Mile Beach with Pamela and Vic to try out a matshed as they are thinking of buying one, and had quite a nice afternoon, although Vic was stung (not badly) by a jellyfish.

Monday, six of us went in Foster's car to his shed (including Mr. Tubbs) and that also was quite nice, except that our feet are a bit tender from cuts through throwing a ball about on the beach. Later that night we went round to Owen's for a drink and a yarn as it was his birthday. Tuesday evening (last night) I went to the Walkers' for chow, so I have done quite well just lately. I go to the Walkers once a week – Vic calls

---

13. Beach-hut

for me and brings me back in the car – yes, they are really decent. I have been to the Smiths' once or twice but they are the only two places I visit. The rest of the time I just stay in or go to the pictures. What do you do with your time?

Now dear, I don't want to worry you any more than is necessary, but I want to know your views about our position if I should go home. Nothing more officially has cropped up, but rumour (the lying Jade) has it that a conference was held today about reductions and that now names are being picked. What I want you to do is to consider the position should I go, and if you have the choice of remaining in Australia for the duration.

I'll admit I'm selfish enough to want you with me but the boys couldn't stay with us in Pompey, so that sometimes I think for their sakes you should stay where you are if we can afford it on Home rates pay. Other times I think that they won't be worse off than all the other kids. Anyway, will you think it over, as you know how things are when we move – all last minute decisions and little time to communicate with you. Well, having got that off my chest, I think I'll leave my letter over for a while and see what transpires, so good night dear.

Friday 6th, evening

Dear,
It's Friday evening and time to add a bit to my letter before supper. I've just come home from a Chargemans' meeting, had a bath, and here I am. I've read through the early part of this letter and apparently the last part need not have been written, but still you might consider it in case it is ever needed. But let me explain.

The conference about reductions of staff was duly held and a lot of people are going and have actually been warned that they will be moving, but no dates are fixed yet. (All departments I mean). I never heard anything and eventually saw Mr. Tubbs who said that my name never even came up for discussion as a candidate for moving, so apparently I am not going.

Two draughtsmen are for Singapore and two other chaps for Simonstown, South Africa, if they want any fitters or if not, home. One more might go and it is apparently between Bassett and Sully. That is the position at the moment and the future depends on – well, one just can't see the future these days. Stanley Smith is going to Singapore, but I believe in his case it depends on whether Eve will be allowed to go. Will let you know later about them.

Yes, tonight also I got your letter (dated August 25th) and was I pleased? It's a treat to hear from you and to know you are all well and that David is also better. Perhaps in your travels you may eventually strike on a climate that will cure him – and that alone would make all this worthwhile.

You speak of sending the sewing machine. Do you really want me to if another free freight goes to Sydney, and is there anything else you want, as I don't know how I shall be placed in the future?

Davis is going to Simonstown somewhen in the future and so unless I can find another lodger (and they are all fixed up now) I shall have to store the furniture and go in with somebody else. By the way, I was a bit disappointed at not going, as there might have been a chance of getting to Simonstown (as a fitter) but I wouldn't have minded that as there was a chance of you being able to join me there. But as everything is so in the air, I think on the whole it's as well to stop here. Besides, it leaves a few countries for you to visit later.

Mr. Tubbs informed me today that he has received instructions from his wife to pay me $22 for their son's piano lessons with you – he hasn't paid yet and I will tell you when he does.

Yes, dear, they do seem to be having a bad time at home. But everybody is safe, so far and apparently the actual casualties are very small.

Well dear, that's about all my news this time. I think I've answered most of your letter and I hope you have got some of mine by this time. One (the first) was addressed to Brisbane so I don't know when you'll get that – the second was addressed c/o Mrs Bethel and the third and this to "Cremona".

That's all for now dear, so Goodbye and All my love to you,
from George

P.S. You certainly make me envious describing all the spring flowers, but I am glad, dear, you like it all. Enjoy it, dear, and then come back to me.

September 6th 1940
C/o S.E.E.D., H.M. Naval Yard, Hong Kong

Dear David,
That was a very nice letter you sent me and not a bad sketch of Sydney Bridge. You certainly described all your adventures in, shall I say, condensed form, and I like the way you end up, suggesting that because you are finished hopping about from country to country that "things are now pretty quiet". You, my lad, can settle down "pretty quiet" in school for a while.

Are you still saving stamps as now is your opportunity, now that you are a world traveller?

I hear you have been chasing the girls again – Ah well, that's our David all right. I suppose you will soon be bathing again, but mind, no diving off that there Bridge.

That's all for now David, so Cheerio and
Love from Dad.

P.S. Tell Edward I want to see if he can write a better letter than you. I don't think he can.
Cheerio.

Friday September 13th 1940
C/o S.E.E.D., H.M. Naval Yard, Hong Kong

My Dear,
Friday night and I am only just starting your letter so I suppose I must look as though I don't love you so much this week. I've had a bit of a cold this week and my intention of writing to you last night was wrecked by my falling to sleep out on the verandah – then I thought there would be plenty of time tomorrow, but of course today I had a rush job and had to work until 7 o'clock. But at last I have started after placing in front of me a nice glass of medicine.

I haven't had your letter yet but as the plane only came in late this afternoon I shall probably be lucky tomorrow morning, so I will finish this at work tomorrow morning – putting it off again, you see.

Actually, nothing fresh has happened here, so I have no startling news. Mr. Tubbs has paid me 22 dollars – one of the few occasions when it's nice to have a music teacher for a wife.

Saturday September 14th

Dear,
Saturday morning now and the mail didn't come in yesterday – it's due tonight instead, so that means I won't get it until Monday morning. Also, now that I haven't your letter to answer I am really stumped for news.

While I think of it, let me get on to you. Do you realise that our wedding day has gone by and you never even mentioned it in your letters. Never mind dear, I hope next year we won't be writing to each other about things like that. Yes, I admit that I thought of said Wedding Day through reading your mother's letter.

Stanley Smith is not going to Singapore now. He is no longer an Engine Fitter chargeman but now he is Engineer of the "Wave", a tug and water boat. It doesn't leave Hong Kong but runs about the harbour – I don't think Eve is very pleased. The money is good but even when he goes back to England he will be on tugs.

Well my dear, Mr. Tubbs came in with a job and I have to push off. He has no consideration for us letter-writers, but in any case I am afraid that is about all my news.

I am glad you are getting some tennis in, on grass I hope too. I should think it must be very nice playing on grass with a nice sunshine and yet cool weather. I hope the boys are still keeping OK and are enjoying themselves.

Well dear, I must finish now, so Goodbye my dear, and good luck to you, Cheerio
George.

P.S. I've just heard wives will not be allowed to Singapore, even if husbands are appointed. Cheerio
George

Friday September 20th 1940
C/o S.E.E.D., H.M. Naval Yard, Hong Kong

My Dear,
Yes, it was just as I thought last week. The post closed on Saturday for Australian mail and your letter that should have arrived on Friday came on Sunday instead. And so once more I've sent a letter to the address you have just left.

A thought has just struck me. You get married and live all those years in number "37" and moving was far from your thoughts and now – well a month in one place must seem a long time to you. Actually, I heard via the grapevine that you are now living at Double Bay – so I take it that you have moved. I should get my weekly letter tomorrow morning (if the plane arrived) so perhaps I shall know more by tomorrow.

Yes, I am glad you sent your overnight "thoughts" on. It is quite true that in the morning it seems too much of "a bit of ourself" to let another person see – that I suppose is the English trait in us, but in any case let us forget that now – those huge things of yesterday have been made very small by present day happenings. One day, if we remember, we will talk about it, but in leaving it, let me repeat what I think I told you then, that throughout that "period" I didn't love you one bit less than I do now and believe me, dear, that isn't just a little bit either. Reading through the last paragraph it struck me that it might be nearly a month between your writing and getting my answer, so in case you are mystified, I am referring to what you call "the row".

Well, in my last letter I suggested you move to some place more permanent and apparently you had done so before you got that letter. Does this rent rise in the summer? One other point – have the boys had to move to another school again? I am glad they are with you and they are as they are.

This week my activities have been as follows: Sunday to the beach; on Monday I played in a chess tournament – I played 3, won 1 and lost 2; Tuesday I stayed in and read; Wednesday I went to the pictures at the Star; Thursday, to the Smiths' new flat at Happy Valley.

The flat is fairly similar to the one they had in Nathan Road. The two front rooms are quite nice but the bedrooms at the back aren't nearly so good – there's only a tiny verandah and while they can see the racetrack at Happy Valley the immediate surroundings are not much. While I was there three fellows (English) two flats further on, being a bit happy, spent a pleasant half hour throwing bottles out of the window to smash in the road and while I don't suppose that is an everyday occurrence, I am quite sure it wouldn't have happened at the Smiths' old flat.

To continue my recital, tonight I stay in and write to you and tomorrow it's the Walkers'. The Smiths are going so we will drink a toast to you, my dear. Yes, that group all together brings back memories and I know that I shall miss you very much tomorrow night.

By the way, in my last letter I spoke about your considering what you would wish to happen if I had to go home. Well, we had a signal to say that our families must accompany us to wherever we go. The day I leave Hong Kong your allowance stops and if you stay in Australia it is entirely at our own expense, and if it lasts more than twelve months you forfeit the free passage home – so that is that. If I go, you go, and I am glad.

Are my letters censored? All yours have been and I enclose a portion of your last letter to show you the bit that he had the bloody cheek to cut out.[14] What did he think you were trying to convey? Let me know what you think of him too.

Well, that is all for tonight dear. I will finish tomorrow morning and perhaps a letter will be waiting for me. So Goodnight, my dear, and I hope you sleep better tonight and not do any reaching out to an empty place as I sometimes do – Goodnight dear.

Saturday morning now, and again the mail has been delayed, so this will have to be posted without waiting for it.

Yes, they are certainly having a terrible time at home now. If it goes on for very long, I am afraid there will be many places we won't recognise when we return.

Well, that is about all my news this week, so I'll say Goodbye again. Try and enjoy your Australian visit, dear, and make it an interlude to look back upon because I expect when we do go home, we probably won't move again.

Goodbye then, dear, love to the boys and Cheerio
George

---

14. Hilda's letter has not survived.

Sunday September 22nd 1940
C/o S.E.E.D., H.M. Naval Yard, Hong Kong

Dear,
I posted my letter to you yesterday, and then today received your not very happy letters of the 9th and the 12th. Yes, I know exactly how you feel, dear. It comes over in waves at times and all you want to do is curse. I am better off than you in some ways, because at least I have to go to work and do something during the day, but, dear, and I mean this, I found that the news that I was stopping here went a long way towards resting my mind. At least it is some of the indefiniteness gone. So remember, dear, I am staying in Hong Kong and you are coming back sooner or later and even if plans alter and I have to move – well, you are going with me, come what may.

I hope by the time you get this that your cold will be gone and that you will feel happier and will have settled down in your new house. You say you haven't had a letter from me for two weeks – well, I wrote two the first week you were in Australia. The first was addressed to Brisbane (as told to do this end) and then one a week since, so you shouldn't go one week without a letter, let alone two. This is the second letter to the Wallaroy Road address and is only a quick answer to your letter as I've just had one from Winnie[15] and will send it on. Everybody is O.K. up to August 16th anyway, and what did surprise me was the fact that Auntie Hillie and Uncle Fred have stopped on in Pompey after the first big raid there.

Yes, like you, I think the High School would be the best for David if he can get there, at least for the present. Things are so topsy-turvy at the moment that it's hard to say what the future holds, but I feel sure the children at home can't be doing a lot of schoolwork just now.

Well dear, this is only a quick letter and must be short to get Winnie's[16] in – I will write my usual weekly letter in addition. Goodbye my dear,

---

15. George's sister, in England - in Isleworth, Middlesex.
16. Winnie's letter has not survived.

I do hope you feel happier now. Always I am thinking of you and waiting for news of the day when we will meet again –
Goodbye dear
George

Thursday September 26th 1940
C/o S.E.E.D., H.M. Naval Yard, Hong Kong

My Dear,
I have just listened to the 7.30 news and now have half an hour or so before supper, so will make a start on my weekly epistle. As I told you, I got your letter last weekend after I had posted mine, so I wrote a couple of pages and enclosed Winnie's letter and caught Tuesday's post, only to see in the next day's paper that all air mail is cancelled until future notice, owing to the trouble in Indochina.[17] So I suppose that means more delay in our letters.

I haven't very much to tell you in the way of news, but I know that doesn't matter a lot, it's just getting a letter from me that counts – though I says it meself that shouldn't. I had my usual weekly visit to the Walkers last night – only a quiet yarn but quite the best evening of the week, with Vic bringing me back home in the car about "twelvish".

We have just had four days of very hot weather, temperature 90° – you know how it runs off my arms – and there's no sign of it getting cooler yet. It's the last kick of summer I suppose, as it should be getting down to my tennis weather in a week or so.

There has been a very bad outbreak of cholera here the last six weeks, especially in Kowloon City, but it is going off now. It was so bad that when it was at its height Amah went on her own to be inoculated as she properly had the wind up, so you can guess it was bad. Fortune tellers, "etc.", told the Chinese that the cholera would last until Chinese

---

17. On September 22nd 1940, Japanese troops invaded northern French Indochina (present day Vietnam, Cambodia, Laos).

New Year, but they quite easily got over that by bringing the New Year forward. So this week they have been going round the streets with dragons and lions, beating drums and carrying burning joss sticks with all the people throwing crackers, apparently to make the devils think it already is New Year and time to depart. Still sometimes I think we as a nation are just as good in deceiving ourselves as the Chinese.

Well dear, I'm continuing my letter on Monday now and the post would normally close tomorrow, but I don't know what is happening now. I think letters go to Singapore by ship as and when a ship is going that way, so I don't know when you will get this. I started this letter Thursday and then went on overtime on a job that had to be ready by Monday. Well, we were ready and Monday (today) started a 60-day trial that once it was started had to be continuous – but all the plans of mice and men, etc. The No1 signal went up at 5.00 tonight and the ship had to go, so now we will have to start all over again when the "blow" is over. This is the reason why I am able to finish my letter tonight.

The weather has been very hot for a week now, so the typhoon will at least cool it down a bit and it may be too late in the year to get so hot again. I went for a bathe yesterday at Repulse Bay and the water was easily the warmest this summer – far too warm to feel any benefit from a bathe. Have you, or at least have the boys, done any bathing yet? Or is it too cold for you hothouse plants yet?

Davis is still with me and apparently it will be two or three weeks before he goes, so I still have my "problem" to solve. I put my notice into Wing On every month now, so that I can move at the end of any particular month.

How are you getting on now? Have you made any new friends yet, and the boys? And does Double Bay suit you better than Manly?

Yes, dear, I'm afraid they are going through it at home and I am also afraid that we out here are inclined to get that "All quiet on the Western Front" outlook – you know a glance at the paper and the thought, "Nothing important, only another raid on so-and-so", but I should imagine those raids must be hell, especially in London where they seem to be more or less continuous both day and night. Yes, I think we should be thankful that we are out here, if only for the boys' sake and we can only hope our people come through safely.

Mrs "O" is still in Cape Town and must stay there, and so far they have received no help financially at all. I think Gerald is sorry he was in such a rush to get back home. Oh, by the way, I spoke of Davis going, but I don't' think I told you where he was going. He was more or less promised Simonstown but now has to go to Trincomalee in Ceylon.[18] I shouldn't fancy that a lot myself, but it has one advantage that I should fancy and that is that his family can join him there.

Well, dear, I am afraid I am not an "inspired" letter writer tonight so I will finish for tonight and if I have time tomorrow and can find something to write about I will add a bit more before posting.

Tuesday now, and only a few minutes to spare, but I want to be ready in case the post goes. I have no further news at the moment, in fact this letter is not what you can call a "newsy" one.

I am quite O.K., dear, and my finger is practically normal now, just a little bit tender but I expect that will take some weeks to work off.

And now, dear, I'm going to close and hope you don't have to wait too long for it. Goodbye my dear, all my love to you
George

---

18. Present day Sri Lanka.

Matshed.
(Referenced in the letter of August 28th 1940)

Hilda, David and Edward with other evacuees at the Guest House in Pampanga.

October - December 1940

...quite a lot of our chaps, this being Hong Kong, have taken unto themselves a temporary wife, Chinese of course, and I tell you, there won't half be a scramble if the wives suddenly return from Australia.

Monday October 7th 1940 (and onwards)
C/o S.E.E.D., H.M. Naval Yard, Hong Kong

My Dear,
I have two letters from you on the table in front of me as I write – one of September 17th and the other written three days later where you start, "Weren't you pleased to see this letter so soon after the other". Actually I got that one first, by a few hours, today, and that is the first Australian mail we've had for 17 or 18 days, owing to the Indochina trouble. Anyway, the mail seems to have resumed again now, for a while at least, so perhaps we will get them more regular.

I'm glad to hear you are settling down more. In fact by the tone of these two letters I judge I shall have a job to get you to come back. But really, dear, I am glad you like it better now. And as regards that old complaint – loneliness – well, I think you are bound to get a few attacks of that. I had one tonight when I walked past the corner of Lock Road and the old chap selling chestnuts had just taken up his pitch for the winter, and I naturally thought of David. But I resolutely put the thought behind me and hurried on – yes, dear, some of these moments are bad but patience (damn it) and then ----!

Now dear, I have a bit of bad news. I didn't intend to tell you but I just can't write. I have unfortunately another whitlow, this time on the first finger of my right hand. It started last Saturday and came up badly on Sunday. Monday, I wrote the ink part of this letter and had to rest my hand a half a dozen times just doing that bit. Well, it's got steadily worse since then and it's Thursday now and pretty bad, so it's either I tell you or you get no letter.

It's not nearly so bad as t'other one and they are trying to get rid of it without sending me to hospital, although I think I would sooner go as it's not very nice trying to work under these conditions. However, it no doubt will go the way of all whitlows. What worries me is the question of why I have had them. I couldn't get any help from "our quack" who just laughingly said that, "you good husbands don't get rid of the badness in your blood now your wives are away," but I'm afraid I wasn't in the mood to appreciate humour. Anyway, on the supposition that I am run down a bit, I bought, after going all over the place, what I think must be the last tin of Sanatogen in H.K. and I'll try a course of that. The weather is much cooler now, just nice in fact – and that I think will go further in curing these things than anything else.

Well, I've heard of worse things, Mr Caplow for instance. Yes, he's gone at last, as perhaps you have heard, and while it's better that than linger on as he was doing it's rotten to die all on your own like that. His wife was on her way to H.K. having been sent for but I believe she will be stopped and returned to Australia for the present.

That is all now, dear, but I will enclose a letter from your mother[19] to make up. Goodbye my dear – don't worry about me. I want you so tonight and am trying hard not to say so. Goodbye
George

October 11th 1940

Dear,
Friday morning and the post closes for Australia today, and on my arrival at the office this morning there was a letter from Winnie for which she had paid 5/- to come air mail via America. It is the very latest news from home, as you'll see by the date so I thought I would send it straight on to you.[20] The other bit from your father came out with your mother's letter so I'm putting a bit in each envelope to even up the

19. Letter has not survived.
20. Letter has not survived.

weight. That address from Auntie Hillie – well I think you had better use your own discretion, but it would probably please them at home for you to call. Well, can't write any more.

Finger just the same so Goodbye dear,
George

Sunday October 20ᵗʰ 1940
C/o S.E.E.D., H.M. Naval Yard, Hong Kong

Dear,
Another Sunday and another week gone, and dear, that means another week nearer our meeting again. It seems such a long time now that you've been away, and the trouble is there is no sign of them allowing you to return yet. Last week they were listening to appeals, in court, from women who didn't want to be evacuated – the majority weren't granted and apparently they will have to go. Yes, these are women that just didn't obey the order to be on a certain boat at a certain time – they have been here ever since and now those of them that haven't wangled a permit one way or another will have to go. But anyway, that doesn't look hopeful for your coming back yet, does it? Oh, and by the way, just to make matters worse, the air mail is suspended again, for a time, between here and Singapore so that means delays again.

Well dear, first of all, my finger – it wasn't anything like as bad as the other one and has now reached the healing-up stage. I've still got it bandaged but that won't be for much longer and I hope I don't get another. Anyway, I have been fairly busy just lately, in spite of a bad finger – in fact I didn't finish until 8 o'clock last night (Saturday).

Davis has left Hong Kong as I told you and Jim Dawkins has come to live with me. As Eve Smith says, don't I pick 'em out, but in both cases they asked me, and it's a case of any port in a storm – actually we have got on all right so far and I expect will do so in future. From a grub point of view we live just about the same as when you were here so don't worry on that score; each night I tell Amah what I want for dinner the next day and she buys it and I settle with her the same day – the only book I keep going is the compradore's[21] and I pay that weekly.

As regards sending stuff down to you, I can't quite make my mind up – the minimum you can send by sea is 40 cubic feet for 49/- sterling, so that black box would cost about £3 to send, including cartage by the time you get it, so I think I'll see what the parcel post is like. I have heard that a carved camphor wood box fetches a good price down there, so if you hear anything let me know and that would pay for the carriage cost.

Well dear, this is Wednesday now, and let me confess I missed the post. I took my letter to the yard to finish and then we had a small panic job on Monday, and I could just not do it. And of course, to heap coals of fire on my head, two of yours arrived together. I'm sorry about missing the post though, dear, for I know what it is like to wait for a letter and not get it.

I was glad to get a letter from Edward and as regards his requests – well the bike first. Like you, I am not keen for several reasons: I don't know Sydney is one, they must be very expensive in Australia is two, and that they will be a nuisance in future travelling is three. I don't say they can't have them, but I think it would be very much better if they wait until we go back to England and I promise to buy them one each. Now for his birthday, I enclose with his letter a 10-dollar note, since he asks for it in H.K money, but if you have any difficulty changing it, send it back and I'll send Australian. If it is not enough for what he wants, give him a bit more.

I am glad you are more comfortable now and judging by your suggestion of trying for a job in Australia after the war, I should imagine you like it very much. How does the place agree with David? Is there any hope of Sydney being the place we have been looking for to cure him? For, if so, that alone would make all this worthwhile – and you, how are you now dear?

---

21. At the local grocery store.

But surely that is not right, that you can't have a piano? If you didn't sign anything, I don't think they can stop you playing, only if you play at unreasonable hours, so I should enquire a bit further about that.

Now dear, it has just struck me that I'm going to be overweight with the $10 note so I must finish, but I'll write again quickly to make up. Goodbye then dear for now, I still love you even if I did miss the post. Cheerio, George

Dear Edward
Thank you very much for your letter; it pleased me very much to open Mum's letter and find one from Edward in it as well, and I'm glad that now and again when you are not busy playing monopoly you do miss your Dad a little bit. Still never mind, when we all get together again, we'll have a lot more fun.

I'm glad you like it in Australia, but you know, in your letter, you forgot to mention school – now I wonder how that came about? Do you like this school? I think you must, because mum says you play cricket for Form 5; but in your next letter you tell me if you are in the arithmetic team.

Now Edward, don't be disappointed about the bike, but I don't think I can grant that request; but don't give me that cold shoulder you promise, and you shall have one directly we get home. If you had one in Australia, I would go dreaming of you riding it over the edge of Sydney Bridge.

However – on to better news! I'm glad you reminded me about your Birthday, as perhaps I should have forgotten it, like I did David's. So Many Happy Returns of the day and I hope you have a happy day. I enclose 10 dollars in H.K. money and tell David I owe him the same for his birthday. Buy something nice (a pair of shoes) and have a good time, and that is all for now, so Goodbye Edward,
And love from Dad.

Sunday October 27th 1940
C/o S.E.E.D., H.M. Naval Yard, Hong Kong

Dear,
I haven't had any further letters from you. The last one was dated October 7th and arrived last Tuesday, but I might get one early in the week – so I have just been rereading the last two or three I've had from you. I'm afraid I still curse every time I think of this business and as for settling down to just wait for your return – well that is impossible. You seem to feel the same when you speak of that suspended feeling and as you say, we must look forward and I keep on saying that to myself but somehow it doesn't do much good. I want to be with you, dear, to love you and yes, sometimes have a set-to with you, but anyway to be with you.

No dear, the end of October and I haven't played tennis – I haven't even looked at my racquet. For one thing, the weather has been very warm and sticky up to this weekend, and nobody appears to be interested. The courts haven't been got ready yet. However, this weekend we had a sudden drop in temperature, so perhaps a move will be made – so you see your picture of gents' doubles all Saturday afternoons was all wrong.

I had a yarn with Mr. Tubbs on Friday and he tells me that the latest from Mrs T. is that she has had to move and so has lost the piano, and away go your lessons – but no doubt I shall hear about that in your letter. He also told me that Mrs. T said you have a very nice house and that the boys look very well indeed – they have put on a bit of fat and are a very nice colour. Is that true dear? I hope so – but really I was glad to hear it, because only two nights previous I was introduced to a chap who, in the course of conversation, most of it quite nice about you, said "Oh, of course, it's you that has the boy that suffers so badly from asthma." I told him that David had had a bad attack soon after getting to Sydney, but that I understood he was keeping fairly good now. How is he really, dear? I know I asked in my last letter, but I am anxious about him.

I had a letter from Auntie Hillie last week and I'll enclose it with this. I hope the censor will let it through as it wasn't considered harmful on leaving England. So, number "37" was O.K. up to September, but the chief thing I thought about her letter was the tone – for an old lady her age going through that, I think she's great, but there, they all are.

Yes, I started on my third year last Tuesday October 22nd as it counts from when I left home. Two years gone quickly, and I wonder what another year will bring – but I won't start that again.

I went with Eve and Stanley to a Whist Drive to celebrate that anniversary (October 22nd) and of course Eve and I had to share the first half price. She got the first prize for top score for both halves ladies, and I got 2nd for gents, but as there were very few there the prizes (cash) were very small.

Wednesday, I went round to Owen's with Mr. Dawkins for cards and darts, and Friday I played billiards, and of course Saturday it was the pictures ("Susan and God") with Mr. Dawkins again; so you see we spend our evenings somehow.

Well dear, that is about all my news and I want to enclose Auntie's letter,[22] so I'll stop. If I get one from you before the mail goes, I will write a bit more. So good night dear.
George.

Monday October 28th 1940
C/o S.E.E.D., H.M. Naval Yard, Hong Kong

My dear,
I've just had my tea, a bit late it's true, and as I am not going out tonight, I thought I would start my letter to you. We had a farewell "do" in the office tonight, but I left a bit early to catch the post, which leaves to Australia tomorrow. I haven't had your letter yet so will answer that later in the week – only as the air mail comes from Singapore by boat now, it seems to arrive any time.

---

22. Letter has not survived.

What do you think of the news in Winnie's and Auntie Hillie's letters that I sent on to you – what a frightful time they are having, although I think it must sound worse than it really is or else they couldn't write like that. All that was six months ago too, so our old town is probably much worse by now. But as I mentioned before, it's so many thousands of miles away, if it wasn't for our people involved it would just be a case of, "No news, only another raid on so-and-so". I have thought over what you said about leaving the boys behind and I don't quite know what to say – if I go, I want you to come and if the boys could stay with us I would want them but I suppose they would not be allowed in our town – anyway leave it for a time as at present there is no sign at all of my going.

Hong Kong is still just the same as when you left, except that there are not so many functions – I do really miss our dances, dear. They were jolly good fun, weren't they?

Well now dear, that is all I am going to write tonight but I will continue later in the week. Tomorrow and Wednesday evening we have a blackout lasting in each case all night, so I suppose we shall have to go to the pictures to pass the time away.

Friday evening now, dear, and of course directly I got the writing pad out, I found I had left my fountain pen in the office – pencil isn't too good on air mail paper but I hope you can read it. Well, we've had a fun two-evening blackout – I went to the pictures the first and spent the second evening at home playing chess with the light well screened. Yes, Mr. Dawkins plays chess – we have had two games so far and won one each, so that will pass an hour or two away.

Last night we had a meeting at the club and the chief item from our point of view, and that only came out in answer to a question put by me, was that owing to the high cost of tennis balls they are going to propose that members provide their own balls. The danger as I see it, is that that rule combined with the lack of interest this year will leave the courts empty and as you know the Yard has been after the site for some time – however, we will see.

I had one surprise tonight – as I left the Yard, I had a note handed to me, and I don't think you could guess from whom it came. There is a "boat" at one of the buoys in the harbour and the letter asks could I go out to see him or make arrangements for him to meet me – now come on, guess? Remember Tom? Well, he's in the Navy now and they must have sent him straight out here. I'll try and see him tomorrow.

And now, talking of letters – into the office I walked this afternoon, and there was one with Australian stamps on. Dear, what can I say? I want to tell you lots of things but the only words that come to me are "damn the evacuation". Four months tonight you've been away dear – four unnecessary months, and yes, I'm afraid I'm getting fed up with this life.

But it doesn't do any good to write this, so I'll get on to something else. Well, I am glad you like it down there now and dear that was a treat to hear about the boys, especially the bit about Edward not swanking about his singing voice. His swimming too must have greatly improved and if David has improved as much I won't stand a chance with him the next time we go bathing together as I had to go all out to just keep my nose in front when he was in Hong Kong. Really, I am glad they are getting on so well, though, and you too my dear, although I think you might go and look for a job as I hear that Mrs. Owen has a job in a shop at I believe 30/- a week – she will soon be making him an allotment. (Meow).

Well dear, that is all now except that you must buy thinner paper. I won't say write less, as 1/10 for postage is disgusting, but it was worth 1/10 to see that letter on my desk.

Good night then, dear, and for a few days, goodbye – I still love you just the same, unfortunately, but like you I'm still hoping – Goodbye George

P.S. Did the letter containing $10 arrive safely, and did I say right about the bicycles?

Thursday October 31ˢᵗ 1940
C/o S.E.E.D., H.M. Naval Yard, Hong Kong

Dear Winnie

Thanks for sporting the 5/- on my letter and it was a real treat to get some fairly up-to-date news. It arrived in my office during the morning of October 10th (posted September 17), and as that happened to be mail day for Australia I put it in another envelope with mine and sent it straight on to Hilda. I paid another 3/- for that, so that letter cost something didn't it? Anyway, it was worth it just once, but don't make a practice of it, will you? By the way, if anything should happen, you can send me a service cable for 5/. Ordinary air mail letters are now reaching us in from six to eight weeks and sea mail from eight to ten weeks – we have had sea mail via San Francisco come out as fast as by air.

Yes, you certainly are living a "fast" life these days (or is that the wrong expression) and I'm glad you can live up to it as you seem to be doing – are the people really taking it as good as the papers and wireless speakers say they are? Anyway, remember your letters have never been censored. It wouldn't be so bad if you could only see the end in sight, but you can't yet – but I suppose it is some consolation to hear that we are "giving" just as much as we are "receiving".

Well Winnie, it's four and a half months now, since the evacuation and I can tell you it's getting pretty deadly. Most of the social affairs are a wash-out this winter of course with the women away, so we have to amuse ourselves the best we can, and there aren't many ways ("nice" ways I mean) of doing that in Hong Kong. But apart from all that, the desire to do anything seems to be missing. Even tennis has lost its attraction – here we are with six weeks of our tennis season gone and only four games have been played on our courts. I haven't played yet, through a water blister on my foot – this by the way is one of the things you have to put up with in hot countries. You suddenly get a large water blister come up that must be looked after or it will turn septic, apparently due to overheating of the blood. Anyway, mine is better now and I shall play next week, and as I was elected tennis representative at the club annual meeting last night I shall try to wake things up a bit, although I think that might be a bit of a struggle.

By the way, about the "nice ways" I mention up above, quite a lot of our chaps, this being Hong Kong, have taken unto themselves a temporary wife, Chinese of course, and I tell you, there won't half be a scramble if the wives suddenly return from Australia. While my socks aren't always black now, I'm not quite modern enough for that yet.

At present, we have no idea how long the evacuation will last. The way the Japs are acting it looks like lasting some while, but perhaps America can keep them quiet – in any case they wouldn't have things all their own way (no, I'm not thinking of the Dockyard Defence Corps[23]). By the way, we're just had one hell of a row about the evacuation. You see, everybody was ordered to get out except those doing necessary work (nurses, ARP, etc.), so of course those with push got their girl friends a job. Army, naval and dockyard wives then went followed by the civies – well a lot refused to go. Boats were chartered and sailed half empty and then, when most had gone, they had the remainder in court, refused their appeals and chartered another boat. Then some bright soul found out that the government can't do it legally, so the evacuation is now voluntary, and nobody else is going. Then, of course, there was a mass meeting of husbands demanding their wives back, and I think if only the Japs would pipe down a bit, we might get them.

I suppose that you will wonder what we have to moan about out here and thinking of the way you are living, I wonder too. But there, we never know when we are well off. I had a letter from Hilda today, and she's quite well and comfortable and David has just sat for the High School. She also told me that she had just sent a parcel off to you and one to Mum, so I hope you get it for Xmas. How is Mum sticking it now? The more I think of it, the more bewildered I get – it's most difficult to imagine all that going on in London, but I've seen (on the screen) pictures of the big stores in Oxford Street burning fiercely and the whole place seemed in ruins – is it really as bad?

_____

23. Earlier in 1940, the situation with Japan had been considered serious enough for employees in the dockyard to be asked to join a Dockyard Defence Corps.

Yes, I'm still keeping the flat going but I've got another fellow in with me and we share expenses – I shall keep going as long as I can. This week I had the piano packed in a case and it sails on Monday to Australia. I'm not sure if Hilda will be pleased or not, but she will have to sell it if she can't use it – I couldn't sell it here; with everybody wanting to sell you can buy one for a few pounds, while in Australia they are very dear I believe.

I'm going to send this sea mail, as there is a fast mail via San Francisco tomorrow (November 15th) and while I can't wish you a merry Xmas, I do wish you a Happier New Year. (I've just said the same thing in a letter to Auntie, but that is a most sincere wish.) Also, Winnie, if Mum hasn't written for Xmas, do try and persuade her to write.

That's all then, Win, so goodbye and the best of luck,
From George

All my best to Sid.

This letter is a bit disjointed, I'm afraid – I stared October 31st, and finished November 14th, but I've spent so much time lately over sending and packing the piano to Australia.
Cheerio,
George

Tuesday November 5th 1940
C/o S.E.E.D., H.M. Naval Yard, Hong Kong

My Dear,
November 5th today and no kids to make me go up on the roof to let off fireworks, or didn't I want much making? Anyway, it's a good deal more quiet here tonight than November 5th last year. Do they have fireworks in Australia on this day? Or perhaps in any case they are banned during the war.

Well, how are you all now, and how do you like Australia now that it's warming up? I hear that the actual temperature gets as high if not higher than in Hong Kong, but that it's not so trying as the humidity is a lot less. Have you done any bathing yet? I know the kids have, but how about you? The thought has just struck me that you will be having two summers this year – you wait, my gal, you'll feel an English winter when you go home – but there it will be nice to feel you cuddling in.

Well dear, I saw Tom on board his ship for about ten minutes and then last evening he came over to the flat and spent the evening here. He has only been out here five weeks and was in our town when they had their first big bombing raids, so you can guess he was full of news. From the point of view of actual damage he couldn't tell me any more than I knew, in fact I told him some that he didn't know as Auntie's letter was written after he left home, but there is a big difference in just hearing a place has been hit and hearing what it looks like after being hit. Still, there is one thing, everybody seems to be sticking it well and just carrying on more or less as usual.

Tom himself – well he is just the same old Tom, quite a nice chap with a few foolish ways. I almost said simple ways. For instance he has only been in Hong Kong five days and during that time he managed to hide his money (not much, but all he had) in one of his shoes, forgot where he had put it and sent the shoes to a Chinese boot repairer. Strange to relate, it wasn't there when the shoes came back – but that is typical of him, go very careful to save a bit of money and then do something like that.

We still haven't had any tennis, as it was a wet weekend, but in any case I have a blister on my foot that's not quite nice to walk on so I won't play until that is better. I don't know if everyone else has blisters, but I think they must have.

Well dear, so far on Tuesday evening and then supper arrived and after supper Dawkins and I played crib. I thought I had the rest of the week for your letter but the paper only shows a mail going out today, Thursday, and then nothing until next Thursday – I expect there will be one in between but I didn't like to risk it so I am finishing off in the office and will post today.

Yes, I have one piece of fresh news, but I should imagine the Australian papers will carry it long before you get this letter. All the women that have dodged the evacuation so far, have been in front of a court of appeals recently and had their appeals refused – well now they haven't got to go. The evacuation for all who remain is now voluntary – while they are still advised to go, they haven't got to go. Women who have left Hong Kong are still barred from returning.

Well, I suppose that is a step in the right direction, but only a very small one, but I bet there is an outcry now from the civilian women that have already been evacuated – anyway, what do you think of it?

Oh, and one other piece of news; I can already hear you saying, "I told you so" – last weekend we had a burglar in the Yard. He broke a small window, reached through and opened a large one and got in our shop, and then forced two drawers belonging to Cummings and two of Baker's. In Cummings' he found $100 and nothing in Baker's – actually Baker was very lucky as he had $800 in another drawer in preparation for going to Simonstown. Anyway, you needn't worry as far as I am concerned. My drawer is empty – now.

No fresh news from home dear, but in my last letter I mentioned hearing from your mother and that they were O.K. There was a bit about John starting a (what I thought) dance, but on rereading it I find the word is divorce, which is more the "end of the dance", but I'll send it and you can see for yourself – is he really going to do it at last?

And now, dear, I think that is all for now – that one small step I spoke of earlier has revived hopes in spite of "reasoning" – and how I hope!
Goodbye my dear,
George

P.S. Have you visited Aunt What's-is-name or are you going to give it a miss?
G.

Monday November 18th 1940

C/o S.E.E.D., H.M. Naval Yard, Hong Kong

My Dear,
Once again I'm making a start but as it's only Monday and the post goes Thursday, I don't suppose I shall finish tonight – we'll just call it Chapter I. Perhaps Chapter II will be an answer to your letter if I'm lucky enough to receive it.

Well, I'm still wondering what you thought of the bombshell in last week's letter[24], about the piano – did I do the right thing or not, only the offer of the cheap freight was such a temptation and it seemed a pity to have the thing here rusting while you were piano-less down there. Of course, to make matters worse, your last letter that arrived on Friday contained the story of the person upstairs suggesting the boys could make less noise. Anyway, weigh up your wishes on the matter and don't let those sort of people influence you too much.

And, now, these are the instructions. Look out a good piano firm, and then when you are notified that the cases are ready for collection, get them to go and collect it, take it to their factory or workshop or whatnot, and unpack it and see if it has been damaged. It has been insured against damage by breakage and damage by fresh water, that is rain, and I will forward the insurance papers. Also, when you select your firm it might be as well to ask if they are prepared to buy the case – it cost £3 sterling, so you ought to be able to get from £1 to 30/- Australian. If you decide you can't keep it (the piano, I mean) then see if the firm will store it awhile and then sell it for you. Get it valued in any case. (Your name and present address are painted in big letters on the case.)

And now the other case; you'll have to collect it of course and then your next bother will be to open it – if it's in good condition, try and save it.

---

24. Letters were lost in the post at times during the war, and a few of George's letters written during this period have not survived - the letter containing the "bombshell" either undelivered, or missing from the collection.

First, you must prise the nails out of the iron band just to clear the lid and bend it back out of the way and then unscrew the lid. I don't know how you are going to do all that yourself, but that is one I know you can solve.

Well dear, after all those instructions, how are you and the boys? I suppose David is relaxing from the mental strain of his exam. So, he found the papers easy, did he? Hmm, I'm afraid that's a bad sign. I was at the Smiths' on Saturday night, Stanley's birthday, and speaking of the boys, I told them that one, about David finding the papers easy as an example of David's philosophy and that it certainly wasn't to be relied on as a token that he had done well.

We held the Club General Meeting last Thursday, and I've never been so disgusted before – and unfortunately, I wasn't the only one to think so. I say that because having spent nearly two hours on "election of officers" – and having got a fairly good committee the whole affair then collapsed. You see the bar was open all the time, and, well two hours is a long time and when a meeting starts with bad feeling it's openly expressed two hours later and although the collapse sobered some of them I think, others were beyond any effect less than a mallet.

Having elected the officers the Treasurer announced that the last half hour had proved to him that he could never be an officer of a club of this sort, it would be too degrading, resigned and walked out. There, that's nice, isn't it, but wait – they then proceeded to elect one of the "Old Guard" to the empty post, and then the Secretary, a good chap too, said he was sorry but now he must resign, as he couldn't work with that man, in fact he had never seen him sober enough to be on any committee and then he walked out and another Old Guard was elected.

What a club!! Warren and I are the two tennis representatives, but as they passed a rule that all players provide their own balls (on that court) and as there is no interest anyway, I don't think we shall be overworked.

And that, my dear, brings Chapter I to a close – Amah has just brought my supper in and I look round the room and it's just the same except there's no piano and only one plate (Dawkins out tonight). Dear, I can't tell you what it's like at times – but that's all taboo, isn't it. I'm all right, dear, and still loving you so – Goodnight dear.

Thursday evening now and the post closes tomorrow, not today, as I said at the start of my letter, so I'll just add a tailpiece and finish as I want to enclose the insurance papers for the piano. It tells you where to go for survey and payment in the event of damage (by fresh water or breakage).

I don't think I have any fresh news for you, and I can't answer your letter as no mail has arrived from Australia this week.

I played my first game of tennis last night but it wasn't too good – the light was poor and I felt like the cow with the musket, and also the place was filthy, but anyway we're going to hose it down before playing again. Warren and I were talking today of advertising the first tournament for next Saturday week – we don't think we shall get enough entries, but I suppose we must give them the chance. Have you played any more or are all the tennis folk still at Manly?

The people going to Simonstown still haven't gone yet, but I believe they may leave about the first of the month, and no, the Singapore people will not be allowed to have their wives with them – yet!

Yes, that was quite a good idea of sending those parcels home – I don't quite know how much they are rationed, but if they are short of those things they certainly will be appreciated, for as you say, our folk, mine especially, like their cup that cheers.

And now dear, I'm going to bring Chapter II to an end, and no doubt, directly I've posted it your letter will arrive – I hope so anyway. Goodbye dear George

P.S. About two letters ago, you said you were sending me some photos by sea mail – did you send them as I have not received them if you did. G.

Monday November 25th 1940
C/o S.E.E.D., H.M. Naval Yard, Hong Kong

Dear,
Hello again to you dear – it's Monday of another week, so once again I'm starting my letter to you. I haven't any startling news for you, and I haven't had a letter from you for ten days – and we pay air mail rates too. Perhaps this week I shall get two, and that will be twice as good.

I went over to tennis last Saturday afternoon; there were only five of us, so one dropped out every set. We had five sets each and although the weather was threatening all the time, it was well worth going over. Mr Field was one of the five, and directly I entered the court he greeted me with, "Are you all right, your wife wants to know." Apparently, you get my letters just about as regular as I get yours – I send once a week and haven't missed that any week.

I don't do a lot these days so I can't tell you about that – tennis early evening and then perhaps darts and crib with Dawkins or else pictures comprises most of our evenings. Owen and Peters are coming round again to us on Wednesday evening for another Hillwood Rd V Hankow Rd match – more excitement.

I had three letters from home this week, from your mum, mine and auntie – yours asked me to forward one to you as she had lost your address – it seems she sent it (your letter) to my mother for her to read without first taking the address and then never got it back. My mother says she returned it at once, but it never arrived – bit involved what.

Auntie in her letter said that Lily is trying for a divorce from my brother Eddie but didn't think she could get it – but Mum doesn't mention it, so I suppose I wasn't supposed to know. Other than that, I don't think there was any other personal news, but I'll forward them on after I answer them.

And now I'm going to pack up for tonight. Dawkins has just arrived and we have decided to go to a "Grand Concert" at St Andrews Hall.

It starts at nine and we have ¾ hour to get ready and have some supper – so cheerio, dear, I'll tell you about it later. Goodnight.

Tuesday

I have just had tea and Dawkins hasn't come home yet so I thought I would add a bit more. First of all, let me say the "Grand Concert" was putrid and we crept quietly away at half-time, so that was that.

Secondly, just as I was leaving the Office tonight, two of your letters arrived, dated the 11th and 14th, and that was certainly too bad you having to wait three weeks to hear from me. No wonder Mr Field enquired if I was all right on Saturday.

One bit of news I was glad to hear, and that was your intention to get a piano if you had to stay there any length of time – that relieved my mind considerably as I was still in doubt as to whether I had done the right thing in sending ours and you can guess I am eagerly awaiting your reactions to my letter containing that news.

I am glad you are booked up for Christmas Day and I hope you enjoy it dear, as it would be rotten on your own, that day. Another thing I am glad for is that you can speak of the boys as you do – you do make me want to see them, though. So Edward had a good Birthday and certainly seems to be doing well at school and David has passed for Randwick – congratulations, David, but you're not to ease off now, keep it up and you'll find yourself one up on the boys at home when we return.

Yes, I suppose there was great excitement over the latest "evacuation moves", but really, while I don't want to disappoint you the only thing they have got from the Government is the promise that the position will be reviewed later on. Still, that is something to know that it isn't necessarily for duration, and for the present we might hope for an improvement in the situation. Meanwhile dear, try and be cheerful cos in years to come you'll want a pleasant Australian stay to look back on.

And that I think will do for tonight's quota; I am now going to play darts with Dawkins, so once more, dear, I say goodnight to you.

Thursday night now, dear, and time for me to finish my letter as the post goes tomorrow night and I want to post first thing tomorrow to obviate delays by the censor. I played tennis again tonight. The weather was quite cool, in fact good tennis weather – if only it kept light longer. I wasn't busy at all today so this morning in the office I wrote to mum and your mother as there was a good sea mail, going via Vancouver, only to find tonight that the Government had commandeered the ship so that mail won't go I'm afraid.

One other bit of news – whilst writing this morning, the phone went, and it was Eve to invite me out for Xmas Day. So now I also am booked for that day. Well, that's all dear and as I want to enclose your mother's letter[25] I'd better finish. Cheerio then, all my love,
George

Monday December 2nd 1940
C/o S.E.E.D., H.M. Naval Yard, Hong Kong

My Dear,
Monday, and just five months ago that we chased you down the harbour in our motor boat, trying to see the "Empress" once more, before she was lost in the rain. You've travelled a long way since that day but you're still very near to me – I come home sometimes and think you're just out for a bit and that you'll be walking in presently – and yes, perhaps you will one of these days. I hope, though, there isn't another five months to wait.

Well dear, I haven't received this week's letter yet. It's a bit too early in the week but I believe a mail is due in tomorrow so you can bet I'm hoping – anyway, I'll tell you later this week.

---

25. Letter has not survived.

We had that first tennis tournament of ours on Saturday and it certainly seemed strange without the ladies, but it was quite all right and I think everyone had an enjoyable afternoon. It was a cool but bright day, just nice tennis weather and as you said in one of your letters, gents' doubles all afternoon. We suffered from lack of numbers of course. There were only ten entries altogether, so we arranged that each one had a different partner as well as different opponents. Everybody played six sets each and Warren and Ewart were the winners – Warren I think is improving fast and I shall have a job to beat him if I have to play him this year.

Yes, Mr Dawkins and I get along quite well together and the fact that we can stop in of an evening and play games, and like it, is very helpful. He goes to the Club playing bowls until dark nearly every night, so it's about 6.30 or later that he gets home, but I appreciate an hour to myself sometimes. By the way, his three years are up next September, but he has to put in today for his relief to be sent out to enable him to sail next July, so that means I've got to look out for yet another lodger – but that's a long way off yet; in fact Dawkins himself doubts very much as to whether he'll get away in July. He thinks it more likely about the spring of 1942. Anything might happen before then – we might be gone ourselves.

You asked how we get along for gear. Well, we just manage with what we have. I haven't bought a thing. He has his own bed in the boys' room and as regards table things, well we have enough for just us two. It's true we only have tablespoons for desert but that is the only thing we are short of. Kim is still the same, still has fleas, but we manage to keep them under control. He probably doesn't get so many walks as he used to, but there, it's a dog's life for all of us.

Well, so far on Monday evening, and then we had an early supper as D had worked late and had had no tea, and then after supper a game of darts. It's Thursday morning now – I left it till now as we heard there would be a mail in the morning; and so there was, but the only one I had was from your mother. I won't send it on to you as it only said that they were all well and was posted October 8th. What we want to know is if they are O.K. after this last turn out – but I shouldn't worry, dear, apparently it was all the centre of Southampton that suffered and that is a long way from their home in Spring Road, and so hope for the best. The High Street seems to have caught it badly, not a lot left now, and they'll have to build the Civic Centre again.

Well, I'm afraid this is rather a short letter this time, but I will make up for it next time. The thought has just struck me that if the mail should be delayed again, this might be your Xmas letter, so dear I'll wish you a Happy Xmas just in case and mind you try to think it a happy one. (You know, mind over matter.) Well, that's all then, dear, so Goodbye again. George

Friday December 13th 1940
C/o S.E.E.D., H.M. Naval Yard, Hong Kong

My Dear,
Yes, this is a letter really in haste and a tale of woe too – all our bad luck happens on Friday 13th, doesn't it, David?[26] But let me explain.

Last week I had no letter from you, so Monday I started mine and then left it, hoping to be able to answer the two letters that I expected. Well, the mail had to be posted 10.30 on Thursday morning, but early morning we heard that Australian mail was in, so I decided to miss my mail, answer your letters and then catch an air mail via Rangoon that goes today. Well, I waited all day and had almost given up hope when we heard the mail was in, and we duly collected letters at about 5.15 and, yes, I had two of 'em. So home I went and finished my letter and, tho' I says it myself, it was a nice letter for Xmas, as you should get it in time going Rangoon way, and I enclosed two Australian pounds for Xmas for you and the boys. And then I gave it to Dawkins to post as of course he goes to work later than me and could post it early morning.

Unfortunately, we had burglars during the night and Dawkins lost his jacket and of course his letter and mine. I don't think there was anything else of value in his coat, so apparently, he lost a coat and I lost

---

26. A joke, referring to David having been born on Friday 13th (July).

£2. I didn't know until a little while ago when Dawkins phoned me, so here I am writing in a scramble to get done in time. If I can I'll also get two more pounds, but if not you'll have to take the wish for the deed. You can either buy presents, £1 for you and 10/- for the boys each, or else you can use it for spending money for the 6 ½ weeks holiday.

Well, I'm going home to kick our Kim at tiffin time as he was asleep in the armchair and then started barking after the bloke had gone; it seems as if thy Kim Bearman now sleeps just as sound as the rest of the "B" family. Dawkins says he saw the bloke, and said, "All right, Amah?" to him and then a few seconds later the dog barked. I was out on the verandah in seconds but there was nobody there then. Ah well, it could have been worse, but I was annoyed at losing the letter – but enough of that and I will tell you of any developments (if any) later.

Well, I wrote my letter spread over the week and there wasn't any important news – just a few items of interest and gossip. Pamela and Vic aren't leaving and are still here. In fact, I told them you were writing to them, but they haven't heard yet. I haven't been up there for a few weeks as they have had another fellow with them – the Indian representative of Vic's firm, but he's gone now, and so the Smiths and I are going to dinner with them next Thursday and then on to St Andrews Hall as Pamela is in a sketch to be done there. I think the chow is only a way of making sure of getting an audience – I told them that anyway.

It was a treat getting two letters last night, also to hear that Edward is a boy with outstanding ability, although that's old stuff. We knew that, if it was just that he forgot it in Hong Kong – still it's nice to be told so again. David too seems to be getting on well. In fact, the thing that struck me about your letters was the fact that the boys are settling down so and that Australia as you say, is proving to be good for them both with regard to health and education.

I'm glad I did the right thing about the piano – I knew you would want it, but I wasn't sure if you could give it house room and also I didn't want to saddle you with it if you were going to be on the move again.

Of course, you'll have to sell it before you come back but don't worry about what it will fetch, just get what you can.

I am quite all right, dear – not doing a lot of things – I play tennis twice during the week as a rule and then again Saturday afternoons, but there still seems only a few interested. Wednesday, we had Owen and Peters round for darts and crib, etc. Not exactly exciting, but I like games and it passes the evening pleasantly. We have started our training again as soldiers and I've got one amusing story over that about Mr Tubbs, but I'll spin that next week.

And that, dear, is about all I've got time for, except of course to wish you All the best for Xmas, and that we are united again fairly early in the New Year.

Goodbye then dear, and my love to you all.
George

Dear Edward.
That was a very nice letter you wrote to me – complete with funny story too so you can guess I was quite bucked to get it. If it wasn't for an occasional letter from you two, I should forget I had two nips.

And now, how about those requests of yours – first of all I'm afraid I can't send coins as it's not allowed, but if ever I send another box I'll enclose some then – by the way, you know there are only three don't you – a one, a five and a ten. Bus tickets are easy of course, but stamps, what sort do you want? For swaps? And will it do if I put different sorts on mum's letters? Next time you write, tell me how the collection is going on and did you get any in Manila?

So you like the sand on Bondi Beach, but if you dig too deep a hole you'll meet one of those other holes you left on Southsea Beach in Portsmouth. But I did hear that if you dig a hole about two feet deep and put your ear on the bottom you can hear the bombs going off in England – anyway, you try and let me know.

Kim is all right, and his fleas are O.K. too, but what a dog to let a burglar walk past him.

Well Cheerio, Edward and love from
Dad

Monday December 16th 1940
C/o S.E.E.D., H.M. Naval Yard, Hong Kong

Dear,
As I told you in my last letter, the via Rangoon one, I would write an intermediate one so that you wouldn't be without one for a whole week, well this is it, only, once more "the nicely laid plans of mice and men" etc, as you see the mail that was advertised to leave tomorrow has been cancelled and now there isn't one until Friday. That, I'm afraid, will mean you going without for one week, unless, yes perhaps I will send another one via Rangoon, anyhow I'll see how it works out. Anyway, I can now answer your letters of November 20th and 27th more fully – I received them December 12th.

Yes, I suppose at least on washdays you have a fairly full day and the clock was always your enemy wasn't it? But it will all help the time to slip by, and also it will prevent you from becoming rusty on those housewifely duties. I bet some of the folk down there have found it hard work, although "that" sort usually manage to evade work wherever they are.

I've just reread those letters of yours, and once again it struck me how well the boys seem to be settling down and as I said (I think) in my Rangoon letter, a few more months would do them a world of good – on the other hand, of course, I think a father's hand is essential with boys, so you had better come back.

Before I go on, let me say that I'm writing under a difficulty; I find it difficult to remember what news I put in the letter that was lost and in the hurried one I wrote on Friday morning, so if I repeat myself at all you must forgive me. I was wild about that letter – I spent a long time on it Thursday evening because I thought you would get it for Christmas; put the Australian notes in and gave it to Mr Dawkins already for posting bright and early in the morning – and then that had to happen, with Kim there too.

It appears that Dawkins was awake and saw a head come round the screen (the screen that was in the hall now screens his bed from the drawing room) and thinking it was Amah, said, "What belong, Amah?"; and he says that three seconds later the dog barked. Of course, he was out of bed quick enough then, but I beat him to it – I think I was on the verandah within a couple of seconds of the dog barking but there was no one there then. The dog had been fast asleep in one of the armchairs and I expect that was the trouble, it's a bit too comfortable there and he goes too sound asleep. I should think that the burglar made off when Dawkins spoke and made a noise on the verandah, probably going up those spikes and it was then that the dog woke up and chased out on to the verandah. I ridiculed Dawkins when he said he had seen the burglar – I didn't think it possible with Kim there and thought he must have dreamt it and it wasn't until 9.30 the next morning that he phoned me to say that he had lost his jacket and my letter. Well, that's over now and I was able to replace the notes and get them off in time. So I hope you got them all right.

And now, Miss Payne,[27] let me say that I was deeply grieved and shocked with regard to your suggestions about drinking – horrible thought, taking you into the Peninsula.[28] In some other letter, you speak of smoking too. Ah me, I'm afraid it's not only husbands that are going to the dogs.

Well, Hilda, I believe in my last letter I said I had a humorous story to tell you about Mr Tubbs in connection with our training which I think I said we had started again. You know that at the completion of the afternoon's work there is a general stampede for the canteen for a drink before the boat leaves. Well, last Monday we had some training,

27. Hilda's maiden name.
28. The Peninsula Hotel, Kowloon.

interval, lecture (held in the canteen) and then more training. Now imagine that interval and everybody standing about smoking and then the instructor said, "Everybody carry on smoking and make your way to the canteen," and Tubbs replies, "No thanks, I'd rather sit out here in the sunshine." Instructor then laughs and calls out, "Lecture in canteen," and Tubbs then sheepishly gets a move on. I don't know if that will be as funny to you as to me, but it was a big joke here and was all over the Yard the next day.

Well dear, I had quite an energetic weekend this week – tennis Friday evening and Saturday afternoon on our courts, Sunday morning on the army grass courts which was very enjoyable and then again tonight in the Yard. Oh, and Saturday night we went to the Alhambra and saw a really great picture, "Pride and Prejudice" – acting is very good indeed and the spoken English is beautiful. Have you been to the pictures lately – what are they like down there?

Tuesday morning now, and today's mail is going after all, so everything will be O.K.; so I must finish this morning and post at midday.

Well my dear, I suppose your hopes of returning, in the near future, have been considerably revived with all the yarns and rumours floating about – we hear them this end too but actually there is no news at all except the promise to reconsider the situation in the future. Personally, I think that America and Britain are acting together in the East and the evacuation of both countries' nationals is meant to be a gesture that appeasement is over, so that while America is still evacuating their womenfolk I don't see how we can bring ours back. Yes, I know I was always, shall I say cautious, but that I think is better than senseless optimism. If the position is the same in say, three or four months' time, then I have hopes – but there, I'm like the fish in the Atlantic Ocean – small meat, and might be altogether too pessimistic, so hope on dear.

And that dear, is how I'm going to close. A New Year and new Hopes that at least we'll celebrate your birthday together on May 19th. All my best wishes to the boys for the New Year and my love to you dear.
Goodbye
George

P.S. The Egyptian news was good this week, wasn't it?[29] Just the bit of bucking up we needed.
Cheerio
George

Monday December 23rd 1940
C/o S.E.E.D., H.M. Naval Yard, Hong Kong

My Dear,
How familiar those two words have become to me. I greet them as old friends as each week I see them standing up at the head of my letter. That familiarity though is not just one of sight, of recognising a phrase; but a thought, a prayer and of knowing just how true it is. Those are the two words that would be found engraven upon my heart, for I whisper them in all sorts of places, under all sorts of conditions, when I'm miserable and when I'm – well not so miserable and how I mean them, my dear.

And I suppose you'll read that far and jump to the conclusion that I miss you again, and, Yes, Ah me, you're right. I suppose it's a combination of circumstances of which Christmas is one, a big one too, but not the only one. Last week I wrote to you giving my reasons as to why I thought you would not come back yet, and airily spoke of insane optimism; and then the answer came back from England that the husbands' petition[30] had been turned down and turned down hard too, and although it said what I thought it would say, it pushed me down too I think.

---

29. Egypt gained independence from Britain in 1922, but in 1940, because of its strategic importance and to guard the Suez Canal, the British military was in the country in force. In September 1940, the Italians attacked Egypt from their colony Libya, reaching and taking the Egyptian port Sidi Barrani. On December 9th 1940, the British launched a counter-offensive, re-taking Sidi Barrani, and having taken prisoner by December 12th, 38,000 Italians.
30. The husbands left behind in Hong Kong had formed a relatives' evacuation committee shortly after the evacuation took place, with its aim to secure the evacuees' return. This petition had demanded their immediate return and included a formal complaint about the many women who had dodged the order. The petition had also argued that the evacuation was racial as only British women and children had been selected. Ironically, there was much bitterness in Hong Kong, particularly within the Portuguese, Chinese and Indian communities, among women who felt slighted at not having been deemed worthy of evacuation.

Friday was a bad day, and then in the evening I went shopping. I wanted to get two presents, for Eve and Pamela. I thought I had better after the number of times I've been to their places, so I wandered around and of course saw nothing suitable and well – you know how happy I get shopping under better circumstances – so that ended with my returning home empty-handed and ready to commit a couple of murders, and I'm afraid that was how I felt all Saturday. What creatures of mood we are and what a delightful companion I would have been to anybody on Saturday. Well, Sunday morning I went out, determined to get the "present" job off my chest, and bought two things – one I like still and one I don't, but they're bought anyway. I decided on that crystal glassware and bought a cream jug, which really is nice ($13) and a bowl with lid ($9) that I was told could be used for butter or powder, which isn't so nice but is not bad. I would really like the jug to go to do Pamela but in view of the fact that I am at Eve's Xmas Day it's going there.

But Hilda, I've only told you what I bought, not the things I thought or the number of times that I whispered those two old familiar words. To see the shops all dressed up, and the people buying presents and the kids carrying parcels – but there I'll sum it all up and say I felt the spirit of Christmas but was not of it.

But, why do I write all this? I know you are having your bad moments too and my efforts should be directed towards cheering you up. But dear, just think that you're to blame for all this, for just being as you are and making me want you so.

But, enough of all that. From now on it's, "Away dull care", until after Xmas Day – tomorrow night, Xmas Eve, I'm going with a crowd over to Hong Kong to Japanese chow and so I'll tell you all about it later, and that Hilda is all for tonight, and so once more, I say Goodnight my dear.

"Happy Christmas," to you Hilda. I say that knowing you won't read it until 1941, but it's Christmas morning now and I'm just saying it to the "presence" of you that still lingers here in this home of ours. My dear, how I've loved you this week, but it is I know Xmas and its associations bringing back our togetherness, and when it's over I shall try to get back to the thought of you being away on a short holiday. It's not that I haven't things to do, to take my mind off it, but just that my mind won't be taken off – if I do anything good I think of you and want you there and if I'm bored I still want you there for company.

Ah, Well dear, what a miserable letter this is going to be, but it's no good starting again for I'd only write another like it, and in any case the post goes early tomorrow so I have to finish it today.

Yesterday morning I arrived at work to find a parcel awaiting me. You couldn't have timed it better, could you? And many thanks for the tie and pullover. Yes, I can do with a long sleeve one, we have had some quite cold spells and the tie, I like it. The photos enclosed were not too good, though. Hilda, in one I can see just about 1 inch of you, and in the other a lovely back view – that was at Manila wasn't it? The boys' picture wasn't so bad – quite good of Edward, but David is staring too much.

And then yesterday afternoon, just after I reached home Warren brings a letter up that had arrived in the Yard very late in the afternoon. And that had two more pictures of David with the Scouts and they were quite good. I thought that a very nice picture of David. I've now got hopes of him being a nice boy after all.

Well dear, Dawkins is waiting for me now – we're going to the K.B.G.C.[31] for Christmas Tiffin and then this afternoon he's going to Owen's for a bachelor party, they couldn't think of anything else to do, and I'm going across to the Smiths' – I shall dine tonight, two Xmas dinners in one day, what Oh! my tummy. Anyway, I'll tell you more in my next letter so Goodbye dear. I'm now going to try to forget you (if I can), but you wait to next Xmas.
Goodbye
George

---

31. Kowloon Bowling Green Club, an old colonial club in Hong Kong.

9.11.40
83 College Road, Isleworth, Middlesex[32]

Dear George
This letter is my Xmas present to you this year. As I can't send you a present, I'll have 5/- worth of air mail, I don't know if this means you get it any more certainly or not. I did send one about a month ago. I wonder if you got that one. A letter arrived from you a week ago to Mum, and still you seem to have had no letters from us. I don't know where they all go to, as I have written several and Mum has also written, however your letter was dated September so maybe you have got some by now.

A letter arrived this morning from Hilda. She seems to be settling down nicely now. I won't say happily, as of course nobody can be happy under the circumstances. Sometimes I think mentally it is worse for you both to be separated as you are than for us, Sid and me, facing the bombs together. That looks a bit like heroics written down, but one does feel better together. I find that on 'home guard' nights, of which tonight is one, I simply loathe it. I have a friend up to sleep with me, and we are already ensconced in the air raid shelter, hence the pencil. I brought a fountain pen with me, but I was a bit delayed in coming out, and then a Nazi plane appeared and the guns thundered out so I took to my heels and on the way in my haste I dropped it, and as it is past 'black out' I can't look for it 'til the morning, as they are very fussy over using torches nowadays.

Well, you ask for all the news in Mum's letter. I haven't got it here so I can't answer it properly, but I expect she may have already answered it. We went down to Upham to see her last weekend. It was lovely to take our clothes off and sleep in a real bed. We sleep in the shelter every night, as we have had a lot of bombs dropped in this district, and quite a lot of damage has been done. Practically every night they drop a few round about us, but of course we are not one of the worst districts by any means. I expect the people in the East End would think we have

---

32. Letter from George's sister, Winnie.

had nothing. I have not been up to London since the Blitz started, but people tell me it is pretty awful up there. I don't want to see the lovely buildings damaged and destroyed. It is bad enough to see the houses around here.

Our most exciting night so far was when we had about 60 incendiary bombs dropped on us. First of all we heard four HEs dropping and we lay on the floor of the shelter. They dropped very near and we thought we heard the blast immediately afterwards and the pap-pap-pap of the tiles coming off the roof as soon as the noise stopped. Sid poked his head out of the shelter and then he jumped about like mad, calling out 'it's fine', and so I looked out and sure enough it looked as if our house was all right. So I got out as well, and then I saw that whichever way I looked fires were springing up. Sid was nowhere to be seen and so I ran indoors and looked all over the house to make sure the house really was all right – and it was – the flames were from a bomb that fell just outside on the pavement. Everybody rushed out and most of the fire was extinguished within a few minutes with buckets of sand and soil, but a few bombs had fallen on roofs and had to be dealt with by the fire brigade. When the excitement had died down we remembered there was still a raid on and we popped back into our shelter and then I realised that we had not felt a bit frightened, and so if they only don't drop HEs on us, I think we can tackle the incendiaries.

Well George, so far thank God we are all safe still and by the papers it seems as though the tension has eased a bit in Hong Kong. We are sorry you are bored with no women to entertain you. It seems rather superfluous to wish you a happy Xmas, but anyhow, if we are still spared we shall be thinking of you and hoping you will have the happiest Xmas possible under the circumstances and we'll all look forward to the time when we'll all be together again. I hope it is not too far off. Cheerio
Your loving sister Winnie

19.11.40
Dear George,
I wrote the enclosed letter a week ago and did not send it, and I lost it, but have now found it again, but as the paper is so thin I think I could put in another page, I'll try anyhow.

It was home guard night again Sunday, and as we had a simply awful night Friday night, I thought I would pop down and see Mum, so I started out before it was light Sunday morning. The guns were going while we had breakfast, but the 'all clear' had sounded before I left. I got to Waterloo at 9.30, then the siren went again, but no one seemed to take cover, so I didn't. From the platform we could see the trail of white smoke from the German planes, but they were a long way off.

I got to Winchester at 11.25, had two hours to wait for the bus, but I spent the time looking round there. It is a pretty place and I enjoyed it. Mum was very pleased to see me and I was glad I went, but we could hear the guns there all night. The next morning, I was waiting for the bus at 7.30 (it was still moonlight) when a man came along and offered me a lift all the way to London. I was in the house at 9.30, as he had to go down the Great West Road and dropped me at the Osterley Hotel. What luck!!! And I still have my return ticket, so I gave him 2/6 for petrol.

Cheerio. The very best wishes for Xmas
Love, Winnie

Monday December 30th 1940
C/o S.E.E.D., H.M. Naval Yard, Hong Kong

Dear,
Monday evening again, and I'm starting a letter that will have been written half in the Old Year and half in the New. The mail goes on Thursday 2nd January, so actually this will be my first letter of 1941, and I only hope I haven't many to write to Australia during 1941.

Well, it's all over now, Xmas I mean, and I suppose it was as good (or bad), as could be expected – I'm not sure which of those two words is the right one. A Xmas of heartaches, of trying to forget and never succeeding – but there I want this to be a bit more cheerful than the last letter, so I'll get on with an account of my activities.

We really started our Xmas on Xmas Eve with that Japanese chow I told you we were going to. As you know, I wanted to go to a chow of that sort and I was quite looking forward to it and as it turned out it wasn't a bad evening at all – certainly interesting although the chow itself was disappointing. We met, twelve of us at the hotel between 7.30 and 8.00, and had a drink, Japanese beer down below and then chow was announced as being ready, so we all trooped upstairs into a proper Japanese room. The floor was entirely covered with what might be matting covered mattresses, and you must remove your shoes before entering. There was a long low table about 10 inches high one end of the room with mats placed around for sitting on. The Japs of course just sort of kneel but we sat and put our legs under the table, but however you sit it gets mighty cramped after a bit, especially for a bloke with a big tummy. We had seven geisha or sing-sing girls and these sat down amongst us and waited on us and showed us how to use the chopsticks and all this with not a word of English between them. The chow, well, a tiny basin of bits, all fried up together in front of you, although I think perhaps "fried" is the wrong word – braised, is that it? Anyway, it was very tasty and everything of real first class quality – bits of chicken and pork, mushroom and hard-boiled egg and all sorts of veg (no spuds). After a bit I got my chopsticks to work and then soon emptied the bowl and was ready for the next course, which turned out to be another dish of the same – and that's all there was – just as many dishes as you liked, but all the same. Then of course, more beer and smokes while the geisha girls entertained us, singing and dancing, all national dances of course and very interesting indeed. These girls are the real thing you know, and quite respectable – no messing about with them – plenty of the other sort down below, but these appeared to be educated, a different class altogether. Dressed in kimonos of various colours with the lump (?) in the small of the back, but the chief thing was their hair – it must have taken hours to do. It was piled up high in various shapes and kept in place with huge combs. It looked more like something they were wearing, and yet they could move and dance without it even getting ruffled. At least four of them had real charm and that mind you, without being able to speak a word to us. On the whole quite a "banzai" evening – just airing one of the two Japanese words I remember, that one means good – the other one is yam-sing meaning "bottoms up" (glass ones of course, not the other sort).

And then Xmas Day – a lazy morning – bath and finished your letter and then I was Dawkins' guest at the K.B.G.C. for tiffin. About 40 people sat down to the usual Xmas fare of turkey and Xmas pudding and as you know it's a nice club and I think it was a really good idea us going up there. And in the afternoon, Dawkins, Owen, Peters, two others and me made a rink up for bowls – my first game ever. I didn't do too badly, either, once I got the hang of it and it passed the afternoon nicely and then of course straight from there, across to Hong Kong to the Smiths, about 6 o'clock. I had another real Xmas dinner, and was I blown out – in fact I was so full up that I couldn't do justice to the drinks during the rest of the time. We listened to the King's speech and then had a bit of a sing-song with Eve on a harmonium that has now replaced that terrible piano – I don't know which was worse, the harmonium or the piano – a rotten sing-song anyway, and then some card games and a few card tricks and it was then three-ish so we made our departure. I had to cross the harbour in a wallah-wallah[33] and arrived home about 3.45 – not too bad I suppose, but it never got going somehow.

Well my dear, the above is from the old year, a thing of the past, for now it's Wednesday evening, January 1st and the mail goes out tomorrow. I'm glad the old year is finished. It wasn't too good a one for us, was it? Firstly we made mistakes and it took an evacuation to prove to us how futile such things are and secondly, half a year without you – but that's all behind and I'm hoping for better things from '41. "Happy New year" to you all and hope for the best.

Your Christmas parcel to me couldn't have arrived better, could it?, for me to get it Xmas Eve. The pullover is just right and I have already

---

33. A small motorboat operating as a water taxi within the harbour.

worn it – it's just right for those chilly evenings indoors when it's not worth lighting a fire. Tie also O.K. Bought to wear with pullover, Eh! I only hope my box arrived in time for Xmas – I think it should as I hear from the others that some of the wives had been notified that boxes would be delivered by the shipping company and no doubt I shall hear in your next letter. They've forgotten my letter again this week, but perhaps there will be another mail in at the end of the week. Also, I hope you got the £2 and my rush letter in time for Xmas, and it's just struck me that you'll be going "up in the Hills", to the Blue Mountains, about the time you get this letter, so good luck dear and have a good time.

Speaking of the £2 I sent makes me think of burglaries of course, which reminds me of two things – first the insurance company has paid out Jim Dawkins' claim for loss through burglary and so he has stood half my loss so that wasn't so bad, was it? And secondly, we are not the only ones to have 'em – the Walkers thoroughly enjoyed the joke of my having visitors, but this week it was their turn. Last Sunday night it was and when they awoke in the morning, they found a drawer of the dressing table and their clothes had been taken into the drawing room and ransacked. It said in the paper that jewellery and money to the value of $480 were pinched but I believe there was very little in actual money and as they are insured they shouldn't have a great loss – I know Pamela lost her bangle and watch.

Ah, well, I think that is about all for this letter and so 1941's first letter comes to a close.
Goodbye then, Dear.
George

Hilda, David, Edward - December 1940.

Hilda, Edward, and friends, Palm Beach, NSW.
(Referenced in the letter of February 10th 1941)

January - March 1941

We had some more rain yesterday, so no tennis again,
bed in the afternoon and pictures in the evening and I'm going
to see some football this afternoon.

Monday January 6th 1941
C/o S.E.E.D., H.M. Naval Yard, Hong Kong

My Dear,
This is my second letter to you this week as I wrote one yesterday, only to find that they had unexpectedly brought the mail date forward one day, and so I missed the post. However, perhaps I'll send that via Rangoon and then you'll still get it before this one.[34] This of course is only being started tonight and will be added to later on in the week, although even then I expect I shall have to post just before I get yours – it usually works out that way.

Well dear, Christmas is a long way off again now. How did you spend yours, on the beach with the Tubbses as proposed? If you did I hope you bathed so that later on when we are home you'll be able to say (as we crouch round the fire and the temperature is below zero outside), "I once bathed on Xmas Day." Still, I do think that if you went out like that it did take some of the sting from our separation – yes, I can guess there were plenty of bad moments. I had them – just sentimental association, that's all. Damn it!

So, you found that distant branch of our family. Well! Well! Well! Won't Auntie Hillie be thrilled? So be sure and write in much detail to her – if you enclose a bit of the garden gate or a sample of their whatname paper, it would be in the best family tradition. And so he wanted to

---

34. Previous letter was not received.

know what the new "Mrs B" is like – you don't want me to answer that one do you, but apropos that remark, somebody met a woman here apparently upset at being cut by some of our people, but she said, "You wait, I've got to return to Australia in February and I'll tell the wives what the men are all doing." Unfortunately, she returns to Melbourne, otherwise you might have had a bit of "fun" – still she could and probably will cause a lot of trouble.

So, you have a few more pupils. Well, that's the style and it will keep you out of mischief, and when you have enough, you can make me an allotment.

Well dear, I'm just about stuck for news now – so I'll end now and hope for your letter later this week – and so Goodnight dear.

So far on Monday evening and now it's Thursday, but still no mail in – they're all adrift again this week. The mail I thought I had missed early this week did not go and now Thursday's usual mail goes on Friday and they have an additional one on Saturday, which after all can only catch (or miss) the same plane at Singapore. Anyway, I want to mail tomorrow and then perhaps the chances of missing will be less – it is possible though that this letter will arrive while you're on your vacation and in that case will be waiting for you. If that is so let me say, "Hullo! Nice to have you back and I hope you're all nice and brown and that you had a jolly good time."

Well, dear, I still haven't a lot to write about and of course no letter to answer, We've stayed in this week, Monday writing letters, Tuesday reading and games and then last night it was our turn to entertain Owen and Peters, so as you see nothing to write home about in that.

I did have a long telephone chat with Pamela today – the first for a long while and of course it ended up with an invitation to chow for next Monday.

Well, it seems a long time ago that we were in the Yard at Kowloon and they were handing out the twenty pounds – I've been paying that back at the rate of sixteen shillings a week and tomorrow is the last payment.

However, we still have to pay something toward Manila cost –
£2-13-0 I believe, so I suppose they will go on stopping that until the
end of the month. I've heard a lot of objections to paying anything at
all for Manila, but I think some of the women had a very rough time
and think they should be paid for having to stop there. Still, as far as we
were concerned, you were comfortable for three weeks, so I suppose we
can't grumble too much. What do you think? How, by the way, are your
finances? Still going strong? And do you have to draw on capital at all?

Everything is about the same here – still not very busy at work and of
course we still go for our training once a week, although I believe we
now only have twice more to go and this season's course is finished.
Actually, it's quite interesting and I rather like those afternoons.

Well, I've reached the stage when I start scratching about for something
to say, so I had best come to a finish. One of these days, I'll be able to
throw the pen away, knowing that the last letter has been written – may
that time come quick – as it is I had better keep it for next week, so that
once more I can let you know that I still love you and want you back
quickly.

Goodbye dear,
George

Dear David,
Many thanks for your letter containing all those greetings and good
wishes and between you and me, I rather like conciseness. It's only
these women that write as they talk that object.

Well, you don't seem to have done so bad at Christmas and I certainly
would have liked to have been there – but then I suppose you wouldn't
have had quite so good a time – that's the worse of dads, they will
interfere and spoil all the fun. In any case, I expect it was very noisy
with you and as it was, I had a lovely quiet time. But really, I am glad
you're having a "bosker" time in Australia but don't forget you mustn't
like it too much, as you'll be leaving one day and we don't want to leave
too many broken hearts behind, do we?

Hong Kong is exactly the same as when you left, but we now have a skating rink being built in Nathan Road, on the left-hand side just before you get to Austin Road, so when you come back – but we won't talk about that. Well David, that's all so Goodbye and love
Dad

Tuesday January 14th 1941
C/o S.E.E.D., H.M. Naval Yard, Hong Kong

Dear,
I'm starting my letter this week Tuesday evening, instead of the usual Monday, owing to having an evening out yesterday. I had one of my old evenings with Pamela and Vic – nobody else was there and it was very pleasant to just sit and chat. Do write to them – if you haven't already done so. I explained that judging from one of your recent letters you had apparently misunderstood me and thought they were going home. Anyway, Vic is expecting plenty of work in the future and seems as firmly entrenched in Hong Kong as ever. By the way, I don't go there every week as I did at one time – I suppose it's my fault as I know I'm quite welcome, but I don't like dropping in, as I know they do a fair bit of entertaining and also of course of having chow – the result anyway, is that now and again I get a phone call to say as I haven't been up lately, how about so-and-so night – still perhaps it's better that way.

Well dear, we had no mail at the weekend but this morning we heard it was in, and sure enough about mid-morning along came the boy with a big pile and, yes mine was there. I'm glad you had a – shall I say pleasant Xmas. At least you had plenty of children and I'm sure they must have kept you busy. By the way, what a crude way you have of putting things – did I get drunk? Of course not – but if I had done on one glass of port and lemon I would have been too ashamed to say so – or is there any catch? What was the size of the glass?

In your previous letter, you told me all about the arrival of the piano and then at the bottom of page 7 said you didn't have room to tell me how you opened the small box. Well, what's the tale? Also was the said box broken at all?, as a lot of stuff has been that's been sent down.

Music OK? And did the shoes fit? I got the man to make them a shade larger than the previous ones he had made, but of course it was a bit chancy – and the tablecloth I saw in the shop when I bought the other things. It's not a good one as you can probably see, but I thought it might be useful. But there, dear, I expect all these questions will have been answered before you get this.

Well, I still haven't played tennis. We've just had one of those miserable weekends – <u>very</u> dull with occasional drizzle and very cold, so I wasn't very tennis minded. As you know, Warren and I have been running the tennis – well I'm only the assistant. Anyway, we've had the entry list from the tournament up nearly a month and have now closed them. We persuaded quite a lot to enter and now have more entries than last year – 26 against last year's 22.

I had a letter yesterday from Auntie Hillie, but won't send it on to you until I have answered it. Everybody is safe so far – and now they have just had another bad raid. Oh, her date of writing was November 11th. No. "37" was still going strong so we can still hope for the best.

And now dear, supper has just arrived – prawns and do they smell good? And so I will say Goodnight to you again.

Well Dear, it's Thursday morning now and very early at that, as I have to finish your letter and go out and post it before eleven o'clock. I unexpectedly worked late last night – the first time for a long time, so your letter never got finished last night. And also, I must confess I am not an inspired letter writer at 7.30 a.m. (if ever), so I'm afraid it must go as it is. I didn't go out Wednesday evening, so have nothing to tell you since Tuesday evening.

Goodbye then, Dear, as I want to scribble a note to each of the boys.[35]
Goodbye
George

---

35. Letters have not survived.

Monday January 20th 1941
C/o S.E.E.D., H.M. Naval Yard, Hong Kong

Dear,
Monday evening once more, and again I make a start on your letter, this time though it's being written in the office as I'm stopping until 7.45 – only for six days and that's the first time for months. It's a pity we aren't more busy than we are, but that is in keeping with other things, that I should have to work late when you were here and then get off early every evening now.

Yes, it's January 20th and knowing your plans I've just been visualising your climbing all over the mountains today – no hardly that perhaps, but a good hike and you and Mrs Tubbs every time you stop to look at a fresh view, saying, "Wouldn't George and Frank like to be here". Well, you must tell me about it one day, and won't I be all ears to hear about your wanderings and my dear, all those other things I want to hear. Still, I do hope that at this minute you are all happy and that you are enjoying your holiday.

And that, of course, brings me to the news that you'll be losing Mrs. Tubbs as I suppose she will be going to South Africa. Perhaps you will have heard it all from her before you get this, but Mr. T has been appointed Acting E.E. at Durban and I understand will go as soon as possible. I haven't heard this from him, but the story is all over the yard today – it will mean temporary promotion, but of course the main thing is that he will have a HOME again. My dear, I can just imagine the joy in that household in Sydney – wouldn't it have been great if the news had been just a little bit different, but there, it's not to be apparently. This, to some extent, will be a blow to you, as I know you get on well together and of course you lose two pupils. But cheer up, dear, your turn will come one of these days. Actually, from our point of view here, us staying I mean, I think it's as well he is going. He is good technically and that is a help when we are busy, but now he is not much wanted in that respect and in other ways he can be, and is quite often, a bit of a nuisance. Of course, I know that saying, "He soon got another, far worse than the other", but I believe that only applies to husbands – but we shall see. He has lived entirely on his own since July and has become more of a misery than before but no doubt he will get us all drunk before he goes. Oh Yeah!

Two clerks are also going.

Well dear, we've just had another week of very doubtful weather – cold and a fair amount of rain. It poured all Saturday afternoon but that I didn't mind as I stayed on – but then yesterday (Sunday) I was in the team, tennis, to play the Royal Engineers and of course just about one o'clock it had to pour down and washed out all idea of tennis. Anyway, Dawkins and I went to see a football match at Boundary Street and there met Mr. Little and returned with him to his place for tea. And yes, we heard the record she made in Sydney and sent him. Of course, I was told what a pity it wasn't Mrs. Bearman playing, but I'm not so sure about that. What exquisite self-torture to put that on as a cure for one of those lonely spells – I think I might smash the set as well as the record. When you're in the proper mood, yes, it would be very nice, but you would certainly have to pick your time.

Well, the time is getting on now, dear, and I must see about locking up, so I'll say Good Monday to you. Goodnight Hilda.

Dear,
Wednesday evening and the mail goes in the morning, so I must finish tonight. I'm still staying on late, but this is the last night. Yesterday I had to go a-soldiering and it rained; I'm afraid I'm only a fair weather soldier and like the Chinese will want an umbrella in one hand during bad weather. I went home afterwards and changed and then had to return to the office and got wet again. Anyway, I soon returned home, so of course your letter didn't get finished. And now tonight I'm afraid I have a further handicap as I went to a farewell do this afternoon (with all the frills) and then to another tonight, so you can guess I'm not 100%. However, I want your letter to go and for you to know I'm all right – it's evenings like this when I want to go home and for you to just laugh at me – as it is I only feel more miserable and miss you more. Still, I guess you'll feel pretty miserable when you hear Mrs. Tubbs is going to join her husband, but cheer up, dear, it will certainly be our turn one of these days.

Well Hilda, I've had no letter this week and by the papers won't get one, but still I'm hoping. Anyway, it's no good hanging on any longer, so I'll say goodbye to you again. Goodbye then dear, all my love.
George.

Monday February 3rd 1941
C/o S.E.E.D., H.M. Naval Yard, Hong Kong

My Dear,
Another Monday, how they roll by! I think the length of this evacuation will be judged by the number of Mondays, for it's then as I start your letter each week that I think "another week gone by, another week wasted". Particularly, I think that applies to last week with two days' holiday on the Monday and Tuesday – oh, we manage to amuse ourselves but that's the rub, knowing that is all we are doing. This weekend wasn't too bad and passed quite pleasantly, thanks to tennis – Wednesday and Thursday I umpired tournament matches, Friday it rained but Saturday was fine and cold so I played all the afternoon and then the pictures, "Mice and Men", in the evening. Sunday, I had a lazy morning and then played tennis until dark at the K.B.G.C and had some really good games.

Well, that's all my doings for this week, but here's one bit of news. On Sunday morning Amah went out to buy the meat for dinner as usual, but missed asking me what sort for the first time. Upon her return she refused to let me see it and said, "Last year I buy missie flowers for Chinese New Year, this year I buy the dinner" – and so she did – chicken, green peas and the spuds, and even the fruit for 'afters' – not so bad was it?

Well dear, after receiving three letters from you last Tuesday, of course I'm not too hopeful this week – in any case I shall have to post this one first as mail goes on Wednesday this week and the incoming mail isn't due until Thursday, so I shall have to drop back to last week's three for discussion. First of all, let me point out the fact that apparently I have to be a bit miserable to write a really nice letter so look on the bright side of things always, and then when you get a rotten letter, think, 'He's not so bad this week,' – you know something like Sam backing against his club, Pompey, so that he was pleased whatever happened.

Sorry you were disappointed over the lodger, but I certainly agree that it would be better not to have Hong Kong people. There's one little group of three I know living together, (the first two wives of people in our office) because it's cheap, and apparently there is a good deal of bickering goes on and each writes to hubby about it – nothing serious but just a lot of cattiness, and of course each one talks (when the other isn't there). Financially I am still sound and will be so all the time somebody is living with me. I have been able to pay my way each week and with enough over to pay for such things as sending the piano, the things in the box and the Xmas presents here, and next pay day we pay the last of the Manila expenses so I shall be $12.80 in pocket each week after that – so if you want any let me know – I don't think I would change the travellers cheques unless they are a nuisance to look after.

You ask about the pullover – well it was quite a decent fit, the sleeves being just right – I've worn it quite a bit just lately as at times it's been fairly cold, especially evenings indoors as only once have we lit the fire so far and it's considerably warmer with the long sleeves.

Yes, dear, I guess it is pretty rotten to hear every now and again that yet another of the women is to join her husband, and I suppose Mrs. Tubbs going is the worst blow of the lot. Still never mind, dear, our turn will come.

I've heard from this end, and I guess you have, that Mrs. Taylor is to be allowed to return immediately to Hong Kong. I think it's cancer they found in Australia and there is not much hope, so they're letting her return to be with him – I'm afraid that won't be a very happy homecoming.

Well, I'm getting near the end of my news again, so I'm afraid this is not going to be one of those inspired letters. By the way, the boys will be going back to school again by the time you get this, so I hope they get down to it, for I want two more jolly good reports at the end of this term.

That's all then, dear, and as I have to post early this week I'll finish and get it off.

Goodbye then, dear, my love to you all.
George

Monday February 10th 1941
C/o S.E.E.D., H.M. Naval Yard, Hong Kong

My Dear,
I was more than pleased to get your letter – your holiday one of the 20th January last Friday; I knew the mail was in and had made up my mind that there wouldn't be one for me, as of course, I knew you were away. Anyway, returning to the office, prepared to be disappointed, I found it waiting on my desk for me, and so it had an even warmer welcome than usual.

Well, dear, I am glad your holiday has turned out so nice and more than glad that you were both in ignorance of Mrs. Tubbs' impending move, as I feel sure that would have spoilt your holiday. And you walked around the wishing tree, too, not knowing it was already granted for one of you, but there, why must I remind you of that again.

Your description certainly makes the country seem to be grand for a holiday and with the right company to enjoy it, for they all like walking, kids and all. That walk that you described in Katoomba, to Echo Point, down the Giant Stairway, and then up again by railway is I believe a very famous walk. Do you remember that Australian engineer that I got chummy with? Well, he had described that walk to me on one of our hikes, and I recognised it directly I started to read your description. I hope you enjoyed all the later walks as much as that first one and you certainly ought to arrive back in Sydney feeling better for the trip, although judging by the bathing picture you were OK before, especially Edward – what an infectious grin he has. By the way, you say your chin isn't really like that – I should think not, for not that you're getting so tough I should imagine you have developed the chin of a 'he-man'. Anyway, it was nice to see your faces again.

I trust you have had better weather than we have just lately, as it's been fairly cold with a good deal of rain – not heavy downpours, but a steady drizzle. Fine evenings I've been umpiring matches, but my own game on Friday was washed out, as was also our monthly tournament on Saturday.

Well dear, you mention in your letter about a year's extension and while I believe I have spoken of it in other letters – what do you think? At present I am in favour of stopping here, or at least of putting in for the extension, and it's fairly certain to be granted. If I go, I shall want you to go with me, and then what of the boys? Australia, or go home and be evacuated? Auntie says don't come home to Portsmouth and since then they have had it bad – the Guildhall and the greater part of Commercial Road has suffered badly and I don't suppose it will get better yet. The submarine campaign is also likely to get worse before getting better – still I don't know, perhaps all that would be better than staying here. What do you think?

Well Hilda, I started this Monday evening, added more on Tuesday evening, a little more in the office today, and must finish tonight. You see, we have rather been upside down this week, as that long promised "do up" of the flat by Wing On did really materialise this week. Monday, we arrived home to find everything in the dining room or on the verandah and Tuesday it was divided between the two bedrooms. Still, it's all over now and we are just beginning to find things again. The whole flat has been done, including bathroom, Amah's room and the kitchen and even the verandah, which is now cream by the way, no longer advertises popsicles and fudgicles. (I think there must have been children living in the flat a long time ago.)

I'm glad to hear you've got somebody for your spare room and I hope she was still there when you got back from Katoomba – if so and if you shouldn't get on with her, well, tell her to go. At least be comfortable.

We're entertaining Owen and Peters again tonight – no chow, we have ours early and they arrive about eight – a few drinks of course and darts and various card games and then they go just after eleven. And so, dear, as I want to bath before our chow, and in any case I think that's about all I have to say, I'll finish up now. Goodbye then, dear, I'm glad you enjoyed the trip – I might mention I told everybody you were on holiday in the mountains (swank), but that's nothing to that other trip you're going to enjoy one of these days.

Goodbye then, dear, all my love to you.
George

Tuesday February 18th 1941
C/o S.E.E.D., H.M. Naval Yard, Hong Kong

My Dear,
Tuesday evening, and I'm one day later than usual in making a start with my letter – I did get the pad and pen out last night only Dawkins wanted me to have a game of chess and reminded me that a mail was due in, in the morning, so that Tuesday evening I could answer it. However, the mail never arrived. It's due tomorrow now, and also I believe the outgoing mail will be a day late this week. That, by the way, is the one thing I have against Dawkins, he never "does anything", not even reading a book, and he says he doesn't sleep too well – the result is that he always wants to play something or go to the pictures, and then when I go to bed, sits down and writes his letters. Of course as the weather gets better, he plays bowls every night until dark, which I may say suits me better, as I like a little time to myself – still, as you see, he makes a fairly good companion and you know how I like games.

Yes, Tuesday evening. I've been to Stonecutters[36] this afternoon and it's rained hard ever since midday – we just had a lecture indoors today, but we got pretty wet from the knees downward coming home. We've had really bad weather here now for about a month – not every day, it's true, but most days, and when not raining it's very dull and cold, just about like our English weather. Our tennis has properly been washed out lately – I think games have been played only two nights in the last

---

36. A small island close to Kowloon and home to various British Army units.

ten and nobody troubles to arrange their matches now – we are just waiting for a bit of sun.

Before I leave the weather, how nice it sounded at the start of your last letter – you had just got back from Katoomba, and on the Sunday morning were sitting on the verandah writing to me, on a "glorious morning, sunny and warm", but there I suppose it's only a little while and I'll be complaining about it being sunny and warm.

Yes, I received your letter last Friday morning and I'm glad you had a good holiday and I hope you all feel better for it. By the way, the mail arrived in late Thursday evening and Mr. Todd (you know how I like him) got his letter then as he was working late – well I met him going home from pictures late that evening and he knew you had "been up in the mountains", but the way he said it, it sounded as though something catty had been said – also he told me, that Mrs. Tubbs had received a telegram halfway through the holiday and insisted on returning to Sydney at once and that you went with her – anyway, when I got your letter next morning, I found it altogether different.

Well dear, I suppose you have been a bit alarmed this week with all the reports of trouble coming in the Far East,[37] but don't take it too seriously yet; it looks a bit to me like another July 1st 1940 evacuation scare, and if America remains firm, and she seems to be, I think it's very doubtful whether Japan will start anything. In any case my dear, should there be any trouble here, keep a stout heart and try and not worry and pray that we will be united again very soon. Personally, as far as us husbands are concerned, I think boredom is more likely to be fatal than the Japs.

You spoke about having used some of your capital, so this week being remittance week and I having some money by me that I didn't want to

---

37. Japan had previously withdrawn from the China/Hong Kong border the troops which had sparked the 'evacuation crisis' in July 1940. On February 3rd 1941, Japanese troops again re-occupied the area in a further effort to cut off the British supply route between Hong Kong and the Chinese Nationalist government. Australian troops had been sent to reinforce Singapore and Malaya, and the British had mined Singapore waters, plus there was growing tension between the United States and Japan.

bank, I went down to the cashiers and remitted it to you. I don't think you'll get it until the end of the month or the beginning of next – $400 it is, or £25 sterling, which should work out to about £31 in Australian money, so let me know if you get it all right.

News of another one going home – this time to Rosyth in Scotland. I'm not sure that he was very keen on going home as I believe he has been having quite a good time – he says so, anyhow and also said quite openly that he wasn't the only one in his family.

And that, I think dear, will have to be the end for tonight as supper has just arrived. I haven't any further news anyway, but perhaps your letter will arrive this week in time for me to answer. Goodnight, then, my dear – I too want you, to talk to, to be with, to love, and yes, it does make you want to damn the Germans and the Japs too. Goodnight dear.

Well Hilda, it's Thursday evening now and time for me to finish your letter, but the mail did come in today, and much to my surprise there were two letters, January 31st and February 7th, waiting for me on my desk this morning. The last one was postmarked February 8th at Sydney and this is the 20th, so that wasn't too bad.

I'm glad you like your lodger and if she is nice it's far better, as you say, than having somebody from Hong Kong with you – still you haven't had her long enough to tell, so we'll wait a little while and see what you think then. Yes, I know just how catty they can be down there – I heard a bit today from Mrs. O that Mrs. T was going to move to a larger house now that she's an inspector's wife – my reply that even a chargeman's wife could afford more than one room didn't please. Anyhow, if they think like that, they must have wondered who's been keeping you in your big place.

Congrats. to David for starting at his new school and I was glad to hear he was above Graham, and I hope he keeps it up. You give me the impression when you speak of them and school that David is more keen than he used to be – is that the case or is it too soon after the holidays to tell yet? I suppose that meant more schoolbooks and the like for Randwick didn't it? Not that I begrudge that if there's the slightest chance of the school doing him good. The curriculum does sound like a Tec one and should do him good – how does his French stand? Was the bit he learnt in Hong Kong of any use?

Bit of bad luck the shoes were too small, and the maker said he made them larger than the others he made to allow for growing – I'm afraid they haven't my dainty feet and I can see I shall have to look out for my shoes the next time we are all together.

So even the thought struck you that our third farewell party might be a wild one. By the way, who said that wives should have farewell parties – that's not right you know! Anyway, I hope you behaved yourself.

I went to a fairly hilarious do last Saturday night – a fish and chip supper at the K.B.G.C. Of course it was, the supper part, a fairly posh affair, all laid out nicely and I should think that at least fifty were there. I was with Dawkins and had quite a good feed. After supper they had various people to do the entertaining, including some very good army people – one chap, a sergeant, was very good and sailed well into the wind – proper barrack room jokes some of 'em, but it was an all-stag party so it was all O.K. After the turns came the inevitable community singing and it was quite a change to have a good sing – Oh! Yes, there was plenty of beer, but we managed to walk home all right when it broke up about two o'clock. But it was quite a change from the pictures.

I've had a very quiet week since, in fact last night was the first time out – we went to the "Star" and it was a terrible picture and I nearly went to sleep.

Well dear, that's all again for this week as I've reached the goodbye stage. Amah has just brought supper in, boiled beef. It's the first time we've tried it and it's a bit tough. How long should you boil it by the way – a piece about 2 lbs, as we're going to try again?

That's all then, dear, so Goodbye again,
George

Tuesday February 25th 1941

C/o S.E.E.D., H.M. Naval Yard, Hong Kong

My Dear,

Tuesday again and my letter to you not even started. How quickly these Mondays and Tuesdays come round – do they to you? We seem to be living an unreal sort of live, just suspended animation, one of waiting, waiting – and then Mondays or Tuesdays when I start your letter I seem to come alive for a few minutes and I get that sinking feeling, when I think of the way the weeks are slipping by, of the amount of "our" time that is being wasted. Nearly eight months now, and our hopes of an early return are all gone, and I suppose hopes of a return at all aren't too bright. Ah me, I'm afraid I'm a bit of a pessimist tonight, but it does seem a long time sometimes.

Well, again, this week has been very quiet so I have very little "doings" to report. More very poor weather. In fact yesterday, Monday, has been the only passable day since I wrote last week. I just went to football over the weekend and pictures in the evening – I saw "Tom Brown's Schooldays" and I think the boys would like it, if it hasn't already been to Australia. I've stayed in all the other nights as starting tomorrow, we have a three-day blackout – won't that be nice? So I expect I shall go to the pictures three nights too. (I nearly started a moan again then.)

Last night I umpired a match early on and then came home and wrote to Winnie and short notes to the boys so that I can post tomorrow Wednesday February 26th, the first day of issue of Hong Kong's Centenary stamps. The envelope of this letter complete with its stamps, I want you to keep for me and tell the boys not to swap theirs either – I'll send some on future letters for swaps. Winnie's letter is of course for Sid to have the stamps, although as I said in her letter I expect stamp collecting must seem a very trivial thing to them these days.

Well dear, the Eastern crisis seems to have faded just a little bit this week and that I suppose is how it will go on. And by the way don't you go hoping for that transfer to Australia as that is most remote. Alf Pope has been waiting to hear all this time where he had to go, and now has just heard – Simonstown and will probably go with Bell. Some people have some luck, don't they? But why is it that all, or at least most of the people going to Simonstown are those that say they don't want to go, they're quite satisfied with Hong Kong? – yes, Alf Pope is another.

Well dear, I'm afraid this isn't going to be a very interesting letter – it started off all wrong and now I've run out of subject matter (that's good) and of course, to make matters worse, I have to finish tonight as the blackout the next three evenings will make it impossible to write letters. Anyway, I'll write a nice gossipy one next week, especially as I haven't told you the yarn about Mr. Tubbs yet – only I've been waiting until I thought missie would have left Sydney. Dawkins and I, by the way, rarely refer to our wives, although I suppose she must speak of you in her letters – just occasionally he might say, "The wife mentions that yours called on such and such a day," and I'll reply, "Yes, so mine tells me," and there it ends.

We have a new makee learnee[38] now – a girl of nineteen. She seems a fairly bright girl but green of course and not a word of English. She's not bad looking, either, and Jim and I are going to toss up for her.

Well dear, I'm only scratching about now so I'm going to finish up now. Hope everything is well with you and the boys and dear I too am just living for that yarn together that you talk about – it is the absence of those things that leaves such a gap in our lives, but who knows, it may be just around the corner. So, goodbye dear, and keep cheerful, and don't let my miserable letter get you down.
Cheerio, George

Sunday March 2nd 1941
C/o S.E.E.D., H.M. Naval Yard, Hong Kong

My Dear.
Sunday morning, and Dawkins is at the club and I have a few minutes to spare before tiffin (lamb today) so here I am making a start with

---

38. As help for Amah.

your letter. I've just returned from the hairdressers and compradore's so I'm all smart again and no debts, except of course the rent, gas, and electric light. We had some more rain yesterday, so no tennis again, bed in the afternoon and pictures in the evening and I'm going to see some football this afternoon.

Well dear, I got your very miserable letter of the 14th February and I'm afraid I haven't any news that will cheer you up. Everything remains the same, so all that we have is still just hope. Yes, I know those moods well enough, everything seems to be hopeless, but try and keep your thoughts off it and like the song, "Live just live for today" – yes, I know that's useless advice too, but cheer up dear. You say people down there are getting the wind up now, but don't you go doing that, as that would just about make it unbearable for you. No, just cheer up and hope for the best.

Well dear, I said I would tell you a yarn about Tubbsy – the truth is that we weren't very friendly for many weeks. In fact he never spoke to me for three, but he did come round before he went away and even gave me a tin of 50 fags for Xmas. You know each night we take it in turn to be responsible for locking our office – that means windows closed, lights switched off, water off, etc, door locked, keys hung up at the gate and then you sign a "Fire Book" to say everything is safe. Well, I left the lights switched on one Saturday midday, my first offence in two years – and remember this is a thing that happens in some office or other at least twice a week. Well Tubbsy rings me up to ask me if I had left them on as the police had reported it and of course I replied that he would have to accept the police version as if I knew I had left them on I wouldn't have done so. Then two days later he informed me that "my punishment was being considered," to which I replied, "That's very nice," and up to that point that's the whole of the conversation.

Now, there's a paragraph under "punishments" which says, "All lights must be extinguished or the offender can be deducted one day's pay," so Tubbsy goes to the Cashier and asks could I be deducted this day's pay and Cash says, yes, he thought so, but it had never been done in Hong Kong before. Tubbsy goes away and returns to ask, could I be deducted ½ day's pay as the Chief thought a day's pay too much – but the Cashier said, "No, it would have to be a day or nothing."

Well, after another conference they decide to let me off, and it wasn't until I was let off that I decided I wanted to say something – so down to Tubbsy I go. It lasted one hour and ten minutes and opened by my asking whether they were crazy or just childish and you can guess it waxed rather strong after that. At one point he said I wasn't very grateful for him getting me off and I agreed I wasn't – he said he did his best for me and when I asked him how many times I had been charged with any offence he didn't know – so I pointed out it was my first in two years, and he hadn't troubled to enquire and that was doing his best? And then after all that we argued on the legal aspect, and on further examination of the punishment clause he agreed with me that the lights extinguished part referred to naked flames such as gas or candles and our interview petered out then, but as I said, he never spoke to me for three weeks.

The above story is a bit involved and of course it's my point of view, but certainly somebody was childish over the affair and I think it was Tubbsy. I haven't told you before as you were so friendly with Mrs. T and if she hasn't gone, don't give it away – I don't suppose he has told her in any case, and whether any of the others mentioned it in their letters of course I don't know.

Well dear, the weather still hasn't improved very much, but I don't think we've had quite so much rain. But when it's not raining it's very dull or cold. I played at last in the tennis tournament, in fact twice last week – Thursday Mr. Field in the championship and Friday in the handicap, and of course those nights would be warm but very damp and dark. I beat Mr. Field 6-2, 6-3, but it wasn't a very good game – but there, we don't get enough tennis these days to get very good. On Friday I won 6-3, 6-0, but meet Warren in the next round of the handicap and he is a much improved player.

Last week I sent your letters via Rangoon, so I hope you got them safely and have saved my envelope for me – you ought to have seen the scramble for stamps last Wednesday – both Post Offices were packed out all day so we sent the boy to queue for ours.

Well my dear, that's all for now, but I'm going to finish tomorrow night and mail Tuesday so goodbye until tomorrow.

Monday evening now dear, and having read over my "story" I'm not sure that I ought to send it – but don't think I'm in "bad" at all – I'm not and everything goes along just as it always has. That was just one of those things that I've wanted to come home and yarn about and generally let off steam, but we'll save it all up for when this bl---y war is over.

And now the rest of my news, which is from home. I've had two letters, one from your mother, which being only one page I may be able to get in with this one, and one from Auntie, which I want to answer before forwarding on to you. Ena's husband, Will, at Bexhill has been killed by a bomb which fell on his shop – they had been sleeping at the old peoples' place and he had gone on to the shop to get early morning papers out and Ena was to follow. They haven't any air raid siren at Bexhill and the first they knew of the raid was the bomb; but it seems strange that with all the relations we have in such targets like London, Pompey and Southampton, that he should be the first to be killed, in a little out of the way place like that.

Your mother had all the shop windows[39] broken, but nobody was hurt and no news as to how it happened – that was in Auntie's letter, but your mother says she hasn't any news.

Well dear, that's all. I've just had to rewrite the whole of this page as my letter was much overweight – that's this new pad, and now they have brought mailing time forward to 9am and it's now 8am on Tuesday. Try to keep cheerful dear and it will make the time seem shorter. All my love to you Hilda and don't forget that you always have that.

Goodbye
George.

---

39. Hilda's mother had a tobacconist's and sweetshop.

P.S. <u>To the boys</u>. After being on sale for five days all the 4 cent stamps are sold out. There are supposed to be some more coming out from England, but you never know, they might not arrive, so don't swap any <u>4 cent</u>.
Cheerio, Dad.

I'm afraid this is a bit heavy so I cut the bit at the bottom off.

Friday March 7th 1941
C/o S.E.E.D., H.M. Naval Yard, Hong Kong

Dear,
This isn't really a letter. I posted on Tuesday, but having answered Auntie's letter I thought I would post it on to you, with her news about Ena.[40] I also wrote to your mother this week just to reassure her that we are all right and caught one of the San Francisco mails last Wednesday – it's much quicker that way. She seems to have been unlucky with regard to letters, as I have written several and I suppose you have – she said she had been writing every week to your Manly address. Have you been getting them? By the way, when was it you sent the parcels home? None of them appears to have got them yet, certainly your mother hadn't by December 13th.

Well dear, I can only give you this page, but I haven't any news anyway – Mr. Haywood is going to Trincomalee is the latest movement. She can join him there I think but I don't think the place is too good, or doesn't that matter? Pope and Bell left Hong Kong yesterday.

Horrid damp warm weather today, everything wet through. Wish I was in Sydney and how I love you my dear.
Goodbye
George

---

40. Letter has not survived.

Monday March 10th 1941
C/o S.E.E.D., H.M. Naval Yard, Hong Kong

Dear,
Monday evening once more, and this time it's after supper as I stayed on to 7.45 for a rush job – I'm going to interrupt my letter writing presently for a bath, before the water is turned off and then I want to finish as there is a mail going tomorrow. This rush job, by the way, was responsible for my missing a post on Saturday – I posted my (or rather your) letter last Tuesday and then Friday evening I answered Auntie's letter and then thought I would send it on to you, so I wrote a short note to put with it and took it to work with me Saturday morning to post on my way home. Unfortunately, the rush job cropped up and I worked late and didn't remember your letter until too late – anyway I posted yesterday, but I expect you'll get that one and this together. This job will probably last until Wednesday night, but then it's all grist to the mill and we don't get enough these days.

I have nothing much to report except the darn weather is still bad and as the rainy season appears to have set in, I don't suppose it will improve – yet. We had an hour's sunshine last Thursday at midday that kidded us to take our racquets in, but it was almost raining again by 5 o'clock. However, we played and had quite a good game, and that was the only tennis played last week. I was going to play in a football match on Sunday morning and they said, "rain or fine", but come Sunday morning and they decided they couldn't play in that rain. Other than the tennis, I stayed in all last week until Saturday, when we went to the Alhambra to see "Virginia" – not too bad, but not exceptional.

And now dear, a little surprise (I do love surprises) – Mr. Dawkins announced last week that he was sending a box down as she had been getting on to him to send the cream-maker and he wanted to send some gear to the boy, so I thought I could include something. I immediately thought of those shoes so I got "Siki" to come over and explained the others were too small and he said he could make them both a size larger and let me have them Saturday. Saturday came and no shoes, and the same on Sunday morning, so three times Amah phoned, the last time to tell him that if they didn't arrive that evening, I didn't want them. Anyhow they arrived, but I was disappointed, and I know David's won't fit him. Edward's look larger but David's are only about ½" longer than Edward's and I know there is more difference than that. Anyway, they're coming, so if they don't fit, that's another pair you'll have to keep for Edward, but get them to stand on a piece of paper and go round their feet with a pencil and that would be some guide to go by if any other opportunity occurs.

Well, that's two pairs of shoes and then there's some stockings – six pairs that I thought you might like – you have a birthday coming and if you're not back in Hong Kong that may have to be your present; of course if you come back, well, Hong Kong is yours. That's all I bought to send but there was still a little room in the box so I included a very nice full-sized sheet for your bed – it's quite new but might need a darn in one place. Then there's a writing pad for one of the boys, and that's all.

By the way, as regards other things, if you think by sending me sizes I could get anything made, I'll have a go – shirts for the boys, for instance. And possibly a costume for you, or do you think that's too risky? But I thought if you sent sizes and a picture of the style and some idea of the cloth it might be possible. Ah Me!!!

Well my dear, I found your letter of February 29th awaiting me when I returned to the office this morning and I'm glad the "fed up" mood has passed (for a while). So you have started tennis again too. Well that will do you good as you might get fat and lazy and I don't want that sort of wife to come back. Keep smiling my dear, even if it isn't May, and I'm afraid I'm not so optimistic as that.

So Mrs. Tubbs hasn't sailed yet, but where is she staying as I understand that Mesdames O and S have taken over her flat? Mrs. O has asked Mr to send the piano down as she wants girlie to start – with you, I believe – won't that be nice. Anyway, he's enquiring the price now, but perhaps that might frighten him yet.

Well Hilda, with your letter this morning came two others – from your mother and Winnie. They still complain of no letters from us and apparently nobody has received those parcels. Do you think it would be any good enquiring at the shop to see if they have heard anything? January 6th is Winnie's letter, and January 14th your mother's. Everybody is O.K. and Winnie's letter quite interesting and of course I'll send them on to you. Your mother said your father has forgotten all about his operation and is all right now.

Well dear, I'm writing on the back of this page as I still haven't got the weight of these new pages off yet and I want this to be the last. My eyes are nearly closing in any case – yes, I've had the bath and it's now 11.45 pm, so off to bed I go.
Goodbye dear
George

Wednesday March 19th 1941
C/o S.E.E.D., H.M. Naval Yard, Hong Kong

Dear,
I expect you've been cussing the postal people again, over the non-arrival of this letter earlier, but this time it's my fault as I missed the mail. There was one went out Tuesday (yesterday) morning, so of course it had to be written Monday evening, my usual letter night – however we were particularly busy that day, in fact I even had to go without tiffin and never arrived home until about a quarter to ten, so you can guess I didn't feel much like letter writing then. We are still fairly busy, but tonight I got home at 8.15 – I don't know how long this is going to last, but whatever it is it won't be too long for me as it very nicely solves that what shall I do problem. There is one thing though Hilda about this working late business – in spite of the long interval, every evening as the ferry nears the landing-stage I look to see if you and Kim are waiting for me – and you never are.

Ah me, how the evening goes. I got that far, then had a bath and supper and the news on the wireless (not in that order) and now the time is ten past ten, so once more I'm writing against time. By the way, speaking of supper reminds me that Amah managed to cook the pork all right this time – I had tried a piece of boiled pork before and boiled beef twice, but each time it's been as tough as old Harry. However, it was delicious today and was very nice cold for supper, so now I shall give the beef one more try as she should be able to get that tender if she can manage the other. She is still very good, mind. It's only me trying new dishes that she hasn't done for a long time that's the trouble.

The bad weather continued all last week again up to Sunday and then it changed and now we've had three perfect days. I haven't played any more tennis and I suppose must wait until the overtime finishes – the tournament at present looks like petering out – the bad weather almost killed off what little enthusiasm there was, but perhaps a spell of sunshine may revive it.

Yes, as you said in last week's letter, a year's extension is our solution. We can't volunteer to take the nips home as things are at present – if we're sent it's different. I saw some pictures last week of the old town after the big raid 10-11 January and it's terrible – I can't say just how it makes you feel to see pictures of places you know so well treated like this, but I tell you some of the fellows were coming in to see the pictures and then walking out without speaking. One picture shows the Guildhall with the tower afire – there are only four walls left now, and I believe that applies to all the buildings of any size in Commercial Road. There were pictures also of the mass burial – yes, a year's extension even if it has to be spent apart is much preferable to the worry of that. There's been another six-hour raid on the town since then, so I don't suppose there's a lot left now.

That's rather a gloomy paragraph, isn't it, dear? But I'm afraid the news of the bombing in the next few months is going to be gloomy. I only hope we can return it, but let's get away from that subject.

I met Stanley early this week and he tells me that Eve now has a new job. Apparently there was some trouble with the other job as he said, "They served her dirty," – however, I haven't heard details yet. I expect you'll be as surprised as I was, as I didn't think the A.R.P. could get along without that lady. I believe this is a secret at the moment as no one appears to know about the change of jobs – not even Owen and there's not much he doesn't know.

Well dear, my eyes are nearly closing now and that's about all my news, so I think I'll finish and go to bed. If I'm not working though I will try to get another letter off next mail (Monday next I believe). I still love you my dear, even if my letters are short. That's all then, dear, so goodnight and goodbye again.
George

Sunday March 23rd 1941
C/o S.E.E.D., H.M. Naval Yard, Hong Kong

My Dear,
Feeling a bit miserable tonight, and yet I don't know what to say to you; I seem just empty of words except those two, oft-repeated ones. I wouldn't be though, under difference circumstances – if only you were here to yarn with, it would be like heaven as you suggest. Like you, I feel very pessimistic as to when that yarn is going to take place, though; at present I can't see any future date that we can sort of hang on to and hope about. There, that's a nice start to a letter. If I go on like that all I'll do is make you miserable too. But wait, I have one small reason for being miserable tonight, so perhaps I would moan even if you were here.

I played in that several-times postponed football match this morning, and was it hot? One of those hot humid mornings with not a breath of air – and as you know, those Chinese nippers are very quick and make us "steam" in more ways than one. Actually, I think we had more of the game than they did except in just the goal scoring as twice they broke through and scored, all against the run of the play. When I left the field, about ten minutes from time, the score was 3-1 for the Chinese – yes, I say when I left the field, 'cos I unfortunately had my face banged by another bloke's head as we both went to head the ball. I had a rather nasty cut over the right eyebrow and left the field, not so much through the cut as – well, you don't know what you can pick up on Chinese fields, especially at Kowloon City.

One of the team ran me up to Kowloon Hospital in his car and they put one stitch in my eyebrow and an anti-tetanus injection in the buttock.

Anyway, at the moment I look some guy with the usual patch and crossed strips of plaster – I have to go next Thursday to have the stitch removed. I remember David saying his injection made his leg stiff – as is mine stiff tonight, especially in the groin and behind the knee. Anyway, there's no need for you to worry about that – I shouldn't have told you anything about it if there had been any cause to worry.

By the way, speaking of injections reminds me that we have already had this year's cholera injection – there's been quite an epidemic already, and in the cold weather too, so it might get bad as the weather hots up. Full of good news – ain't I?

Well dear, you've had my "rushed" letter of last week, and I know it wasn't too good a letter – my own fault partly. I should have written Sunday, but I never expected Monday's job to crop up and thought I was going to have my usual Monday evening letter writing. I'm making sure this week, although again I'm not expecting to work late tomorrow. Just two weeks the overtime lasted and there is the prospect of a little more sometime in the future.

Let me know how the shoes fitted and don't forget to send a plan of their feet and if there's anything else I can get let me know and supply sizes – shirts for the boys, even a costume for you if you think it could be arranged. Then I could get some things together, and send them on as opportunity offers.

I liked that bit in your letter (dated March 2nd) re the article that about 100 women are still in Hong Kong and are having the time of their lives. I should say the number is more near 1,000 than 100 and while no doubt the 'Peakites'[41] are having a good time, the rank and file like Pamela and Eve are fairly quiet – they don't get about anywhere near like they used to, and I know they have only been to one dance all the winter. Dawkins and I are going along to Pamela's next Thursday evening, providing of course she doesn't mind me with a lump of plaster over one eye, although it shouldn't be a very big piece by then.

---

41. Hong Kong's smart set, from Hong Kong Island's Victoria Peak - known locally as The Peak.

Well dear, your letter never reached me last week but there is a mail in today, so I'm hoping that there's a letter waiting for me in the morning. Anyway, I'm going to finish now and leave the rest of this page for tomorrow evening. Writing to you has lifted some of my miserableness, so I'll leave it at that. Goodnight my dear.

Monday evening now, Hilda, and I've just discovered that I left my pen in the office – hence the pencil. Well, my hope re the mail was justified and your letter (10th March) duly turned up, although I will admit they had their usual game – everybody had a letter but Owen and I, and upon enquiry Main Office said they were all out and then half an hour after they turn up.

The boys certainly seem to be "enjoying" their schools more now, judging by your description and I'm glad of that for it shows they are part of the school and will get on much better that way. Your little "views" of the nips are quite refreshing (this week it was of you round the dinner table, laughing at some story) and I can quite picture you all. Apropos what the masters call Hong Kong boys, remind the nips that if you want to insult an Australian, you want to tell him that his great-great-grandfather was a convict, sent out from England.

As regards the gossip you speak of, I think I have told you that two or three spoke about you being "in the mountains", and I could tell by their manner that "something" had been said in their letters. Whatever were they supposed to be warning Mrs. W against – what is it they think is dangerous in you? – you know sometimes I think that "O" would be highly delighted if he could write something about me to Sydney, but there, you know I don't like him, so perhaps that is only prejudice.

How unfortunate about your mother's cable, and she certainly seems to have been unlucky over letters too, although from what I can hear of it, the majority of letters sent home don't seem to be getting through – the parcels you sent also appear to have been lost. However, to go back to your mother's cable a minute, when I replied at Xmas I put "All Happy" etc, and you'll notice in one of the letters I forwarded on to you your mother wants to know did the "All Happy" mean only me or did it include Hilda and the boys as well? So you see, even if she hadn't had any letters, at least she should have known you were O.K. Write fairly often to all of them, as if your letter is lost when you do write, it makes such a hell of a time before they do hear from us.

Well dear, I don't think I have any local news to tell you, except that two more are going to Singapore sometime in the near future, but that's only Singapore and won't affect the ladies.

I went over to Kowloon Hospital this morning just to show them my cut, as he said if I could spare the time he would just like to see it was all right and as far as I was concerned it made a change from the Yard and didn't cost anything but the bus fares. Anyway, it's all O.K. and I have to go Thursday morning to have the stitch removed, so this time next week it will be all over – I hope it doesn't leave a scar, though, although that was the reason for the stitch. So I suppose it shouldn't, but will tell you next week how it's getting on.

Thanks for the cookery tip. I'll give the boiled beef one more go as it will make good cold dinners like you suggest.

Well my dear, that I think about brings me to the end of my letter – this is the first evening for a fortnight that I haven't worked and of course it's raining quite hard outside – and I had hoped to see some of the colony tennis tonight. Jim Dawkins has just told me that Cummings will hear in the morning that he has to volunteer for Singapore – notice the "volunteer".

That's all then, dear, so once more it's Goodbye again for another week. Cheerio then
George

Tuesday evening now, and I've just come in from the office at 8 o'clock. I've been carrying this letter with me all day but never had the chance to buy the stamps – anyway I have them now and will post at 6.30 AM tomorrow; the post doesn't close until 10.30. I haven't any more news though, except that you remember I told you Dawkins had put in for his relief so that he could leave here about June? Well, today he got a wire from his wife saying, "Cancel your request to go home and get Betty out to Australia", (Betty is the daughter left at home in Plymouth) – and he doesn't know what to do now. Mrs D. has apparently got the wind up, and you can't blame her after reading the news of the last raid on Plymouth. Fancy going home to that. On the other hand he's hoping that by asking for his relief he might get South Africa and they could all be together, but of course it's just a chance and once the appointment came out, it would be too late to cancel it then if it happened to be the wrong place.

No dear, I don't think I shall hesitate when they ask me if I wish to take on for another year. Cummings has agreed to go to Singapore, but only for the one year remaining of his contract as he insists on going home then – his family are still up near Liverpool somewhere and are O.K. at present.

And that I think is really all – I hope you can read it written on both sides, but this paper is very heavy, and I'll have to return to the old. Goodbye then dear, love to you all,
George

Sunday March 30th 1941
C/o S.E.E.D., H.M. Naval Yard, Hong Kong

Dear,
Sunday morning, and a dreary one at that, although it's not actually raining – yet; I've done all those things that go to make up a leisurely Sunday morning, you know, read the paper, had a shave, bathed and dressed, and now presently I shall have my usual short stroll round the block to pay the compradore's weekly bill, etc. In the meanwhile this half hour will go towards your letter, although while news is nil, it's nice just to yarn with you.

I haven't done very much this week, as I've been working late again – remember last Monday, I finished off your last week's letter, telling you that was the first evening off for a fortnight, and of course it had to rain that evening just when I was going to see a bit of the colony tennis.

Well, for the remainder of the week I worked on, up to Friday night, and of course there was no more rain after Monday. Anyway, I think we have another quiet spell now, so next week I may see some of the tennis. Thursday evening, though, I knocked off a bit earlier, at 7.15, and met Mr. Dawkins who had also been working late, and made a dash by taxi up to the Walkers. We had one of those quiet, pleasant evenings with them that makes a visit there so appreciated. We had boiled beef for chow, which was rather funny as that same day, after passing on your information to Amah we tried again and this time it was very successful, which was just as well under the present circumstances, and the way it panned out we had boiled beef for Thursday tiffin (at home), Thursday dinner (Walkers), Friday tiffin (cold, at home, and very nice too).

There was quite a bit of discussion about that article printed in Australian papers, telling of the enjoyment to be had in Hong Kong, and everybody here is quite indignant about it as it's quite untrue, or at least, grossly exaggerated.

Of course, I had to adorn their table with me patch of plaster over one eye, although that was the last evening that I kept it on. The stitch had been removed only that morning, so I kept the plaster over it until I left work on Friday evening and then threw it away. This morning there is just a line left, above the eyebrow, so I don't think there will be any suggestion of a scar.

Well dear, that's about all the news I have for you, except that we went to the Alhambra last night, "Strange Cargo" was the picture, but was nothing exceptional. Tonight there is a musical turnout in the Rose Room of the Peninsula; Gaston is one of the artists and I had a postcard from him asking my support for his first show as a professional singer – he didn't enclose the two bucks, though, which are about the cheapest seats I believe. The prices are out of all proportion to the abilities of the artists, so I haven't made up my mind yet whether to go or not. And now, dear, dinner is nearly ready – I may finish this tonight, but there is a mail out Monday and Tuesday this week so perhaps I might hang on and hope that your letter arrives tomorrow – anyway for now I'll say cheerio.

Monday evening now, dear, and time to finish up my letter ready for the mail tomorrow – today's mail did not go out as advertised so I haven't missed one by waiting but on the other hand I didn't gain, as the incoming mail is now due tomorrow, so no letter to answer. I wasn't working late tonight so I stayed for the tennis and saw one quite good match – not any of the nobs but still quite good.

Well Hilda, I haven't a lot of other news for you – other than Dawkins is <u>not</u> going to try to cancel his relief as his wife asked – for one thing he says it's very doubtful if he could now, providing of course that they intended to relieve him in the first place. No, he says he'll chance it now and hope that he gets South Africa, in which case he would get Betty out. After Plymouth's bad raid he wired home for news and got two replies, "All Safe", but one was sent from an unknown place and one from Croydon, so it looks as though they were bombed out. By the way, I saw a letter from a Pompey chap, to Mr. Dawkins written after Pompey's fire raid – he gave a good description of home life without gas or electricity during the three days following the raid – their only damage was windows blown out.

Well dear, I don't know what else to tell you – just nine months we've been letter writing to each other now, and still no date to look forward to, except that unknown one, the day on which the war ends. Still cheer up, we may get a surprise one of these days, just when we least expect it. I've just been listening to the news on the wireless, all about the sinking of those Italian ships in the Med.[42] – pity they weren't German as that would be a bigger step towards winning the war. Anyway, the news for the last week has certainly been good and I guess we can do with plenty of that.

And that is all, Hilda, for this week; I still cuss the ruddy war every time I come home and find it empty, for I guess I still love you.
Goodbye dear
George

---

42. On March 28th 1941, British warships destroyed a large part of the Italian fleet off the coast of southern Greece, the Battle of Cape Matapan.

Pensinsula Hotel, Kowloon.
(Often referenced in letters such as December 16ᵗʰ 1940)

Hilda wearing her 'hat with the feathers' and friend.
(Referenced in the letter of May 19ᵗʰ 1941)

April - June 1941

Before I leave you though, dear,
I must say how I like that "dicky" little hat of yours in the photo –
you know the one with the feathers.

Wednesday April 9th 1941
Hong Kong

Dear,

I'm sitting up in bed writing this – and yes, thoroughly miserable too. All the evening I've put off writing, knowing just how happy a letter it would be if I did write it, and now having gone to bed, I've succumbed right at the last – but it will only be a very short note tonight. The last letter I had from you was written March 9th and reached me two weeks ago last Monday. This week's mail was due in Monday and has been put off day by day and still hasn't arrived. Monday evening I worked late and then after supper decided I was certain to get one Tuesday, so would defer writing until then – Tuesday evening I came home early, put off my writing again and went to see a badminton championship match at the Kowloon Cricket Club. And now today, having decided to write, whether I received yours or not, I worked late again and as you can see, arrived home very sweet of temper.

I think the war news was the culminating factor tonight – everything going wrong in the Balkans[43] – once again we seem to have arrived too late; always defending where the Germans are concerned and never getting a blow back at them. I think the news tonight made our date, which was already very obscure in the dim future – fade right out of the picture. There, you can see how happy I am tonight – my dear, how I want you back with me! Goodnight dear.

---

43. On April 6th 1941, Germany launched invasions into Yugoslavia, and northern Greece.

Ah me, it's Thursday now – I worked late again tonight, have had supper, and now both Jim Dawkins and I are each end of the table writing to Australia. I've just read through last night's effort and I think it was just as well that I stopped when I did. I feel a bit better today, but then I received two letters from you today so perhaps that has something to do with it. One of them, posted March 16th, has taken three weeks and four days to reach me – WE are so proud of our air mail!

Sorry to hear of your upset with the old woman overhead, but don't forget if it wasn't in the agreement you have every right to play and sing. If you do move, take your time and select a place that suits you – it goes to show how wise we were over "37", isolated and insulated from everybody else.

So you hope to have a go at the organ, and I get the blame for your not having done so before; but I notice you get a long way away before you say that. However, it will keep you out of mischief, so have a go by all means. By the way, talking of mischief, I'd like to say that I haven't heard of any parties with Russian gals – I wish you'd send me the address. No dear, I think those stories are all exaggerated and apart from an occasional celebration everybody acts quite normal – those that were always a bit wild still are, and the steady ones are just the same, so don't believe any of those tales.

Cummings has gone to Singapore now and Foster has left his job to take his place in the Shop. The Yard, by the way, is not closing for Easter, but the Commodore has expressed the wish that all Europeans have 1 ½ day's leave, so we are taking it in turns. He thinks that owing to the fact that practically nobody has had any leave since the evacuation there might be an increase in sickness in the future if that state of affairs continued. I tossed with Owen to see who should have Easter weekend, and I won, so I'm on holiday now, having tomorrow (Friday) and Saturday morning off. I don't know what I shall do – Jim Dawkins also has Easter but will be playing bowls most of the time – still it will be a rest as I've had a fair bit of overtime lately.

How's the tennis going? Had any more games lately? We played a match last Sunday morning on Stonecutters in a gale of wind, and was it cold. Anyway I always do all right in those conditions, having plenty of control over the ball, and was on form – we won. This Sunday afternoon, weather permitting, we have a match on our courts, with the Royal Army Ordnance Corps, including tea and after two days rest should be full of energy.

"The Great Dictator", Charlie Chaplin's latest, is showing at the Star over Easter, and I think we will be going Saturday evening – I'll let you know if it's any good.

Those two snaps were very good – two good little groups, although as you suggest it makes you look a bit fatter. David doesn't appear to be any fatter, but I don't suppose he ever will be – he's a Bearman, all right; how is he keeping now, any more attacks? Also, in one of these letters you mention a picture of "Edward in the team", but it didn't arrive, so I suppose it was too heavy. Also dear, you don't mention whether you got the money I remitted – have you had it yet?

The Balkan news is bad again tonight and it looks as though we shall be right out of Greece by the time you read this, although we ought to have learnt enough by this time, to know how to stop the Jerries. It's about time we had another Eastern crisis too, but perhaps we're waiting for Matsuoka[44] to get back from Berlin. No, I certainly think you can wash out April as a travelling month, May too for that matter – I've reached that state of mind when I think it's hopeless to attempt to forecast any date, but keep on smiling dear, it's bound to come one day.

That's all dear, but I feel much better than last night, and I'm still O.K. What's up with you too dear, nerves? What, in nice quiet Australia? But take it easy, Hilda, we don't want any sickness. Just think of it dear – three days' leave and nowhere to go to. Goodbye dear, or I shall start cussing again. Cheerio, George.

P.S. Am off to bed now and my lay-in in the morning – coming?

---

44. Yōsuke Matsuoka, Japan's Minister of Foreign Affairs. On 27th September 1940, Germany, Italy and Japan had signed the Tripartite Pact, creating a military defence alliance between the three countries.

Wednesday April 16th 1941
Hong Kong

Dear,

Have this day received your letter of March 30th with the new address – I was certainly surprised, as it was only in your last letter that you first mentioned the probability of your moving. I hope the new place is all right anyhow, although you say you thought the old place might be cold during the winter and now you've gone to live on top of a hill. Also dear, you started off your letter by saying, "Once again the cabin trunks have been hauled out," and although you didn't add, "Blast it," it sounded as though you meant to. Now dear, you must cheer up and try to settle down and not worry about things as much – you'll only end up by being really ill if you don't. Again, you haven't mentioned whether you received the money I remitted – do let me know if you got it all right – I really wanted to know before today as today was the last day for remitting at the end of April – anyhow I decided it probably was all right so I have remitted another £20 (sterling), which should be about £24 Australian money. One snag occurred – I gave your old address, as your letter didn't reach me until late this afternoon – if I can change it I will but I'll let you know about that – and you let me know when you receive it.

Jim Dawkins' letter that he received today was dated April 2nd, three days after yours, and Mrs. Dawkins mentions that she has received notification that the box had arrived and that she was going with you, that day, to see it. I hope the shoes fitted somebody, but let me have the plan of their feet and perhaps I'll have better luck in the future if the opportunity occurs.

I had another letter today, beside yours, from your mother again. She posted one to you at the same time, but if I can, I will send this one on, just in case yours doesn't arrive. It was a special one to say that they had received the parcel and were enjoying the tea and sugar. What a time that took to get home, nearly five months, but still, now your mother has hers, it's possible that the others have reached home too, so we should be hearing. I notice by the way, the tone of the letter was quite cheerful. I think hearing from you has bucked them up a lot.

Well Hilda, I had my quiet Easter last weekend, which consisted of staying in Good Friday and Saturday, writing and reading (and dozing) with pictures in the evening and then Sunday, which was a lovely day, we had the match with the R.A.O.C. on our courts, eight men a side. They had quite a strong side, but we were all on form and just managed to beat them – all good hard games – Warren and I played together and won 3, lost 1. We provided refreshments during the afternoon in the shape of beer and lemonade and the Warrants Club catered for tea – and would you believe it, at the finish of the match, there were still some "live" bottles left, that we returned to the club and got our money back – the only case on record I should think. Next Sunday we have another match over on Stonecutters, but we are the visitors for that and it's only six aside. Back to work, of course on Monday.

You know of course that we do all the usual A.R.P.[45] exercises. Some of us are on first aid, others are fire-fighters etc, you know, the usual things. Well, up to this week I had escaped all of it, but now I've had to take Cummings's place, and Powell and I are now a searchlight crew. Owen and Foster are also on the same job on other lights – we had a practice yesterday evening, but tomorrow is a general blackout and all searchlight crews have to sleep in the Yard all night. I can see us being turned out in the early hours, you know just to see how long it takes to get the lights going – anyhow, they've given us camp beds complete with all accessories which should be quite comfortable, providing they let us sleep in them. The lights, by the way, are only for shining over the water, not for looking for planes. I think David would enjoy this job far better than me.

I met Eve this week. That's the first time I've spoken to her since Christmas Day and I believe we shall be spending an evening there sometime this week – she's going to give me a ring. I also had a yarn with Pamela over the phone today, and we shall be going to her place next week. They both wished to be remembered to you, and don't forget to write sometime – this writing business, I seem to be always writing

---

45. Air Raid Precautions.

to someone and yet always having one to write – during Easter, by the way, I wrote to Winnie.

This week, they have ceased to publish information about the mails, so now we have no idea when mail is going out or coming in – more delay, so now it's possible for me to post tomorrow and the letters stay in Hong Kong for a week, and of course they are still going to charge $1.15 for it.

Did I tell you I had a letter from Auntie last week, dated February 17th? Number "37" was O.K. up to then and they had received a letter card from you – I will answer it first and then send it on as usual.

One last thing, dear, I was very pleased with Edward's letter last week and David's this week was his best ever – very newsy. It's very nice to hear direct from them, gives me quite a whiff of home – I can't answer them this week as I want to enclose your mother's letter[46] but they can look for answers in my next letter. That's all again, Hilda, but don't forget, cheer up and be happy in your new house – it won't last forever. Goodbye my dear.
George.

P.S. I've just remembered how "cheerful" my last letter was, which makes that last bit funny. Ah, me, I hope it's not very long.
Now that I have no information re mails, I'll number the letters on the back so that you can see if you get them in the right order.
Cheerio, G.

Saturday April 19th 1941
Hong Kong

My Dear
Just one half hour I have to talk to you, and then home I go. It's 6 o'clock Saturday evening, and I'm writing in the office while waiting for my

---

46. Letter has not survived.

lads to come back – yes, I've been working this afternoon and now it's nearly time to pack up. I've just been playing that silly game of being sorry for myself – I pictured my going home presently, spotting you as the ferry neared the pier and then the walk home together, some supper and then off to the pictures somewhere – well, I probably will do those things except the seeing and meeting you. Yes, I know that's a most unprofitable game, but we must indulge in dreams sometimes, even if the coming to earth <u>is</u> hard afterwards and, Oh! my dear, how I want it to be true. How I value those things now, just our usual Saturday night trips, and the Lord knows they were sober enough as a rule, and yet looking back they were lovely evenings – did we know then? Yes, I think we did, on most occasions at any rate and I know we will on all those evenings in the future that await us round that corner.

Goodnight my dear, rather an abrupt ending, but my chaps have all come trooping in and we will be away now. Yes, I know I shall look for you now as the ferry gets in and, dear, I know you won't be there. Goodnight.

Tuesday afternoon and I should go right across the Yard to see a job, but it's pouring with rain at the moment and looks like continuing for a while, and so another contribution towards your letter. I'm still working lots so I don't get very much interesting news for you, although as you know, I would just as soon be working under these circumstances, quite apart from the financial consideration and of course that is very welcome. Most nights that I work late I get home about 8.15, have supper and a game of darts or something and then of course a couple of chapters in bed before lights out. Dawkins often wants me to go out to last house pictures after supper, but I'm usually too tired for that and so sometimes he pushes off by himself. Saturday night was just as I forecast it would be – even to the disappointment – we went to the Majestic as it happened, but the picture wasn't great. Sunday, the weather was very hot and sticky – in the morning after a lazy bath etc, I did a bit of shopping, paid the bills and had a haircut; and then in the afternoon, it was to Stonecutters for a tennis match against the wireless station people, and <u>was it hot</u>. Luckily they only have one court, so it meant playing one set and sitting out two, until everybody had played three sets – it was quite pleasant sitting out in the shade, watching the other people perform, but once on court, a couple of services and you were wet through. Anyway, on the whole, it wasn't a bad afternoon: a nice tea was provided and we played until dark.

I did hope today that I would get your letter, but no, not yet – and as I told you last week, no information is published now, so we just have to hope. We had one bit of news that might be good sometime in the future and that concerns a rise in pay – last week we had a cable from home asking us what we thought of the proposals, and they wanted a reply cabled back. Unfortunately we hadn't received them, another letter lost, and so after signals to and fro, we are now supposed to have them, but have not heard officially what they are. I won't say what it amounts to until I get more information but according to rumour it's not bad – there is of course, the usual snag; no date is mentioned from when it would start, but the fact that they asked for a cabled reply and not just a letter, seems to point to a fairly early date. I will, you bet, let you know more of this directly anything transpires.

I told you in last week's letter, didn't I, that I was one of a searchlight crew and that we were exercising last Thursday – quite funny that was at times, but I will say our work was quite effective. A blackout was on, but we certainly lit up the harbour for a couple of hours, and then we slept in the office all night – supposed to be testing sleeping and catering arrangements. Anyway, all was well, although Owen complained of being kept awake by a mosquito diving around him. But I slept all right.

And now, dear, I'm going to leave a little room just in case your letter arrives tomorrow and in case there's anything you want answered quickly, so

Goodnight again, dear.

Thursday now and just as I had given up hope of getting your letter, it came along. I'm glad you think you'll be comfortable in your new house. Is that rent an "all year round one", or is it variable with the seasons? Sorry to hear you have colds, but, now I know where I got mine from – I think I had one about six months ago, but not since. Well

dear, I've been to a Chargemans' meeting and we've accepted the new proposals, which of course is the answer that will be cabled home. I still don't know when it will be started, but I should think it would be soon. It should give me about $20 extra which isn't too bad, is it? I'll tell you more next letter. Goodbye dear, don't let anything get you down.
Love to you All.
George

April 23rd 1941
Hong Kong

Dear David
That was a very nice letter you sent me, certainly the best ever and full of news too and the slang, which always seems to find its way into your letters, gave it quite a homely touch. I'm glad you like the "beaut" stamps and every letter I try to work in some stamps of smaller values, so that you'll have some changers (Oh! now I think you call them swaps, you can see my education is neglected since you went away.) By the way, you might keep a set for me, when you have plenty, besides the 1st day cover that I asked mum to keep.

I expect mum has told you that Mr. Powell and I man a searchlight under the Dockyard Defence scheme, and we've had some fun – I'm sure you would have had a heck of a time. Last Thursday we had to go on the light in full kit, uniform complete with tin helmet, gas mask and rifle and bayonet and we did look a lot of guys. We shine on the harbour, not up in the sky, and as there was a blackout, you can bet we lit up Kowloon, every time we swept the opposite shore.

Quite a good sketch of your bike, but it looks to me as though you've been done, they didn't put the mudguards on – didn't you notice that when you bought it? Also, what's this I hear about falling off? An old hand like you shouldn't fall off, but I expect I've got the story wrong. But seriously David, look after yourself. I want a complete boy to come back to me. That's all this time, so, Goodbye and Love from
Dad.

Monday April 28th 1941
Hong Kong

My Dear

Monday evening and I'm <u>not</u> working late, so this week I'm making an earlier start on your letter. All day I've been looking forward to the semi-final of the colony tennis and then about 4 o'clock it started to get dark and gloomy. We could see what was coming as by 4.30 it was as dark as it usually is at seven – well I got to the gate in the dry and then at exactly quarter to five it dropped. You know just how it can rain in Hong Kong, so of course I hopped straight into a rickshaw[47] and home, and thankful at that to get home dry. It's kept on steadily all the evening, a proper storm with much thunder and lightning, so that means the match postponed until later this week I suppose and I might have to work over sometime later this week too.

I had a fairly quiet weekend except I went to Pamela's on Friday night and Eve's on Saturday – both of them asked me to remember them to you and of course wanted to know the latest news of you. We played cards at Eve's most of the time, but it was just yarning and leg pulling at Pamela's. I told you her mother had been bombed – the house next door received a direct hit and everybody there was killed, and Pamela's mother and sister had their legs badly burned. Her mother must have been fairly bad as Friday Pamela was worrying as to whether a leg had been amputated. Anyway, I saw her again Saturday and she had heard indirectly that it wasn't necessary.

I saw her again Saturday because of you, but first, before I speak of that let me wish you Many Happy Returns of Your Birthday – it's just three weeks to go, so I should be in time, but you never know these modern days of air mail. Yes my dear, I wish we could have last year's May 19th over again; we made a mess of that one – but I forgot, we're looking forward aren't we. Anyway, to go back to my story, I saw something at Pamela's that I thought you might like for your Birthday, so I got

---

47. A light two-wheeled hooded vehicle drawn by one or two people, and one of the main means of getting round in Hong Kong.

Pamela to get it for me and she brought it to me on Saturday. Yes, it's something to wear, but it's not a huge present so you mustn't hope for too much, but the thing is to get it to you. I don't quite know how to send it because of Customs, so I'm afraid you won't get it by the 19th – however, when you celebrate remember that's one present you have. I will let you know what I do about it.

Well Hilda, my best news last week I suppose was about the rise – there is still no further news as to <u>when</u> it commences and I suppose we have to wait for a reply to come out from England – as long as it's cabled I don't mind but I hope we haven't to wait for a letter. Under the new terms we are going to get the same pay as a man of similar status at home plus of course Foreign Service allowance. It will give me just what I was getting before I left home, including the sliding scale, together with 15/- charge pay and 1/- a year rise for each year of service – exactly as home – and of course it's what we've been after, or rather what they've been after, long before I arrived. With the Foreign Service Allowance it will give me, as I reckon it, an increase of twenty two dollars a week and it is backdated to April 1st 1940 so I have a nice little nest egg to come, somewhere in the region of a thousand dollars. Not so bad, eh! Everybody established[48] and all officers are very hard hit through Income Tax – Jim Dawkins pays about £4 a week and just a chargeman with no children pays 35 dollars a week. Hong Kong folk – the H.K people, make quite a fuss when they give a dollar to the Bomber Fund, and moan and write letters to the papers about having to pay Income Tax, one tenth of the United Kingdom Income Tax – I'd like to see them have to pay 10/- in the pound, they'd know then we had a war on our hands. Bob Owen's establishment came through this week, so I don't know if mine is in the offing – but of course his is from another yard to mine. I'm not keen on it just now, of course, but will accept if it is offered.

----

48. There were two types of employee at the dockyard, those who were 'hired' and those who were 'establishment'. The latter had more secure jobs but received less money. Almost half the shipwrights, a quarter of the tradesmen and about one sixth of the skilled labourers were established. At that time George was a hired employee.

Well Hilda, quite a fuss you've had over the box again – what a nerve to try to charge 25/- carriage for a box that size. They apparently expect to make money out of evacuees – anyway I hope you have it now, and are not too disappointed; but I am expecting to hear all about that in this week's letter, when it arrives.

I had a letter from Winnie this weekend, posted March 11th, with everybody O.K. up to then – Mum had gone back to London for a while, but will return to Upham if the raids get bad again. No other news of any importance, except that Eddie has become a jolly good chef (says Winnie) and has been round her house doing cakes and biscuits – funny chap, Eddie!

Well my dear, that is one more Monday gone and now I'm going to finish writing to you and go to bed. How many more of these Mondays have we to endure, I wonder – it's still impossible to guess, and the war news this week – the evacuation of Greece and the capture of Athens doesn't make it any easier to be bright and gay (dammit). Oh well, I'll leave a little space again, for a day or so, in case I have anything to add, so now, Goodnight dear, and once more All the Best for your Birthday, Goodbye
George.

Wednesday

I was going to mail this today, but yesterday I received an invite to drop in and hear the record at Mr. Little's and as we were going tonight I thought I would keep it open and include my remarks about it. However, I had a message from him today to say that he had to go out and then on top I had to work late, so I think I'll mail now and tell you what I think of the record next week. Your letter arrived yesterday, the one started Good Friday – yes, the Holiday made me miserable too, every time I stopped to think – that is our trouble you know, we think too much. But never mind dear, there are more Easters coming. Goodbye dear again until next week.
All my love to you
George

Sunday May 4ᵗʰ 1941
Hong Kong

Dear,

It's Sunday morning and as my lodger has gone up to bowls, it's nice and quiet and a good opportunity to make a start on my letter. It's a lovely day, nice bright sun but a cool breeze and no doubt you can picture me sitting on the verandah in shorts and singlet, with Kim lazing a few yards away with a, "Better to take me out than write that old letter," expression on his face. However, he can help me pay the compradore presently. We haven't actually gone into "short" yet, but the weather is beginning to warm up now, and no doubt a couple of weeks will see the long 'uns put away once more.

Well, first of all I'll tell you what I've been doing this week, although that of course is not very sensational, especially as it was bad weather on the only two evenings I knocked off early – yes, I have been working late again from Wednesday, and so of course didn't see the tennis semi-final.

Tuesday evening, after supper, we went along to Little's to hear "our" record – to tell you the truth, I thought it might bring on a fit of the blues to hear you play again, but no, it didn't. I thought it was very good and quite enjoyed hearing it, particularly the "Ships of Arcady" which has a very nice accompaniment – the other one, I thought was too typically Irish to be 100%, but I believe the song is an amateur one isn't it? It was very easy to "see" you playing, that old and so familiar scene and of course it made me want the reality – however, as I said, it didn't get me down.

Well dear, I've posted off your present to you and as a ship is leaving almost at once, you should get it soon after your Birthday. I had a big fuss posting it, as new regulations started in April, and you have to get an export licence to send anything out of the colony now. I'm hoping they let it through without customs tax, but I'm not sure, so you might have to pay. Anyway, I hope you like it, and it should be warm for the winter.

And now, as the time is getting on, and I have one or two chores to do before dinner I think I had better stop now, so cheerio dear.

Tuesday evening now dear; how the weeks go by in chunks – Sunday morning I wrote the first part of this letter and now it's nearly half way through the week again. I worked late last night, but came home early tonight – we've been doing dynamo trials; you know, absolutely drenched with sweat in about five minutes and after about three hours I'd had enough for one day so hopped off home at 3.15. Anyway, a bath and a doze after tea have certainly brightened things a bit.

Well dear, I told you what little news I had on Sunday and I'm afraid I haven't much to add except that since I posted your parcel, I've heard all sorts of yarns about how much you'll have to pay in duty. Some seem to get things through all right, and others have to pay – I think it depends on your luck, so we'll wait and see.

Poor old Dawkins last week could hardly sit still when the news of those raids on Plymouth were coming through on the wireless, so I don't know what she must have been like down there in Sydney. The town seems to have had it worse than Pompey now and that was bad enough – I often think of that day in the main office at Pompey, when I made him tear up the contract and make another, allowing you to come out here. It would have been nice for me, wouldn't it, listening to the news of the raids and thinking of you at home on your own – no dear, I tried for <u>years</u> to get away, but no they wouldn't let me go until now, so don't grumble too much, dear about being separated. I love you, my dear, and it seems hard to waste so much time apart, but always remember that we are going to make up for it. It's the 6th May today and in four days time the 2nd anniversary of your arrival in Hong Kong. Ah my dear, I think I had better get drunk that night, if that will stop me remembering, but I doubt if even that would.

One thing more, dear, how is it I'm only hearing nice things about our nips – I'm sure they haven't turned into little angels so let's hear about those other things and then I'll know they are really all right. Goodbye

dear, for another week, keep smiling. My love to you dear, and hope you had a Happy Birthday.
George

Sorry I didn't ask before, but how are you – hope you've lost those headaches, but dear, don't worry.

P.S. Did I tell you in last week's letter that I had heard from Winnie and she also had received the parcel so it looks as if they all got home.

P.P.S. As I write the wireless is playing, "Lady Dressed in Jade", remember, Oh! for the days on the river. Dear, we've had some good times, haven't we?

Monday May 12th 1941
Hong Kong

Dear
I had hoped to start your letter yesterday (Sunday) morning – it's nice and quiet then with Dawkins up at bowls, and out on the verandah cool and bright enough to induce me to write a cheerful letter. However, we've had quite a heat wave this last week, so yesterday morning I had to do a bit of shopping instead of letter writing – I ordered some shirts (white short-sleeved ones) and bought some summer pants and vests. Anyway, it's Monday evening now that I'm writing, for the above reasons.

First of all, I'll tell you of my activities for this week and that won't take very long – I worked late three evenings last week, but one of the evenings off was Friday, so I was able to see the colony doubles final. It was quite a good game to watch, in fact very good in parts, but not nearly so good as last year's games. I went with Ronald Foster and so of course had to do it in style – we worked tiffin time and so left the Yard early, strolled along to have a be-ah and arrived in nice time for the tennis. However, Pamela and Vic arrived soon after the start and sat with me, so Ronald didn't get a lot of my attention after that. Yes, dear, in spite of so much company, I still thought of you, as that final had become one of our little trips – it was Pamela's first visit there, so of course I had to tell her that it was the first place you came to, your very first day in Hong Kong. Ah me! That's two years ago – one very good one and one very weary one. Roll on!!

Upon my return to the office this afternoon, I had a pleasant surprise – your letter was awaiting me on my desk and as I wasn't expecting it until about Wednesday you can see it was a surprise. But dear, are you all right? You again speak of having a cold and bad heads – is that the same cold that you spoke of two letters ago? And those headaches? – dear, is it just worry? But you must look after yourself. Why not see a doctor? Perhaps something can be done about it. I'm quite all right at present, but it's a bit early to say if my third tropical summer is going to affect me – last summer I had those bad fingers so it remains to be seen if it is going to affect me this year.

And now, dear, a word about a subject that you spoke quite strongly about in last week's letter and in this week's – you use the word "Probability" in connection with it. I don't like to disillusion you, but just think as to whether I should be allowed to do as you would like. At home, they have brought in conscription of labour and can move you from one job to another whether you want to or not and also you can't leave one job and go to another (even if it's a better one) without first getting permission. Now, as I have told you, we are down to rock bottom in the Yard and nobody else can be spared, so I know I would have little chance of getting down with you. I know of two fellows in outside firms that had jobs to go to in Sydney, but upon making application to leave the colony were stopped by the military. I would be quite willing to get a permanent job down with you, but I'm afraid there is little hope of that – one other point, too, I'm not so sure I would be very welcome either, just at a time when their own men are joining the army and going away – however, cheer up dear, perhaps things will work out all right yet. But don't worry.

Fancy Mrs. Dawkins having to lug that box about herself – her letter was full of just what she thought of Australians – and it's just too bad that after all that trouble the shoes wouldn't fit. No, I suppose I had better not send any more, although in any case I wouldn't have had any more made without the pattern of their feet.

Well dear, part of this was written before supper, and part after and now my eyes are beginning to close, so I'll pack up and finish tomorrow. Goodnight dear.

Well, Wednesday evening now – I intended to finish last night and get this posted, but at the last minute I had to stay on, probably the only evening this week as we are not quite so busy for a little while. Anyway, I can now tell you that I have today paid in to the cashier £20 (sterling) to be remitted to you. That should be about £24 Australian but of course it won't leave Hong Kong until the end of this month – I still haven't heard that you received the two previous remittances, one at the end of February and the other at the end of April, but it's too early for the April one in any case yet. By the way, we've heard that we are getting our rise in two weeks' time, but will not pick up the back money for some time to come – which is just as well for some – Yes, I'm tellen you!

Well dear, I remembered that a few weeks back you suggested I sent some sugar and butter home and now that the other parcels have arrived all right I've been making enquiries and today sent off four parcels – to your mother, mine, Winnie and Auntie Hillie; I thought I had better include Auntie this time as she is doing the house business for us, but they are only small parcels, about 10/- (sterling). However, I will give you details of them next week.

We have just had about ten days of really hot weather, but today has seen a break – some rain and it is now much cooler – just about right now, but of course that won't last very long. Well dear, once again I've reached the end of this week's letter and so I suppose once more I must say Goodbye. Goodbye my dear, keep smiling as always you have my love.
George

P.S. Yes, I remember 10th May, but I didn't get drunk – yes, I'm looking forward to another one. High day or holiday?

Monday May 19th 1941
Hong Kong

Dear
Monday evening again, and another start to be made on the weekly
epistle – this letter writing! Sometimes I can sit down and write away
quite easily and at others I just sit and scratch. It wouldn't be so bad if
I had any news to write about, but usually I'm afraid they must make
pretty dull reading.

There's nothing much to report about last week that I didn't tell you –
I saw two pictures, "Andy Hardy meets Debutante", and "The Son of
Monte Cristo"; not bad, but nothing outstanding. However, yesterday,
Sunday afternoon, we played a return tennis match against the army
people, the R.A.O.C., and had quite a pleasant time. In the morning I
was afraid it was going to be unbearably hot, but quite a breeze came up
after tiffin and made it much better. There were eight in each team and
they just had two courts, grass ones, so that each pair had a rest and
a cool off between sets. If you remember, we beat them on our courts
and this time they had strengthened their team a bit, but we still just
managed to win.

Well dear, I told you last week, that I had sent off four parcels – I made
enquiries and found that there are more restrictions now than there
used to be and only small parcels can be sent to each person – if you
exceed the amount they lose some of their rations at home. However,
the parcels are quite big enough at one go because of the risk of them
being lost en route. Winnie's was 9 ½ lbs of sugar at a total cost of $7.33,
which works out at about 1/- a pound, and as she makes jam I thought
that might be most useful. The other three, to your mother, mine and
Auntie, consisted of 2lb butter and 2lb sugar each, costing $8.85 – I
didn't like to send all butter, as I'm not at all sure in what condition it
arrives home. It's in airtight tins, but what effect heat is going to have, I
don't know – still I'll see what luck we have and if it's all right, I'll send
all butter another time as I expect that would be a real luxury. Anyway,
what is your opinion of my effort? I sent one to Auntie, as you didn't
include her last time, and after all she is going to a certain amount of
trouble for us.

Well dear, I've just had supper and now I've been looking at the writing pad for about 20 minutes considering what to write about next, and so I think I'll finish for tonight and add a bit tomorrow. Before I leave you though, dear, I must say how I like that "dicky" little hat of yours in the photo – you know the one with the feathers. I think it will help make you feel more gay as well as look Hong Kongish. I wonder if you feel better this week? I haven't had your letter yet, but the last two or three haven't been too happy. Cheer up, dear, we've got to stick it out and it only hurts if you dwell on it too much. No, I know there is nothing I can say that will make you feel better, except of course that one thing, for which we hope in vain at present, but dear, do keep on hoping and keep cheery too. Goodnight my dear, and I hope that today for you hasn't been too lonely a Birthday. Yes, I thought of all sorts of things tonight – after tea I went out on the verandah in the cane chair and had a doze and thought of it being your Birthday and of course thought of last year's and even that was better than this one – but dear, I can see this will go all miserable if I go on. I love you dear and once more, Good night.

Well Hilda, Tuesday evening now, but still no mail has arrived, so I suppose I must finish off without its help. I ran into Stanley this morning and he said they had received a nice long letter from you, but I haven't seen it yet – I might drop in there tomorrow night.

Ah me, I've just done what I described earlier in this letter last evening – looked at the pad for about 20 minutes chewing the pen, trying to think of something to tell you, but I'm afraid my mind is not very productive tonight. One thing I thought of though – I remember you saying in one of your letters that you had heard a bad rumour about the ship Mr. Tubbs went on – well, it's <u>not</u> true, but the point is, that we had that story here, a long time ago now, and someone must have included that in their letter to Australia. It's a good job Mrs. T left before she heard it – that would have given her a pleasant voyage wouldn't it? – wondering what she was going to hear when she arrived. There is only one rumour that I'm willing to spread, just give me the chance and see.

And now dear, one last word – I've just read over where I said your last couple of letters weren't very happy ones. Now don't try to write happy letters just to deceive me – if you are miserable, say so, but do try and keep cheerful and I hope you lose those bad heads. How is David keeping now that winter is coming on? Is he still having attacks or is there any sign of it going? Jessop was telling me that his wife had it very bad at Pompey, practically lost it at Hong Kong, and now has a return of it at Sydney. Also, by the way, she gets some tablets down there, which she finds easily the best thing for easing it that she has had, so if you do run into her, ask what they are. Well dear, that is all again for another week, so I'll finish. Cheerio, my dear, and I hope you have received your present by now. I'm still wondering how much you have had to pay on it.

All my love and Goodbye to you.
George

P.S. The old snap is just to show you what I look like.

Tuesday May 27th 1941
Hong Kong

Dear
I'm afraid this won't be a real start to your letter tonight as Jim Dawkins has just informed me that we have a visitor coming and we are having supper early, before the gent arrives. I am still working over, but packed up early tonight owing to A.R.P. exercises, so I thought it was a good opportunity to do my writing. However, I won't get much written tonight it seems.

Well dear, I mentioned last week that your letter hadn't arrived and of course it turned up, about two hours after I had posted yours – three days later, on Saturday, I received another, so you see I'm in clover this week. And dear, just let me say how sorry I am about the organist job – I know it must have been a bitter disappointment to you, after getting the chance, and a sort of personal blow when you found your hearing letting you down. But dear, I certainly agree with you that the job wasn't worth keeping if it was going to be worrying. I expect you had a howl that night, Eh? If so, I hope it got it out of the system – never mind dear. Still keep smiling; I think I know exactly what that meant to you and I am sorry.

I kept my appointment with the doctor today and he passed me as fit for another year and so I suppose here I remain. I only hope we're together long before the end of that year. I certainly never meant to do a fourth year, but I <u>do</u> think it's the right thing to do under the present circumstances.

Well dear, so far on Tuesday, and then I had to pack up for supper and our visitor arrived shortly after – Sellers his name and he's a Lieutenant in the Royal Engineers. I believe his wife is in Sydney; we just sat yarning and as the news of the Bismarck[49] had just come through, I think most of the talk was of the war. Yes, that was certainly a much needed tonic after the blow we had over the sinking of the Hood[50], that much advertised show ship of ours, and to some extent took the edge off our naval losses around Crete[51]. A sorry business that is, and it looks as though we might lose Crete in spite of the sacrifice of ships – still it's not finished there yet and if we only have enough equipment we might pull it off yet – but I expect you will know one way or the other by the time you read this[52].

And now to a more personal subject, very personal – they talk of the Hong Kong husbands, but what do you think of a wife that writes to her husband and says – well let me quote; "I think living alone especially sleeping was bad for me; but here there is a nice secure feeling, two men and a dog and I have slept much better." Well, what do you think of that!!

---

49. Germany's newest and fastest battleship, sunk May 27th 1941, with the loss of more than 2,000 lives.
50. HMS *Hood*, sunk by the *Bismarck* with the loss of more than 1,400 lives on May 24th 1941.
51. When Italy attacked Greece in October 1940, Britain had sent forces to Crete in support of Greece. At the end of April 1941 these forces were joined by Allied troops escaping mainland Greece following Greece's fall to the Germans. By May 1941, Allied troops on the island numbered 40,000, and on May 20th, the Germans launched an airborne invasion of Crete. Initially British ships were able to prevent German ships landing reinforcements by sea, but lost many ships, planes and men, and on 27th May it was decided to evacuate the island. Eighteen thousand troops were rescued during the nights of 28th, 29th and 30th May, but again at heavy cost.
52. Crete surrendered on June 1st 1941.

You ask me in one letter how much the piano cost to send down to you – it was just under $100, or £5 sterling, or £6 Aussie, excluding what you had to pay, but including the cost of the packing case. What became of that by the way – did you manage to sell it? If you can't, you ought to give it away rather than let that robbing firm have it.

I mentioned that I received two letters last week. Well wonder of wonders, I had another yesterday, Wednesday, making three in eight days, and a very nice one too dear, one of your old chatty letters – dated 18th May and it only took 10 days to get here. Fancy those of mine taking a month again, it certainly is too bad for an air mail letter and this week I'm going to try via Rangoon, but if it's just local people holding them up, it won't be much better – anyhow, let me know if it's an improvement.

So you are going to get another 5/- a week for the kids in August are you, but surely they'll pay it to father won't they? I pick up my rise tomorrow, but not the back money and we're waiting to see just how much it is – the back money may not be paid for some time, but I don't mind that. How are you financially now, living within the weekly income? And also, while I think of it, you mention in one of these letters about getting the remittance safely at the end of March. Yes, I suppose it is a perfectly safe way of sending it, but let me know about the other two remittances, as I just like to make sure.

And now that I'm on the last page, I'll let you know what I think is going to be bad news – I believe our furniture in storage was burned on the 9th of March. I can't say for sure yet as I've had no notice, but late this afternoon I had the usual bill, only this time it was for 2 ½ months, 1st January to 9th March, which looks ominous to me. I suppose somewhere in the post (if it isn't lost) is another letter with the official notice. Yes, I echo your "blast", but knowing how things are I've been expecting it – our writing table too – what else was there of value? Anyway, I also had a letter from Auntie dated 3rd April and everybody is O.K. and our house all right up to then. They have been out at Upham and returned for a few days to get their pension, etc. Binnie has been collecting all the rents and she by the way has been unlucky. Her house has been damaged, but Auntie doesn't say how much, and six

houses near her knocked down. I will send her letter on next week after answering it. And now, it's Goodbye again I suppose, damn it – how many more Goodbyes, I wonder? Goodnight dear, and how I want to say that to you instead of writing it. Goodbye
George

Monday June 9th 1941
Hong Kong

My Dear
This isn't even meant to be an attempt at writing a letter – like you I haven't got over the shock yet. I received your letter, containing the news about "37" and your mother's Clipper letter, at midday on Saturday, just as I was going home and have been – well stunned ever since. I had a letter from Auntie dated 3rd April, to say that all was O.K. up to that date – however, I've just received another, dated 10th April, with all the details, and which I'm sending on. Tuesday 8th April was the fateful night and the two kids were apparently lucky to get out alive[53].

Directly I decide to use the Rangoon route they make alterations, with the result that my last week's letter didn't leave Friday as it should – mail closes Monday now, so this should arrive with it.
Well dear, I can't write about it yet, so Goodbye.

Sunday June 15th 1941
Hong Kong

My Dear.
Several times this week I've tried to start this letter, only to end up on each occasion by throwing the pad across the room – and now it's Sunday morning and I've just got to get something down as the weekly

---

53. The 'two kids' were the children of the family renting number "37", and on April 8th 1941, the house was hit during an air raid.

Rangoon Mail closes tomorrow. Yes, it's certainly been a black week this has, but it's come to an end at last.

Last Saturday I received your letter with "the news" and then on Monday that letter of Auntie's with all the details, which I forwarded on a couple of hours later – in the meanwhile my tummy had gone back on me, and you know how pleasant and inconvenient etc that can be in Hong Kong. Jim Dawkins has been the same in that respect, so you can guess we've been a happy pair – something we've eaten I suppose, because there seems to be quite an epidemic of it about. It's much better now, however, although the old tummy isn't "working" quite right yet. Still, I expect when I write next week to be able to say that it's all O.K. again. We've been living on soups and stews right through the week, in fact we have another even today although it's Sunday – Oh! I forgot we had boiled fish one day. And then we've had most delightful weather – a typhoon has been hovering around and it's been most depressing, very warm and damp both day and night, and Thursday night I had to work on a most worrying job until 10 o'clock, so you can see why I say it's been a black week.

I can't write about "37". I still choke when I think of it, but I'm glad nobody was hurt – Oh! my dear – no, it's no good, I just can't think straight about that.

I've remitted another £20 (sterling) to you. It leaves here at the end of June, so I suppose it will be the end of July before you get it. By the way, all those remittances have been out of income (total of £85 sterling) – I haven't drawn any from the bank since you left.

Yes dear, it's Monday morning – I'm afraid letter writing is beyond me this week; it took all day yesterday, at intervals, to get as far as I did – directly I pick up the pen I go speechless and just stare at the paper.

I have just received your letter of 1st June, complete with David's splendid effort. He has certainly shown me up this week – a very nice letter. Yours too, dear, and I think I feel at least 5% better already. I'm sorry, though, that you hadn't received my letter to hear about the furniture, as then you would have known the lot and had it done with.

Well Hilda, I hope to write something a bit better next week – I'm giving up now.

That's all dear, I still love you and want all of you, even if this letter doesn't show it, so Goodbye.
George

Thursday June 19th 1941
Hong Kong

Dear,
Yes, I know it was a wretched letter I sent you last week, but believe me it wasn't through lack of trying – I was just incapable of any straight thinking and even this week I'm afraid I won't be awarded any literary prize. For one thing, I'm so busy being sorry for myself that other things are almost excluded from my thoughts – yes, I know, directly us men get a bellyache we think we're ill.

Anyway, my tummy is far from being well yet – it started with the ordinary "dog", but that very quickly passed and now it seems to have left what I should imagine to be some form of gastritis. I feel blown right out all the time, you know, that after Xmas dinner feeling, only in this case I have it without eating, and all round the ribs it feels sore as though somebody has been punching me. I've seen the doctor and he says something we've eaten upset the stomach and wasn't cleared out properly, so the old stomach is still upset – I have some medicine, nearly all Bismuth I think, to take after meals, but I only started it yesterday, so I must wait a bit to see if it is doing any good. Jim Dawkins has been more or less the same, not quite as bad as me, and today he tells me that he is considerably better – so perhaps mine will soon begin to lift too. I shall certainly be glad when it does, if only from the point of view of meals as it's a ruddy nuisance trying to think of something we can eat – but there, I think I've written enough about tummies for the moment, so we'll progress to other things – dismal ones of course.

One thing about this week is that we've had a little rain, 15 inches of it between Saturday and Wednesday – six inches of it fell on Wednesday

141

morning. We just caught the tail end of it going to work, so you can see that even the weather isn't trying very hard to do a spot of cheering up.

I've just read through your letter again that I received on Monday (and didn't answer), and David's, and his was certainly the best ever. I know exactly what you mean when you say you probably weren't nice to live with "that" week – looking back I wonder what a lot of people thought of me – especially my gang – no, I too certainly don't want another week like that.

So you are beginning to feel the tobacco shortage in Australia – Well, well, well, when we go home we shall have to have ashtrays fitted to the piano like the candlesticks (if we have a piano).

I don't like your taste in books – "The Rape of the Netherlands". I think some nice book, like "What Katie did Next" would be much more soothing to the nerves.

Well dear, so far on Thursday, and now it's Sunday morning and another week is gone – the 51st. Yes, one more week completes a whole year of separation – and what a year – and still no hope of any move in the immediate future as far as I can see. Plenty of rumours during the last two or three weeks and even these have been definitely squashed in today's paper where the Governor's[54] interviewed and makes a statement that there is no truth in these rumours and that the position is unchanged. I'm afraid I, as usual cautious-like, didn't believe the yarns, but even so, at the back of your mind there is always the hope that one day one of the stories will prove true and every time you see these contradictions in the paper it's the death of a faint hope.

There was much indignation here this week, with all the usual letters to the paper, because an assessor appointed to the war department of Hong Kong is a woman. They're going to send her out from England to Hong Kong, at a time like this, when they say that other women can't be allowed to enter the Colony because they might be detrimental

---

54. The Governor of Hong Kong - in June 1941, Sir Geoffrey Northcote.

to its defence. To make matters worse, it was found out that Mr is already here, another assessor, and came out a few months ago – quite obviously another wangle. She will find herself quite famous, or rather notorious by the time she arrives. By the way, the Singapore women that go back just pay their own fare – I mentioned that last week didn't I, but I did think then that it was recoverable – but now I find it isn't and that will be a huge sum to anybody with children; it might be as much as £150 for a woman with two children. It's not good enough. They <u>made</u> them go, at least they should pay for them to return.

Well dear, the old tummy is a bit better now – not cured but anyway going in the right direction. I'll report again next week.

I've just completed one week of "summer time" in Hong Kong as they put the clock on one hour last Sunday. It's no good at all to me, as now it's dark summer and winter when I get up – late twice this week, shame! Who cares, anyway.

Well Hilda, that's all again, so goodbye dear. Give my love to the boys and I'll be writing to them. Goodbye.
George

P.S. They have just brought out 1c notes here now owing to the shortage of the coins, and I enclose one as a curiosity for the boys.

Thursday June 26th 1941
Hong Kong

My Dear,
I hope you don't think I have been really bad, only looking back it seems to me that that is the conclusion you might jump to from my last two letters. I know they were rather rotten ones, especially the first of the two, but that week perhaps I wasn't quite well – not as much physical as mental. Everything seemed so hopeless to me that week, and then the bad tummy on top just finished it – anyway I hope you haven't been worrying too much. I'm quite all right again now, just two weeks it lasted, but last weekend was the turning point and I'm now eating as

per usual. The Walkers invited me again out to the matshed during that fortnight and again I turned it down, in case I should get a chill in the tummy on top of the other – however Vic rang me up yesterday and I think I'm O.K. now, so this Sunday I shall have my first swim of the season.

Yes, dear, the news about our home was a shock, in spite of knowing of all the damage that has been and is being done. I still couldn't visualise "our" house being hit. Have you tried to picture to yourself how it must look now – I have and somehow or other that's a picture I can't imagine at all. Yes, it still hurts to think about it now after all the memories we have of it – presently perhaps I shall be able to think that is only being sentimental and that the kitchen ceiling wanted renewing anyhow. It seems that Mrs. Fenwick caught it a bit worse than ours and I am surprised at that – remember what I used to say, that "37" didn't have another to lean on, and that if it was hit I was afraid it would fall right down. Have you heard since? I had another from Auntie this week with a few more gory details and what looked like a request for money to pay the mortgage. I've answered it so I will forward it on to you. The mortgage has still to be paid, of course, so next month I will remit £20 to her instead of to you. One thing dear, I am glad those kids weren't hurt and when I think of <u>that</u> I'm thankful we are out here, even with you in Australia. I don't want our two to have an experience like that.

Now, as regards the furniture, I think I told you that at present we get no compensation because we were not householders at the outbreak of war. However, the question is being taken up with the Board of Trade, so we want to get a claim registered in case we ever do become eligible for compensation. I still have had no letter from Chaplins, although they told Auntie that they had sent. I have already written to them asking for confirmation that the furniture was destroyed and for a claim form. In the meanwhile if I send you their list of furniture will you have a go at estimating its value and then send it back to me. The way they worded some of the items is not too good from an "estimate of value" point of view is it? Still, have a go. Ah me, I write all this dear, and if I stop and think I want to throw something at somebody it makes me savage, but I've had two weeks of that and I'm trying to fight it now. It only makes it harder to feel like that – and you dear, do you feel better over that now?

Thursday tonight and tomorrow starts our nightmare weekend of a year ago – a year and still no end to it. What a war this is, Russia[55] now and still Turkey stands by, knowing it must be her turn next – one after another they're submerged in turn and still they won't unite. What effect the Russian war will have out East remains to be seen – if Russia could hold out for about four months it would be a tremendous blow to Germany and I should imagine make Japan sing small, but I'm afraid that is being too optimistic.

Well dear, thus far on Thursday and now it's Monday morning – I was at the beach with the Walkers all day yesterday and intended to finish my letter in the Yard this morning. Anyhow, No. 9[56] Typhoon signal is up and no ferries to Hong Kong this morning, and so I'm home and can write in comfort. No. 7[57] went up yesterday (Sunday) morning, but I went up early to the Walkers and we decided to chance it and it turned out to be the best thing to do – hot and sultry all day and then wind and occasional rain squalls in the evening. Anyway, it was a very nice day and I had two quite long bathes. By the way, Pamela was quite pleased with your letter, which I believe arrived about two days after she had posted one to you. Next time you write to her, mention the dressing gown as it was she that got it – actually, it came about like this. Mrs. Basset asked Mr to get one and gave her size and he asked Pamela if she would get it. Well, she got your coat and we all went up to see it. It just fitted Pamela and she was afraid that it would be too small for Mrs. Basset. I had taken a fancy to it by now, and so between us we persuaded Harold that it would be too small for his wife – so I had that one and Pamela bought another for Mrs. Basset. I'm glad you like it, because I did too, very much – I'm also glad you didn't have to pay.

I saw a very good picture last week, "The Philadelphia Story". The acting is good and the dialogue very clear – if it comes your way try and see it.

I went to a meeting on Friday at the Peninsula of all the husbands, but came away feeling that the position is just as hopeless as ever – much

---

55. In 1939 Germany and the Soviet Union had signed a Non-Aggression Pact. On June 22nd 1941, Germany broke this pact and launched an invasion of Russia.
56. Increasing gale or storm force winds.
57. Gale or storm force winds, from north east, and expected to persist.

indignation expressed and some talk of demonstration against the local Government; and I suppose all the good the talking did was to show the bitterness that is growing. Of course, we had the usual promise that the position will be reviewed from time to time and when they can recommend the return they will do so, but that I'm afraid, means nothing. Yes, one year ago this morning, we were dashing around to Kowloon Yard and then across to the other side to the boat and that unforgettable farewell. Well, tomorrow starts our second year – I wonder if this one will be completed too. But dear, I'm afraid that is not very cheery to end up my letter. Goodbye, my dear. I want you all back with me more than ever – this seems such an empty life without you. Goodbye Hilda.

I'll leave out the furniture bit this week, so that I can get David's letter in – I'll send that next week. Cheerio.
George

June 30th 1941
Hong Kong

Dear David
There is one good point that I can see about the evacuation, and that is, that going to Australia has certainly improved your letter writing. Many thanks for that last one and I must say I thoroughly enjoyed reading it. You don't seem to be having such a bad time, for which I am very glad, mind, but I can see that at times you have a bit of trouble with that mother of yours. Still, be patient with her, especially the week that she can't get her fags, and remember it will be worse still when she has a dad to back her up.

Well David, what do you think of poor old "37", the "house where I was born" as far as you were concerned? But look here, when we have it rebuilt, don't you think we ought to have some improvements? You just give a little thought to this and if you can think of any, let me know; in fact you might get out the plans after your college training.

Oh, yes, and talking about you being born at "37" reminds me that it must have been about this time of the year – that (un)lucky day the 13th (yes, on second thoughts I'll admit I think "lucky") and so David, "Many Happy Returns of your Birthday", and I hope you have a nice party. Next year I hope to be there too. And about a present – do you want one? In case you do, I'll send a £1 if I can get one. If I can't you are to ask Mum to give you one and I'll send it to her next week. Goodbye then, David, and if Mum has to pay extra because this letter is too heavy, I can see her taking it out on you again.
Goodbye and the Best of Luck, and

Love from
Dad

P.S.   Don't forget to save me a set of Hong Kong stamps.

Afternoon
Sorry, David, but I can't get your £1. All the shops are closed, and there are no buses or ferries and have I got wet coming to the Post Office? I'll send it next week.

Cheerio,
Dad

Hilda, David, Edward - Botanic Gardens, September 1941.
(Referenced in letter of October 15ᵗʰ1941)

July - September 1941

I was just having my tiffin in the office this afternoon when in walked
the boy with your letter of July 27th – a nice long one,
and was an exceedingly nice third course.

Thursday July 3rd 1941
Hong Kong

My Dear,

Thursday evening, and I have the place to myself for a little while, so I'll make a start on my letter. I'm not working late now, and I haven't done so for a couple of weeks and I doubt if I will have to for a while. I've had a little read after tea and Jim Dawkins went straight up to the Club from the Yard and won't be back for about another hour. Yesterday I got your letter of June 13th, or should I say budget – yes, quite a cheery one, and did I want it. In it, you answer one of mine in which I said that your letters weren't very "happy" ones – and I'm afraid that that letter of mine must have been about the last happy one you've had from me. Somehow I can't find anything to be very cheerful or hopeful about these days – not a very nice thing to say, but all the blows we've had in the last two months, together with this blasted separation has got me down. And you needn't go worrying about me on that account, I shall climb out of it, I don't doubt, sooner or later.

Well dear, that's a nice start for my letter, I must say, but mind, don't worry it will pass. I had a day and a half holiday this week because of that typhoon last weekend – I told you I think that it was due Sunday evening, but we went to the beach and had quite a good day on Sunday. During the night however, it blew up and Monday morning they hoisted No. 9 and promptly stopped all buses and ferries. I arrived at the ferry at twenty to seven to find all services cancelled and so back home, and that was the position all day. I finished your letter in the morning and went down to post it and to try and get David's pound

149

note – that part was hopeless though, as all shops were closed up and after getting pretty wet I had to post without it – anyhow I have it now and will enclose it this week.

I stayed indoors all the afternoon and then went to the pictures in the evening – there was hardly any wind and no rain, but No. 9 was still up. Tuesday morning, however, turned out bad again. The typhoon was not a bad one but was moving very slowly and the wind was again strong enough to prevent the ferries running. They did actually start, I believe about ten o'clock, but I didn't go over until the afternoon.

Tuesday evening, we had a speech on the wireless by the Governor on the evacuation, the first time that any of them have troubled to refer to it. Of course, he tried to justify it, said it was necessary and in his opinion still necessary and gave us a lot of soft soap about patriotism etc, and of course the usual promise about reviewing it when the situation improves. On the whole he left the impression in my mind that you won't be back for a long time – blast him!

By the way, in your letter you mention about "enclosing" some pictures and a letter – they weren't there, so I presume the letter of seven pages was too heavy to permit enclosing them – anyhow perhaps I will get them next week, or are they coming sea mail? So you have given up the numbering idea – I keep two columns on the inside cover of the writing pad, one column for the number of my last letter and date of posting and the other for the date of arrival and number (if any) of your letters – doing it that way, I don't forget to number them and also if you refer to any of them, I can see when that one was posted.

Well my dear, here's Sunday again, and another wet one too – funny weather we've had this week. It started with a typhoon and then got more hot as the week went by, until on Friday afternoon they hoisted the No. 1 again. Saturday was showery in the morning with only a little wind and in the afternoon they took the signal down – and now today it's been pouring with rain with terrific gusts of wind. Jim Dawkins has of course been moaning all day because he can't play bowls, but now that we have Summer Time here they can play every evening up to about eight o'clock. The bowlers are about the only people that benefit from the Summer Time that I can see except a few very hardy souls like Pamela Walker that still have an occasional game of tennis. To me it's no good at all and means I have to get up in the dark all the year round. By the way, talking of tennis reminds me that our Final will now be played in October, when it's a bit cooler – also there is the Doubles to finish off.

I had another letter from you yesterday, postmarked June 22nd, so that was two I received in three days. I see you mention Mrs. Samson and children are going to Singapore – how about that restriction, no children over nine – doesn't that affect them? Or have they got round it? That certainly is a hard decision to have to make if it's true about the restriction, and as you say, I hope that that doesn't come our way.

Well dear, if this letter isn't too long on the way, it ought to arrive in time for me to wish you Many Happy Returns of your Wedding Day. Fifteen years, dear, or should I only say fourteen because I don't think we should really count this last one – still we'll make up for that, with the only trouble being when are we going to start? Anyway Hilda, I am glad of that day, fifteen years ago, and thank you for it, and for all it brought to us.

And now dear, I'll bring this to a finish – I am enclosing David's £1 and also a list of the furniture[58] as they sent, soon after you arrived out here – have a go and see what you can do in valuation and return it to me. You had better keep a copy in case I want to refer to any particular item – and you can have a few weeks to do it.

Now don't go worrying about me, for being miserable, my tummy is quite better now – I nearly forgot to mention that – and no doubt it will all pass directly. I love you dear, you and the boys and all I want is just to be together.
Goodbye dear,
George

---

58. List has not survived.

Friday July 11th 1941
Hong Kong

My Dear,
It's Friday evening and late in the week for me to make a start on my letter – I intended to start yesterday evening and then quite unexpectedly had to stop late in the Yard – and so it didn't get started. Tonight I'm stopping again, but this time I'm only relieving Owen, who had to go out to a ship and so with nothing for me to do, I'm sitting in the office, in just a vest, trying to keep cool. Actually this is the first bit of overtime that's come my way for a month, and between you and me, I think that's one of the reasons why I haven't been so cheerful – no, I don't <u>only</u> mean from a financial outlook, although that counts, of course (tight); but besides that, it means going home, with a nice long evening and plenty of time to think and moon about. I can quite see how that must have been, and probably still is your trouble and of course the only temporary cure is to try and find something that keeps your mind busy – I say "temporary" as I know of a much more permanent one than that – you wait – that will keep your mind busy.

I've stayed in every evening this week, and so I'm afraid I haven't much in the way of news to report, and also, up to date, your letter has failed to put in an appearance. This is the month, July, that Jim Dawkins applied to go home in, but so far he has heard nothing – two other people, however who applied for their reliefs just before Jim have heard that they are appointed to Devonport – but when their reliefs will arrive they don't know, so they may be here months yet. Anyhow, Jim is hoping that he will hear something soon now, but I should imagine it will be some while yet before he leaves. Yes, my old problem will crop up again I suppose when he goes and of course it's harder to get anybody now, but still I won't tackle that fence until I get to it. Actually I don't think he is quite so keen to go now as he used to be and if Betty were out here he definitely wouldn't want to move, unless the boredom here gets worse than it is (if that is possible) and Mrs. Dawkins, I know, has quite got the wind up at the thought of having to go home, not that I blame her for that. I think about 80% of her letters to him consist of telling him of the various rumours she has heard – the date the women are coming back here, the number of people that are managing to slip into Hong Kong and how they do it, and shall she try it, and so on. Every letter is the same. He often reads bits like that out to me – is that what she is like to talk to?

Yes, this certainly is a funny war, and Germany's attack on Russia came as a surprise to me – it opens up enormous possibilities, but they <u>all</u> appear to depend on whether Russia can hold out until winter comes. So far, I suppose the German attack has been a success, more or less, but it does appear as though Russia is putting up more resistance than we thought they could. I rather fancy that by the time you get this, you'll be able to see more plainly what the chances are – personally I think the Russians will break, but then I always was a pessimist. If they only could hang out until winter, I believe it would be the beginning of the end for Germany. <u>We</u> are still muddling along nicely in the Middle East, but I will say our bombing of Germany seems to be coming along – but there, I expect you'll agree that that is quite enough of the military situation for one letter.

How are you dear? I'm always thinking of you and wondering what you are doing. Time doesn't seem to cure me of that, and when you describe the boys' antics I see them so plainly – yes, I want my family with me. I've been writing away, regardless of time, and have just looked up at the clock and am I late, so Goodnight dear.

Monday morning now, and I'm sorry to say I'm in a bit of a hurry. I was going to finish this yesterday and then Jim asked me to go with him to Kowloon Football Club to see a big bowls match (Colony championship) and we never got back home until late, had tea at the club and later went to the pictures. I thought I would have had plenty of time this morning, but of course it never works out like that – I've been rushing about all morning.

There was no letter from you this week, so I expect I shall get two next. A signal came round this morning to say compensation for loss of furniture is only payable to people who were householders in August 1939, so apparently we shall not get any. I still haven't heard from the

firm yet. Well dear, you must forgive me for the abrupt ending and I'll make up for it next week. Goodbye dear, all my love to you.
George.

Saturday July 19th 1941
Hong Kong

My Dear,
In last week's letter, I told you that yours hadn't turned up, and I began to think it was going to be the same this week. However, after waiting all the week, two letters arrived yesterday, Friday – one of them, posted July 6th, only taking twelve days, which wasn't too bad, I suppose.

And of course, the first thing I looked at, was your face – I've looked at it many times since then – yes, I know it only arrived yesterday, and although as a portrait I don't like it very much, it is a treat to be able to gaze at you again. I don't think it does you justice (or have I forgotten) but I certainly agree that you look posh – no wonder they want to sting the Hong Kong women, I can understand why they think you have plenty of money. But really dear, it <u>was</u> nice to get it and gave me quite a funny feeling in the tummy when I pulled it out of the envelope – how long, damn it!

So the story of the wealth of the Hong Kong chargemen has reached you via Mrs. W, but don't be too hard on her for that, because, while I know the motives that prompt the telling of the story, they are really justified in complaining. Assuming that he allows Mrs. W the same as I allow you, then I expect he picks up just about the same per month as I do, or even perhaps a little less – and that is <u>without</u> me working any overtime. I <u>know</u> that is the case with Mr. Ellis, because he told us his money one month, pointing out how he lost financially by becoming a foreman – and he is the same rank as Mr. W. It's true that under the new Income Tax, part of the money they pay is only borrowed, and will be paid back in a lump sum after the war, but it only amounts to about £1 a week – still they are really saving that amount, and of course they never mention that. The story about the £26 is of course made the most of – actually it was true, and applied to about six men for two weeks and you can guess they had to work to ten every night including Sunday – 15 hours a day for seven days a week, but that was very exceptional and the average chargeman working all the week at the usual overtime hours as you know them, earns about £12. I say earns, because he doesn't pick that up – all the Australian allowances have to be stopped which reduces it considerably. I've been working late <u>all</u> this week. In fact I'm in the office now, Saturday afternoon, and I might mention very sticky. It's just five o'clock now, so another 1 ¾ hours and I shall be going home to some chow and then on to pictures at the Alhambra.

Yes, same old programme – when are you coming?

We have rather a rush of work at the moment, and I expect I shall be working over for about a month. Next Monday we start a three night blackout practice – three nights mind you in this weather when it would be impossible to live with the windows covered up; I have some blue lights that just give enough light to move about, and we can eat in the "breakfast" room with the window covered and the fan on. Monday night we have searchlight exercises again, the first time for months, and so it will be late when I get home. I'll have time just to have supper and go to bed, but the other two nights I suppose Jim and I will have to go to pictures.

Yes dear, as you say in one of your letters, I expect feeling is high in Australia against the women that stayed. It is here, amongst the "bachelors", and I've heard all sorts of things, some of them most offensive, said in a loud voice, on the ferry, especially if the speaker has had two or three (or four) at the time. I know it's a cat in the manger feeling, but after all this time, it does make one bitter to see a crowd of them all together going some place, as we wend our way home to an empty flat. Sometimes the "nurses" give a show of some sort – they've just had a swimming gala in aid of the bomber fund, but I don't think any of the "bachelors", at least amongst the rank and file, would dream of going. But there, there's 900 of them, so I don't suppose they miss our support. Anyhow, when you all come back, you'll be so overjoyed as to forget all that – personally, I can't think of a better way of spending an evening than a dance in the Peninsula in the same company as we uster – unless it's just an evening together – <u>Anywhere</u> – damn it!

Well, my dear, it's Sunday morning at home now and I'm glad I started my letter yesterday in the office. All my letters these days seem to be finished in a rush and even this week I'm not much better. Working overtime all the week doesn't leave much time for letter writing, for I'm afraid I'm not in the writing mood by the time I get home and have supper. This morning I've been out paying the bills and doing a bit of shopping and for a haircut and it's nearly one o'clock. I did intend going out to the Walkers' matshed, but couldn't make it. But if I don't feel too lazy after tiffin, I might go this afternoon. And if I do, I'm afraid that will mean finishing this letter in the usual rush tomorrow morning.

You ask if I have heard how the Bakers like it in South Africa. Well, there's been a lot of rumours floating around about them. We didn't believe it at first but now I understand that it is true. I shall probably hear all about it tomorrow, as Brandon has apparently some news of them from his wife in Melbourne. The yarn we heard was that he had been sent home (cause unknown) – his wife left Melbourne, he joined her at the Cape, and they were torpedoed on the way home, but all saved. The story came from a Brisbane paper that published an interview with the survivors and quoted a Mrs. Baker as moaning about losing her bankbook. That certainly sounded like the right Mrs. B., but anyhow we've been waiting for Brandon to hear from his wife at Melbourne, as Mrs. Baker had never joined Mr in South Africa. If I see Brandon in the morning I'll add a postscript, but Owen said yesterday that the story is apparently true, and so, if so, he didn't get on too well, which after all is understandable – he had never worked on a ship in his life (always the shop) and that is the job he was pitch-forked into.

Owen read me an extract from his letter this week – Mrs. Owen was on a bus or tram and thought she knew the boy opposite her and then realised it was David Bearman and he <u>has</u> grown. That was all, at least all he read to me, but I wonder what changes I will see in them.

Oh! one thing more before I finish – I told you last week that I had just had a signal saying no compensation for our furniture. Well, they have now asked Admiralty if <u>they</u> can pay some compensation to those not entitled under the Board of Trade scheme, so we still have faint hopes – and so carry on estimating.

That's about all my news now, dear, and so again I must say Goodbye. I love you, dear, and want you more than ever – damn this letter writing, it's talking to you and seeing you that I want. Goodbye
George

P.S. (Monday morning.)
In the usual hurry, full of work this morning. Brandon can't confirm the story himself, but says Hurren's wife has had a letter announcing the Bakers' safe arrival in England. So, might be true – might not.

I went out to the Walkers' matshed yesterday afternoon – one of their visitors had a yacht there so four of us sailed back at night – Vic and Pamela, me and a bloke named Pullen. We left 14 ½ Mile Beach at 6.45 and got as far as Jordan Road Ferry by midnight, so gave it up there and landed by sampan[59]. But I'll tell you about it next week.
Goodbye my dear.

Friday July 25th 1941
Hong Kong

My Dear,
Friday evening, and like last week, I'm commencing my letter in the office – I've been fairly busy, but now I've done all I'm going to do today (I hope). At the moment I have a job to make a start on the letter, not just because I have no news, that's the same every week, but my mind is still attuned to work. That's one of the drawbacks of writing in the office – but I expect I'll forget work after a bit. So for the present I'll tell you about last Sunday's sailing trip that I mentioned in last week's P.S.

---

59. A relatively flat-bottomed boat, used for fishing and taxiing.

It was about 4.30 pm by the time I reached the Walkers' matshed, having had a five minutes after tiffin, to find that the Walkers had only arrived about an hour previously having sailed out in the yacht. We had a long bathe and then tea, and then I was offered either a trip back by car or in the yacht, after warning me that I might be late home if I chose the yacht. Well, time being no object, I yachted, so at 6.45 pm we set sail, to the cheers of all the beach – Pamela, Vic, me and a sergeant, Bob Pullen, from Kai Tak aerodrome (the chap from whom the Walkers bought the shed), and a Chinese "boy". The first thing we did was to sail backwards for over half a mile (more cheers from beach), but at last got the wind and off we went.

The first 1 ½ hours was rather slow, sailing a bit and then drifting a bit, but then we got a lovely breeze and bowled along in fine style – this part of the journey was very nice, dark by then of course, but cool and very quiet on the water. The wind took us all the way to Stonecutters by about 9.30 pm, which wasn't bad going – and then, alas, the wind dropped <u>completely</u> – if the tide had been against us, we would have gone backwards. As it was, we just drifted with the tide all the way from Stonecutters to the Yaumati Ferry, which took well over two hours, and then having got in some current, we just drifted to and fro in front of the ferry pier. You can guess we had had enough "yachting" by then, so we yelled for a sampan and deserted the boat, leaving the Chinese boy to drop anchor until the wind came up – we landed about midnight, so it was nearly half past twelve before I got home. The last two hours certainly got a bit boring, but on the whole it wasn't a bad trip and made a change at least.

Well dear, I'm afraid that's rather a lengthy yarn, but now I'm working over every night, I'm afraid it's the total of my social activities, since my last letter. We had our "blackout" this week, but only for two nights, Monday and Tuesday, but now that they carry blackouts right through the night, it's awkward getting up in the dark in the morning. Wednesday night, <u>we</u> performed on the searchlights and of course owing to summertime we couldn't start until late, and so it was ten o'clock before we finished.

Well my dear, it's Sunday morning again – I've just read over Friday evening's effort and I'm afraid there is too much "yacht" about it, but when it's the one thing that happens in a week it's a job to keep it out of my letter. It's been raining hard this morning, but is fine again now, and very sticky. In fact I think this week has been the "stickiest" week since I've been in Hong Kong. I worked yesterday until seven o'clock and then we went to the Alhambra to see Mickey Rooney in "Strike up the Band", and wasn't it hot – I came out of there with my trousers sticking to me and my shirt wet through – the warmest evening I've known I think. I can't understand your wanting to come back here – what with sweat, prickly heat (I'm covered with it) and mosquito stings, I think Hong Kong a most uncomfortable place. As regards the mosquitoes, they are rebuilding our battery shed and I think the "mossies" breed in all the rubble and muck lying about, with the result that we have a job to stop in our office, first thing in the morning and last thing at night.

No letter from you this week – to make up for the two last week I suppose, but yesterday there was a mail in from home, and I had one from Auntie. She reports that Reg was lost in the Fiji[60] during the Crete business – remember him? I'll answer Auntie's letter and then send it on to you – probably one or two others as well – only my letter writing time is restricted now with the overtime.

Well dear, tiffin is being put on the table, so I must finish again, but if I have time tomorrow morning, I'll add a bit more. I'm all right again now, dear, just fed up with all this writing, but we manage to keep moderately cheerful. Goodbye dear, for another week again.
George

Friday August 1st 1941
Hong Kong

Dear,
Yes, I'm still working late, and so once again I'm making a start on your letter in the office – this is the third overtime week right off, with

---

60. HMS *Fiji* was sunk at the Battle of Crete, May 22nd 1941. There were 523 survivors, but 241 men were lost.

possibly two more to come, and you can guess it's very welcome. Apart from work, it's been a fairly dull week, so once again I have nothing to report beyond going to the pictures on Wednesday – saw "Dulcie" at the Alhambra and it was quite laughable.

Heard the Hong Kong Husbands' broadcast to Australia last night, did you? And if so, what did you think of it? I thought the best was poor, and the majority "tripe" – but I admit the difficulty of a message of about thirty words. I didn't send a message in, for I couldn't imagine sending one of the sort they wanted, not after all this time – it seemed so puerile (is that the right word?), although I admit that while listening to the others I thought that possibly the words didn't matter after all, and that it's just the sound of a familiar voice that counts. However, I'm afraid I am still not enamoured with the idea – what do you think?

Well Hilda, it's now Sunday again – I was interrupted the other evening and then tried to make another start yesterday afternoon, but one thing after another cropped up and I eventually had to give it up. We went to the pictures in the evening, last house, not much of a picture, and then met Harry Little afterwards and went round to the K.B.G.C. for a drink – quite a crowd round there having a sing-song so we joined in for about an hour and got home one-ish. This morning has brought a change in the weather. No. 1 has just gone up and it's been raining all the morning and quite cool – the first cool spell for a long while. Jim Dawkins is of course like a bear with a sore head because there are no bowls today, but even so, judging by what he tells me, she must be worse than him, every day. He had two letters from her this week and apparently they just consisted of damning everything, the Government, Australian Authorities, Australian people – so much so and in so unmistakable language that the censor had cut a lot of it out. By the way, talking of censors, are many of my letters censored now?[61] Nearly all of yours are. But to return to the subject, if she really is as she writes, then her life must be a misery to her. He has just got our Chief to send a telegram home, asking for a reply to his previous letters, "Re Dawkins' relief", so he might hear something in the future.

---

61. A few of George's letters did not survive intact. But of those that did, and which are reproduced in this book the censor deleted nothing during this period.

Our very "Rev" Higgs has done his duty again, "as he sees it" – he got long leave to go to New Zealand and has now written to say he won't be coming back as he considers it his duty to be with his wife and family. That was in yesterday's paper – in the same paper it was published that Rosenthal, Vicar of Christ Church, was also resigning to go to Australia, as he considered it his first duty to provide a home for his family. Almost like the rats leaving – isn't it?

The Yard is now taking another step to bring it in line with the Services – they are going to give each of us an identification disc with the type of our blood engraved on it – the idea being that in the event of injury they can rush up the right type of blood without delay. To do this we are all in the process of having our blood tested, to see what grade it belongs to, and at the same time they ask if you are willing to be a "donor" – I go next week and I think I will agree to be one.

It appears as though we have another casualty in our department but keep it under your hat until it's confirmed. You remember Kettle, Inspector, well he was bad about three weeks ago and went into hospital for T.B. tests and before he went, he told Jim Dawkins that he was convinced he had it. A week later he said that the hospital reported "No", but that he was going to hospital at his own request under observation – now <u>we</u> have never heard the official hospital report, but our Chief must have, and he has said that he doesn't think Kettle will return to work in Hong Kong Yard again. He, Kettle, has been in hospital two weeks now and if it were true I should imagine he would soon be going home.

Well dear, last week's letter arrived Monday and it looks as though the same thing will happen this week. I'm glad David had a nice Birthday, thirteen now. Eh! He is certainly getting on – unfortunately we are too. It would be better if we could stand still and watch them grow up, wouldn't it? By the way, you speak of the mortgage on "37" – I believe Auntie mentioned in one of her letters that it is somewhere about £90 still – a bit more than I thought. Anyhow, I remitted the £20, not actually sending money, so there is no fear of loss. Also I asked her to see if she could only pay the interest, in which case £20 will last a long while.

Well dear, that's all again for this week. Hong Kong is just the same, although it remains to be seen how this "freezing" order will affect prices[62]. Things are considerably dearer now to what they were, but they might get worse yet. Goodbye, dear, for one more week again. Goodbye.

P.S. You didn't put David's report in last week's letter – hadn't you received it or was it <u>too</u> bad?

Do the boys still want me to put the <u>set</u> of stamps on the envelope – what do they do with them?

Wednesday August 6th 1941
Hong Kong

Dear,
Your letter that I should have had last week arrived yesterday, and I fully appreciate the difficulty of writing letters under these conditions – every week – very few weeks have I any news to write about, especially if I'm working late all the week, and writing your letter is interspersed with many a "what shall I say now". In fact if a loquacious person like you has difficulty in finding things to talk about, then have pity on poor me. Still, it's not what's in the letter that matters, it is just the fact that it's from you and that there'll be another one next week that makes the weeks go by. How those poor devils, whose wives are in England, and they have to wait weeks, sometimes months before they get their letters – how they manage, I don't know. I find it bad enough when the mail is late and I have to go a week without one.

Well I had another complete week of overtime last week and one this, but the job will finish towards the end of next week I think. By the way, Harry Little, was asking after you, mentioned that you had had the flu and said this particular variety ended by affecting the stomach and that everybody was sick for a couple of days – was it very bad? Anyway,

---

62. At the end of July 1941, the Vichy government in French Indochina agreed to allow the Japanese use of their military bases in southern Indochina. In protest, Britain and America imposed a freeze on trade with Japan and a freeze on all Japanese assets within their countries.

judging by your last letter you seemed to have got over it by then, so I hope you didn't have too bad a time.

Saturday now, dear, and I'm afraid I didn't get very far with your letter on Wednesday evening – I've been very busy just lately and even when I get home it's late and too warm to feel like getting down to letter writing. Proper August weather we're having now – hot, but dry. It's nearly six o'clock and the temperature in our office as I write this is 92^0. I went to the surgery yesterday morning for the blood test – they push a needle in a vein in the bend of the arm, just like inoculation, and then draw out the blood, about a teaspoonful I should think – anyway an hour later you have a job to find the spot the needle entered.

I was just having my tiffin in the office this afternoon when in walked the boy with your letter of July 27th – a nice long one, and was an exceedingly nice third course. Incidentally, I think it provided me with my biggest laugh since the evacuation – yes, David's latest invention I mean.[63] I really enjoyed that. Unfortunately, only Ronald Foster was in the office, the others having gone home, but I'll read that bit to them on Monday. What a lad! A few more like him and this war would be won – whatever was the drawing like? I expect if Heath Robinson had seen it, he would have sued David for infringing his copyright. Tell him to get on with some idea for dropping families into Hong Kong, although as you say, things aren't too settled at the moment.

Hong Kong doesn't alter, though, and things are just the same here, although I see in the paper that Hong Kong folk are accused of living with their heads in the sand. Still, the authorities have manufactured so many "crises" in the past, including the one of July 1st 1940, and they've cried "wolf" too often to expect the people here to get in a flutter. Yes, if things settle down, and you do get back, we will certainly buy some furniture here to take home, as renewals will cost a dickens of a lot at home after the war. Actually we are a few things better off than I thought, for I had forgotten you had packed a few things at your

---

63. David had invented a design for a machine to improve weapon efficiency, and which he'd sent to the patent office. A report had appeared in a local newspaper.

mother's. How about the piano – have you heard lately if that is all right?

Not much news this end again – Jim Dawkins is fuming because there has been no reply to last week's telegram, but it looks as though two more people, both Inspectors, will be on the move as a telegram has arrived asking if they can be spared. Mr. Holmes leaves this week for home via Australia, where he will have two weeks' leave before going on with his wife – Admiralty have been asked if this procedure can be carried out with everybody going home, owing to the difficulty of arranging the junction of husband and a family at some place en route. Well dear, time is getting on now, and I'm just off home, so I'll just put the tailpiece tomorrow morning. Goodnight, my dear.

Sunday now, Hilda, and I've just read your letter again and had another laugh over David – I read it out to Jim Dawkins who was much tickled. The bit about his school report, though, comes as something of an anti-climax and you must point out to him, that if he doesn't do better he won't have the technical knowledge to put those imaginative ideas into operation.

I've just been reading today's paper and Australia is apparently taking the Eastern problem very seriously – the papers down your end seem inclined to panic, much in contrast to peaceful Hong Kong. However, don't go worrying about me before it's necessary, and even then, not more than you can help – I expect this will blow over like all the others, though. Well dear, I don't think I have much more news for you, except that this week I bought a dozen pairs of silk stockings for you. I shan't be sending them now, as I bought them just to keep in reserve – anyhow you know you're better off for stockings than you thought you were. That's all then, dear, as I want to add a page for David. Goodbye, my dear.
George

Sunday August 10th
Dear David,
Many thanks for your very breezy letter which arrived with Mum's this week. She told me all about your "wonderful" invention and I had

quite a laugh out of it, with the other fellows in my office. One of them passed the remark, "Brainy kid that", but I didn't tell him about your school report – 40th out of 46 – what was the matter with the other six? Really, though, David, it won't be any good having ideas if you can't make them work through just lack of knowledge, that you should have got at school. No, I don't want this to be a lecture, but don't forget I shall be very disappointed if I get another report like that one, so come on, buck up.

Well, that's enough of that, don't you think, so we'll leave that subject. Yes, I'll try and get the Chinese writing things if I can, but you'll have to wait until I'm sending a parcel – as it's quite a business now you know. You have to go personally and get an export licence for every single thing sent out of the Colony. So you want a picture of my mug do you? Well, I'll see what I can do. Perhaps I'll have a "frowning" one done especially for you, to look at when you're doing your homework (or rather <u>not</u> doing it). Well, cheers, David, I'm glad you had a nice Birthday and write again soon.
Goodbye and love from Dad.

Wednesday August 13th 1941
Hong Kong

My Dear
Wednesday evening and I'm still writing from the office – the last hour has just started, so if I don't get interrupted this will be episode 1. It's still very hot; every day the temperature goes over 90^0; it's been 93^0 in the office all the afternoon and even now it's 91^0. Remember what it's like going to bed these hot nights – it's much cooler having a bed to oneself, I'm all for it.

Well, Jim D. has had a reply to his telegram at last and apparently, he is appointed to Devonport. I say apparently, because the telegram never mentioned his appointment, but said approval had been granted to the boy to continue his apprenticeship at Devonport and free passage granted the family to rejoin him at Devonport or pick him up at Hong Kong at the Commodore's discretion. Anyway, they have now sent more telegrams home – one asking when his relief is coming, as he can't otherwise be spared, and the other asking if he can rejoin the family in Australia. Well, to sum up, it does seem as though he will be going soon now, in a month or two at the most, I should think, but we won't hear for certain until the replies arrive – perhaps next week I'll be able to tell you more.

Two more moves are underway – Singapore again, and both are shipwright chargemen, and I understand they will leave next week. The funny part of this move is that they called for volunteers and had five, and then the powers that be select one volunteer, and add another who wasn't. Of course the other four volunteers who were not picked are kicking up a row about it, but whether that will make any difference I rather doubt – chargemen being the proverbial small meat.

This afternoon I paid a visit to the Cashiers and remitted another £20 (sterling) to you, which will leave here the <u>end</u> of August – it is the limit they will let me remit in any one month or I would make it more. Must go now, so Cheerio, dear.

Ah me! Sunday morning at home now, and as usual I'm all of a rush – I never seem to get time to do all that I want to do these days. It's a combination of the weather and the overtime that's against me. It has been hot this week, and still is this morning, every day this week over 90^0 and of course this is the week we would do dynamo trials on my job – 110^0 in the dynamo room, and after putting in several hours down there during the course of the day, I just don't feel like doing anything by the time I get home at 8.15. I say anything, although by the time I've had a bath and supper is over, there's not a lot of time left. That job I've been working on, by the way, is finished with the exception of a few further trials and now I've started another similar one, so I suppose I shall be working late for about another four weeks now – but as you know I would rather be spending my time in a profitable manner than any other way now.

Oh, yes! Yesterday we had a memo round to say that we would probably pick up our back money on Friday, the 29th of August, and that arrangements were being made whereby we could remit over the limit to Australia if we cared to. Now, I have already made out my remittance for this month, but tomorrow I'll go to the Cashiers and see if I can get it altered, so next week I'll tell you what exactly the remittance is that you can expect. If it's the back money it will be about £80 sterling – not bad, eh! Unfortunately, I shall lose all the thrill of picking up £80 – I shan't even see it, but just receive a chit to say it has been remitted to you. It's all those things, the little rejoicings – I know they don't really matter, but they go to make up our normal life together. All day and every day I miss you, Hilda. It gets worse as time goes on.

Well dear, no Australian mail for anybody again this week, and I have no further news so I'm going to finish. I want to get all the "doings" done this morning again, so that I can go out to the beach this afternoon to the Walkers. I ran into Vic last night, on my way home from work and told him I was coming – that was the first time I've seen either of them for a month, since the Sunday we sailed back, which was also, by the way, the date of my last bathe. Vic said they intended to sail out there today, but judging by the amount of wind this morning, it would be quicker to walk. I am taking your last week's letter with me, to read that bit about David and his invention to them – I know Pamela will appreciate that. That's all then dear, so Goodbye again.
George

Monday midday

Dear,
Your letter has just arrived. I've shown the cutting about David all round, but what a pity his name wasn't on it – I hope you've sent a cutting home. Mum and your mother will be thrilled and Auntie would send it round England. Apparently, the idea was not so daft as I thought. Well, I can't stop now as I'm just posting. Goodbye dear.

It struck me that while I got quite a kick from David's "doings", all I did in my letter to him was get on to him about school. Tell him I think it's very nice to have a son with "big things in this head" and congratulate him from me.
Cheerio, George

P.S. Tell David that when I bought the stamps this week, I was told that they were selling the last of the "4 cents" and that no more would be made.

Cheerio. G

Wednesday August 20th 1941
Hong Kong

My Dear,

Another week, and another letter from the same office, and of course it will be full of news like all the others – yes, like you, I'm getting tired of this letter writing. There, that's a very bad beginning again, but if you're any good at reading between the lines, you'll be able to deduce that I have a rather bad cold in the head. I think those three day dynamo trials last week are responsible; anyhow, a stuffy head this weather is hard-going, especially when you have a lot of work to do, and I think I have been more busy the last two months, than at any time in Hong Kong.

Well dear, it's Sunday morning now, and as you see, I didn't get very far with my letter the other evening. I made one or two other attempts later in the week, but was interrupted on each occasion. I don't think I've written home for a month and I owe everybody letters now, but I just don't get the chance, or at least I had better qualify that by saying that when I get the opportunity it's too darned hot to write letters. Well, my cold is not a lot better yet. It's going through all the usual stages, so I suppose it will soon make a move now – but that and the heat have certainly got me down this week. Small blisters have come up on my toes now, just to make things more comfortable – still, one more week and August will be over and it will gradually cool off from there.

One bright bit this week dear, is about the money – I went along to the Cashiers last Monday. He wouldn't tell me how much I had to come for the back money, so I asked him to remit the whole of it, whatever it was, to you. And then Friday I received a receipt for £97 sterling – so my remittance at the end of this month will be £97 plus the original £20 that I had already remitted, making £117 in all. You'll get something over £140 (Australian) for that, and let me know when it arrives.

Well dear, your letter arrived last Monday, just as I was setting out for home at 12 o'clock, and as I had to post my letter on the way, it was a very hurried P.S. that I scribbled on the back. I must admit that I did get quite a kick from the cutting. It was a great pity that David's name wasn't printed with it – but anyhow I hope he doesn't get a "swelled head" from it all – I don't think he will, he's not that type.

With regard to the picture, I'll send a snap on as soon as I get a chance – and that means when this darn cold is gone – but what's wrong with shorts, sounds to me as though you're having a crack at my legs again.

One incident in the flat this week – late on Thursday evening we found the "frig" wouldn't work and of course that's serious this weather, so we carried out an investigation and came to the conclusion that the fuses had gone downstairs. In the morning, however, we soon found the reason – someone had cut out and stolen about 40ft of the wire that runs up the stairs. I asked Wing On, the robbers, to replace it and they want me to pay $11, so they won't do the job – in the meantime we're running the frig from the electric light until we find somebody cheaper. Hong Kong is a nice place and all the thieves aren't in Sydney after all.

Well, dear, that's about all my news, except that I went out to the beach last Sunday – no, that didn't have anything to do with my cold, or did it? I set out after tiffin, by bus, and arrived there three-ish; very nice out there, considerably cooler than in town and I had two bathes and came home by car about nine o'clock. Yes, I told them all about David's turn out (I didn't have the cutting then, of course) and as I thought, they were very much tickled.

I haven't seen Eve for ages now. I'll have to make a trip out to see her when this overtime finishes.

Well, dear, that's all again for another week. Jim Dawkins still hasn't heard anything with regard to his relief, and that is about my news. Goodbye then, dear. George

Tuesday August 26th 1941
(posted September 1st)
Hong Kong

My Dear,

I received your letter today, and you certainly made me envy you with your description of the Australian winter. It can't be very cold to have the roses blooming, and frosts must be extremely rare or absent altogether, and just about the coldest part of the winter too. Hong Kong could do with a spot of just that sort of weather, although it has been much cooler now for two days – unfortunately, we had to have rain to get it cooler, and I don't think it's left off for those two days. Still the coolness is more than welcome for all that, and my cold, which is still with me, is much more bearable now.

Talking of gardens reminds me that I had a letter from Winnie last week, full of the allotment and its products, for which I expect they are very grateful now. She says Eddie has done his garden "all pillars, and steps and crazy pavement and flowers everywhere, just like a little bit of Hampton Court". She had hardly anything to say about the actual war, which shows how quiet and peaceful a time they are having now, in comparison to last winter. You know, it came as quite a surprise to hear that people are still doing their gardens – I don't quite know what I did expect, but I had the impression that life in England was far too upset to think of gardens and flowers. By the way, Eddie's divorce case hasn't come up yet, owing to bombing of the Courts and congestion of cases – you mention John's in one letter as being under way. How far has that progressed? Oh, there was one other thing in Winnie's letter – how bad it is now they are rationed for clothes. She bought a shirt for Sid for his birthday and had to give seven of his coupons for it. What a game that must be.

Sunday morning now, my dear, and I'm sitting at the old familiar spot on the verandah. Can you picture it now? Or have you been away too long? I often try to imagine you sitting over there on the other cane chair. I wonder if you ever will? I'm afraid I have my doubts as to it being in Hong Kong, but sometime, some place, you will be sitting "over there" – my dear, may it be soon.

Well dear, only one thing of note to report from Hong Kong this week and that is a meeting of the Husbands that took place in the Peninsula on Thursday – I didn't go through work; I was the only one on in our section, so it would have been difficult to get off, but in any case it would have cost me £1 and I don't think I could have done that much good by going (tight). The meeting was called, owing to the action of a committee member, on the committee for only about two months, who wrote to the papers making charges against the committee – the old committee were of course fairly well known Hong Kong people, and one of the charges he made was that in 14 months they had done nothing, and owing to their social position never would do anything. Well, at the meeting, the committee answered the charges, and then eventually a vote of No Confidence was proposed and passed which split the meeting – the old committee and all the "best people" walking right out. Another committee was duly elected, including three "dockies", one of them being Chairman.

Anyway, the others did nothing, except perhaps a bit of personal axe grinding, so these can't do less – they tried to see the Governor the next day, but he wouldn't see them; he leaves the Colony next Wednesday[64], so I don't suppose he cares a lot. By the way, Mrs Governor arrived in Hong Kong last week, to help him pack, and the Press considered it very bad taste that that should be mentioned at the meeting. Ah me, I think you're going to remain in Australia a bit longer yet, although this morning's papers are all full of hints of Japan climbing down – paper talk I expect and they are just as likely to print scare headlines again next week.

Yes, all smiling faces in the Yard Friday when the blokes were picking up their bundles of money – a very nice windfall, eh! But I expect some of them will manage to run through it before very long. There were of course a number of celebrations last night – we called into the club after the pictures, so that I could stand Jim a drink on the strength of it, but I would like my celebration to take the form of a Chinese show if it could be arranged, but you want a party for that. Anyhow, you know

---

64. To be replaced in September 1941 by Sir Mark Aitchison Young.

my celebration will be fairly mild. You can have one too, you know, when you get it – if only you had been here, we could have had a nice shopping expedition – one day dear. By the way, speaking of money, are your travellers cheques still O.K? Are there any restrictions of time or anything on them, do you know? My letter of last week, by the way, was posted or – at least I hope it was, by one of my Chinese as it was pouring hard with rain. So, if it doesn't turn up, let me know. I forgot to number it, but it should have been No. 20, and it contained all the details about the remittance (£117).

Well, my dear, here's the end once again and all that's left is to say goodbye. My cold is all gone from my head now, but I still have a bit of a cough, so I got another bottle of medicine yesterday. The weather is warmer again now, but not nearly like it was. Well, my dear, that's all, so Cheerio and love to you all from
George

27th June 1941[65]
83 College Road, Isleworth

Dear George,
Don't pass out or "chuck a dummy" when you realise that at long last I am writing to you. It's not in commemoration of anything or to mark a birthday – for a long time I've been saying, "I'll write to George – soon." Time passes so very quickly it's hard to realise you have been away from England so long and that such a lot has transpired since your departure. As Winnie writes pretty regularly there's not a great deal of news to tell. The amusing thing about your letters is the references to Winnie's remarks – remarks that seem years old at times. Your letter bearing the set of stamps arrived quite safely – it took as long to come as your previous sea-borne mail. The stamps must have increased the value of my collection by 100%. Anyhow, many thanks for them – they're a fine set and worth having. I still collect the few stamps that come my way but I'm anything but an ardent collector.

---

65. Letter from George's brother-in-law, Sid Haslen, received, September 1941.

Of recent times we've had the weather one longs for but seldom seems to obtain when on holiday. Real June sunshine – no cold winds, and when one desires an open-air job provided one doesn't have to work very hard. After a longish period of wet and cold, the sun wrought miracles in the gardens which are now a blaze of colour, the roses being particularly fine. The sun has brought us out more and instead of doing the garden and other jobs we spend many evenings gadding about. I expect Winnie reported on the exhibition tennis we watched and the dance to finish off the day? On several evenings we've used our bikes to see round some of the local places that we haven't visited before.

Having a day's holiday owing to me in lieu of Good Friday I decided to take it last Tuesday while the weather seemed settled. We plonked for a day on the river and were glad we decided to do so, because the day was ideal and the trip thoroughly enjoyable. We cycled to Whitton; left our bikes at Mum's and travelled by train to Windsor. We were on the river by 11 a.m. and off round about 8 o'clock. We punted downstream – I suppose paddled is the correct word – leaving the harder work for our return. It really was grand. We stopped at Datchet for a drink. We were surprised Datchet was such a likeable place – rather old-fashioned – and made a note to start from there on our next river trip. There's no need for me to enter into a long description of the river, as I believe you know it pretty well. The river was at its best. There was a fair number of boats about, but it was much quieter than upstream from Windsor. We passed a craft – a motor cruiser – named "Andante". Winnie suggested if it were hers she would re-christen it "Presto"!![66] War seemed non-existent – we could have done with some oranges and apples – planes were flying about at varying intervals – a soldier asked (yes!, asked not told) us, when we were just floating near one bank, to kindly go across stream if anyone was about – and just some barrage balloons in the sky.

Then the other aspect – who would think that after nearly 22 months of war we could spend a happy day like that? And only a madman could have imagined that we would be fighting the French and Germany

---

66. Musical terms for moderately slow and quick tempo - Winnie too was a piano teacher, having at one time been Hilda's pupil.

the Russians – what will be the position in six months? A year? Or ten years? I, for one, have given up forecasting future happenings. What a blessing when this b----y war comes to an end.

According to a newspaper advert, Sarah Churchill was playing in "Marie Rose" at the "Q" Theatre for the week commencing 23rd June, so we decided to go along on Wednesday. We bought the tickets, found our seats, and when we opened the programme – what a sell, we were a week too soon. We watched a thriller, well-acted, "Kick In" – and we could have kicked something ourselves, especially when the beautiful weather was laughing at us outside.

Last evening we paid a social call – is that how one should say it? – to the home of a couple of girls from our Tennis Club. We consumed a tea well up to pre-war standard – except that I've given up taking sugar with my tea – and then played cards in the garden for the remainder of the evening – I finished a few bob to the good.

I continue to work late at the office fairly frequently. So far we have five of our colleagues in the forces – one is training to be a pilot. The remainder of us under forty are being de-reserved – and the first man has had his medical exam – with the promise of a rapid call-up. We don't know when, but individual times will come. Have you any vacancies in Hong Kong or would you recommend some other spot?

I'm optimistic enough to put down the last two weeks of August for my holiday. We don't anticipate going away – for my part a holiday at home gives one a chance to do things and go places that are denied us in the ordinary way. Perhaps the war will have been finished by then, then we'll have a chance of making real whoopee – I don't think!

The fellows are being replaced by girls in every walk of life, in addition to offices, bus and tram conductors – labourers in the workshops – a plumber working at our office told me he has been informed that he'll soon have a woman labourer. I saw a gang of women painters renovating a Southern railway station recently – and did they look tough? I should think some of them would make good shock troops.

Judging by the girls in the office I think the girls will find it hard to have to relinquish their jobs after the war.

In a week's time we hope to pay another visit to my parents – hoping our visit coincides with "strawberry time". During the last few weeks a number of bombs have been dropped in the fields near them. We up here have had quiet nights (touch wood) with only an occasional warning. We must thank the Russian business for the decrease in raiding. We have been sleeping upstairs for a long while now; but we still keep a bed in the dining room as our insurance.

I suppose you know we are rationed for clothes. We'll be all right as we grow rhubarb, which I consider more efficient than fig leaves. A shirt and two collars call for seven coupons out of a yearly allowance of 66. But still, I expect the Government will supply many of us with our next suits.

We're anxiously watching the tomatoes in the garden – they're late this year – now beginning to bloom. The price of tomatoes is controlled from last week at 1/2 per lb. Last week the price was round about 3/-. Now there's not so many about or perhaps they're bought up quicker. When you can get them most greengrocers limit you to half a pound. Other things in the garden and in the allotment – allotment sounds too good as I only have about one third of a ten-rod plot – are doing well at the moment. We should really keep our eyes on next winter rather than hope for produce for immediate consumption.

We're now having double Summer Time – 11 p.m. when it's only 9 o'clock by the sun. I like it although it's a shock when bedtime approaches. To a certain extent we follow the old advice, "Early to bed and early to rise, etc," but I don't see where the wealthy part comes in.

I don't know if it's the same with you but we find the time simply rushes by and we can only manage to get through a small portion of the things we want to. Still, I suppose the quicker the time goes the more rapidly will we be at peace again. Or nearer the next war!

Hoping you are getting plenty of sport and keeping off the beer (!) –
I understand that supplies of that commodity are hard to obtain in
certain districts; and at times one queues up for "smokes" – I'll finish
by wishing you all the very best of luck and may the day be near when
we'll be seeing you again.
Cheerio,
Sid

Thursday September 4th 1941
(Posted September 8th)
Hong Kong

Dear,
What a rotten lot of organisers we have in our Post Office – my letter
to you must be posted Monday tiffin time, and over the last four weeks
one letter of yours arrived at twenty minutes to twelve, and the other at
three something in the afternoon. Not that either of us write anything
to which we want a quick answer – nearly every time I finish a letter
nowadays I think, "Well, that's not much of a letter, but I'm afraid it will
have to do," and then yours turns up and gives me a few fresh ideas.
Still, as I say, it's seldom there's anything important in them, and what
isn't written one week gets done the next.

Yes, this first contribution is still being written in the office, but I think
next week will see the end of the job (unfortunately) – I've already had
seven complete weeks overtime, right through the warmest part of the
summer, and quite a good bit previous to that, so a rest won't come
amiss, although of course once you start this resting business you never
know how long it's going to last. Ah! Just talking about resting wasn't
I! Well, our boy has just arrived down here from the office with orders
from the Chief for the Searchlight crews. They will be exercised from
10 pm next Sunday night until 2 am Monday morning – that will be
nice! Anyway, it does say that he will have the motor boat waiting to
take us over to Kowloon when the exercise is finished, so we might get
to bed about three.

By the way, I said I had been on continuous overtime; that is not quite right, as I had Tuesday evening off this week – No. 1 went up in the afternoon, but we didn't see anything of a typhoon, only a very small drop of rain the next day; anyhow, I made good use of the evening by writing to Mum. I've been trying to get that one off my chest for a long time, but it's been too hot – I meant to get it home in time for her Birthday, September 8th. The spirit was willing, but again the flesh was weak; anyway, I've sported a five dollar Clipper mail to help make up a little time.

I had a letter from my brother-in-law this week, Sid I mean. I wrote to him back last – when was it? – the first day of the Hong Kong Centenary Stamps, to let him have a first day set, so I suppose he felt he ought to answer it. He says it's very quiet and they've gone back to sleeping upstairs in their bed, and also that there is a chance that he might get called up – I bet Winnie doesn't stop there on her own if that happens. He had just had a day off (June), so they spent it on the river – train to Windsor and all day in a punt, going downstream to Datchet – we haven't been below Windsor, nor do we know Datchet, but he quite made me homesick describing the old familiar river sights. How would you like this summer, NOW, on the river with the nips!

Well, my dear, after all that, how are you? You started your last letter (the one I received last Monday) by saying "We're O.K. etc," but I don't mean you, but YOU, the inner man, if you get my meaning. Are you getting as tired of all this as I am? Everybody here too are kidding themselves that you will all be back by Xmas, but what it's based on I can't see, and I'm afraid of just hope without reason; the fallback to the depths again is always worse after the uplift. And now that must do for tonight – as usual I've carried on up to the last minute and now have to shave and wash in a hell of a hurry – So, Goodnight, dear.

Well, here we are again, another Sunday morning – how they come and go! It's just two years ago that we stood on the roof, the day war was declared, and watched the Germans being rounded up. Ah me, many things have happened since then!

Your letter of August 24th arrived yesterday, just to put me in the wrong, after saying that they always arrive <u>after</u> I post mine – but I expect we shall make up for it by not getting any at all next week. However, I'll go on with what news I have. Jim Dawkins hasn't been too well this week, been home since Tuesday, but like you say about Mrs. Little, don't pass it on. Apparently the symptoms are like flu, aching all over, but no temperature – doctor thinks it might be dengue fever, nothing serious but rotten for a few days; trouble is that with the warm weather (and the aches) he can't stay in bed comfortable for very long and he's a restless soul at the best of times – I tell you, bear with a sore head's not in it. He still hasn't heard any more about his relief, so his sailing date is still up in the air – as he says, he may still be here at Xmas. My position is that I <u>won't</u> be sent home at the end of my time, but beyond that – well, anything, it just depends on what is required, but like you I hope something transpires during that year, <u>and</u> I don't want it to be Singapore.

As you forecasted, I don't know what to say about David – what Mrs. Little said about Terry is what Auntie always said about Victor – that he wasn't so bad until the doctors operated on his nose and throat. I'm not very keen, I'm afraid, on an operation, but I suppose I'm only unsettling your mind more than ever. Have you seen the specialist yet?

I had a cable from your mother on Thursday, to say that my parcel arrived safely on September 3rd – so I'm hoping that if one got there safely, the other three did. I want to hear how the butter arrived, but I believe that now the parcels are restricted very much again and only <u>very small</u> ones can be sent. Your folk needn't have cabled though, that's another 5/- to add on to the cost and they were dear enough as it was.

Well dear, once more I've reached the end – even of the "tailpiece", so I suppose it's goodbye again. I'm having a lazy day today, which of course includes a sleep this afternoon, in view of our session on the searchlights tonight at 10 o'clock (9.30 we have to be there).

How do you like the "photo"? It was done at a Chinese trade fair last Xmas – the profile's not bad but he's made my head too fat – perhaps though it's a character reading as well. (It's better for me to say it before one of the nips thinks of it.)

And now, that really is all, so I will say goodbye.
Cheerio, my dear
George

P.S. Re stamps.
No more "4 cents" can be bought and they are not renewing. I still have a few left, so I will carry on with sets until they are gone. Don't forget I want two sets kept for me. The boys can keep one set each and then they won't fight.
Goodbye, G

Saturday September 13th 1941
(Posted September 15th)
Hong Kong

Dear,
Saturday afternoon, and I'm afraid that even now this contribution will only be a small one – all the week I've tried to make a start but haven't been able to. Plenty of work this week; with trials on two boats due to start Monday and enough work still to do that when the No. 1 went up at midday today we had orders to carry on, even if the boats went out to typhoon moorings. The result is that presently I have to go out in the motorboat to collect the men – anyway, I'm afraid I am very dull this week for I haven't any news as it's just been a week of work, come home and go to bed. We had our searchlight practice last Sunday night that I told you about – arrived in the Yard at 9.30 pm and left again at 1.30 on Monday morning; everything went off all right and I had an hour off in the morning, getting to work at 8 o'clock. There, I think that's a record of my week and as there has been no Australian mail in, I haven't even a letter to answer.

Our great item of interest in Hong Kong at present is an enquiry that is being held into the affairs of the A.R.P. with regard to contracts for digging tunnels and erecting shelters, etc. Some dreadful things are coming to light. It seems it was one gigantic swindle and so far, Mr Hobbs, the A.R.P. architect has shot himself and another has attempted suicide by poisoning, but a great many more are involved. Has anything got into the papers down there about it? I wish you could read our papers, we get nearly two pages of evidence every day and I have never heard of anything like it before – thousands of dollars appear to have found their way into various pockets but whether the enquiry can prove which pockets is another matter. The Chinese firms just don't keep account of any "awkward" things and questions dealing with those things are always answered with "I don't remember". Well dear, so far I've had two bites at the above, and now it's nearly time to go home – yes, the usual Saturday night programme, chow and then pictures at either the Majestic or Alhambra, so cheerio then until tomorrow.

Sunday evening now – nearly the end of a lazy, yes and lonely day, although that I suppose is my own fault. This morning was spent reading and I am afraid a doze and then a bath and out for a haircut and pay the compradore. This afternoon I intended to go out to the beach – Pamela phoned me yesterday, but after tiffin I had a couple of minutes shut eye; and woke up at 5 o'clock – still, I expect the rest did more good than a bathe would have done, especially as it was just cool enough to enjoy a lie down. The No. 1 is still up, but you wouldn't know otherwise that there was a typhoon about.

Jim Dawkins is all right again now. He's been back to work all this week – had four days off last week, but he is more restless than ever. There's still no news of his relief – that is annoying you know, and I think more upsetting than our position.

Well my dear, I think this is going to be one of my "hopeless" letters. I have just nothing to put down – I think it must be a case of "all work and no play", for I certainly feel dull where letter writing is concerned this week. Yes, I shall be working over again next week – that easing off is still being put back but we're reaching the trial stage now, so it won't last much longer.

Well, that "peace in the Pacific" seems as far off as ever – it still looks, even though things have died down now again, as though Japan will continue sitting on the wall – in fact I don't see that she can do any other. There will be no war here, I'm convinced, unless we are defeated by Germany, and Japan's role at present is still to tie up our forces out here, and the only hope I can see for the "evacuated" is that sometime in the future the ban might be lifted and they might allow the return under the same conditions as at Singapore – pay your own fare, etc.

And now, dear, I'm going to give up this struggle and hope I am more "inspired" next week – we heard the mail came in today, so I'll leave this open until tomorrow morning. Goodbye dear – I still think nice things of you even if I can't write them, and I still love you dear. Goodbye.
George.

Monday morning

Mail is in and delivered, but apparently mine is still en route – it will arrive during the week I expect.
Cheerio, G.

Tuesday September 16th 1941
(Posted September 22nd)
Hong Kong

Dear,
This is Tuesday morning; I haven't received your letter yet, and I don't think that at the moment I am any more inspired than last week. Still, the point is, that our typhoon has developed now as a properly brought up typhoon should; No. 7 is up and it's blowing hard and rain coming down in sheets – the ferry was running early this morning, although they've stopped now, so that we managed to get in all right but have no work as of course all the ships have gone to typhoon positions. Hence, you see we are in the office with a good opportunity of catching up with our letter writing – I meant to get on with one for home when I got the pad out, and then thought I'd start episode 1 of your letter first. Speaking of writing home reminds me that I had a note from your mother the week before last; no news (except that she hadn't heard

from you for a long time) so I won't send it on; but she mentions that she sent some snaps of themselves, hoping they would reach you for your Birthday – she sent me some too, so if you didn't get yours I will send mine on to you.

Well Hilda, I think we're just as daft here as the folk at your end – yesterday morning we heard "for certain" that the ban was being lifted, and that it would be published in the midday papers. So emphatic was the rumour that even an unbelieving Jeremiah like me left your envelope unsealed right until I got to the Post Office in case it should be true – and there I sorrowfully stuck the damn thing down with the momentous P.S. not written. Yes, that yarn is already relegated to the past, as just another of "those rumours". What exactly would be our position if the ban should be lifted, I don't quite know, but I expect the Commodore would issue a statement in that event.

No. 9 has just gone up now and it is really blowing a gale, so I can see I shall be marooned here all day – we shall send the boy up for tiffin later on, and as long as I can get back to Kowloon tonight it doesn't affect me very much. We (Owen and I) have just returned from a walk along the seawall, all dressed up of course in sea-boots and sou'westers and the harbour is quite a sight; really big waves are sweeping up the harbour and right over the wall and from what we hear the typhoon is going to pass pretty close – two ships have already dragged their moorings and gone ashore.

And now Mr. Fewen has just come in for a conference so I must leave you for a bit – you see how my good intentions are shattered.

Saturday now, Hilda, and I'm writing from home, the first Saturday I've spent at home for some weeks – I haven't had all the week off; Monday and Tuesday for the typhoon and now today. Tuesday's blow was fairly severe, but it passed fairly quickly in the afternoon, and I was on the first ferry to run at 4.30. I didn't get all the letter writing done that I intended, only finishing one, to your mother, and I've half written one to Winnie; I try to write to everybody once a month, but that got behind during the hot weather (combined with the overtime) and I never seem to have any news worth writing about – still now it's cooler

I'll try to pick up the once a month again – what do you do? I had letters from Mum and Auntie this week – Mum's great news was that Eddie had got his divorce, or at least been divorced; but up to the time of writing they had no details as to how much he will have to pay – quite a fair bit probably. Mum says Winnie is worried as Sid is the next one in his office to be called up, but she is going to stay on in the house if that happens, and get another girl to live with her. Auntie says "37" has now been pulled right down – ten altogether in Randolph Street, five each side and all the houses round the corner in Kirby Road that Chase built. That corner must look a bit bare, I should think, eh? I don't think there was any other news of interest. Everybody is O.K., but I'll send the letters on.

Well dear, not much other news, but evacuation women broke into the headlines yesterday. The papers published that fifteen women, believed to be returned evacuees from Australia had landed in the Colony that day; the authorities when approached by the press, said the question was a delicate one and refused to make any statement. Another wangle I suppose, although more wangles of this sort will help to point out the ridiculousness of the situation – what a ruddy game it is!

And now I'm getting near to the "speechless" stage again, and not even your letter to answer – yes, that's a fortnight now without one, but Mondays is their favourite day, so perhaps I shall get two then – if so, I'll add a bit this Monday morning if I can. I may go out to the beach tomorrow. It's four weeks since my last bathe and so far I've only been out there three times this summer.

Well dear, supper is on the table now and of course after supper, being Saturday, we shall go to pictures – No, don't say it! I've said all that on many Saturday evenings, damn it! But I wish – !! Goodbye, dear.

Monday morning and your letter of August 31st has just arrived. I can't answer it now but there's just one point I want to speak about. You speak of your weekly money. I'll quote you, "My £4-10-0, £3 government and your 30/-". Now dear, do you mean Australian money or English as in Australian money you should get £3 government and my 37/6 – my 30/- is sterling and becomes 37/6 Australian. Is that O.K.?

Edward's marks at the music festival weren't too bad – at least he's keen and that's the main thing.

I went to the beach yesterday, but will tell you about that next week. Goodbye my dear.
George

P.S. Tell the boys that the "2 cent" stamps have all gone now, so they won't get many more sets.
Cheerio, G.

Saturday September 27th 1941
(Posted September 29th)
Hong Kong

Dear,
This week, I haven't been able to make a start on your letter at all, and now it's Saturday morning and only another ¾ of an hour and I go home. I've been pretty busy again, trials mostly, in fact for three days I was down the harbour on a boat, so you see the overtime is still being stretched out, although this week I had Monday evening off, and even then that was almost counterbalanced by my having to stay until 10.30 last night.

There was a meeting of the husbands on Wednesday, but again I didn't go, although this time I didn't have much choice about it, that being one of the days I was down the harbour. J Dawkins went and apparently there was plenty of strong talk, but no practical suggestion of what to do – well, can you think of anything? They got more personal than usual, and freely mentioned people's names, including some quite high officials, in connection with the wangling, but I noticed that none of these were printed in the Press account next day. They're pressing for an enquiry into the working of the evacuation and also sending a telegram to Duff Cooper[67], but I don't suppose that will have much effect either.

---

67. Alfred Duff Cooper, the Chancellor of the Duchy of Lancaster, was assigned by Churchill July 1941 to report on the situation in the Far East and the state of Britain's defences, arriving in Singapore as Minister Resident in August 1941.

It's pretty certain, I'm afraid now, that you're going to have another Xmas in Australia, but that at least should be the last, as this position can't go on for ever.

Your letter, by the way, arrived on Wednesday, dated September 7th; it was waiting for me when I got back to the office and was I glad to see it. By the way, you mention "our dog" in connection with a story of Mrs. Little – is this dog a new acquisition, as it's the first time you've mentioned him, or is it the dog of the house? This, by the way, is Sunday now – I didn't get very far last night. In fact I stopped in the middle of a sentence so today I've just carried on. We went to the Alhambra last night and afterwards called in the K.B.G.C. with Harry Little, for a singsong and, yes, more to drink than I oughter – but you needn't worry, it wasn't much then, and it's not our usual habit either, just now and again – but of course, don't pass it on. Anyhow, just a bit of a head this morning, so it's a lazy day for me. Last Sunday I told you I went out to the beach in the morning, in fact I arrived before the Walkers, as apparently Vic had had a "heavy" evening the night before at the Police Club and couldn't get up – however, I had a very pleasant day and of course several bathes – the water is much cooler now, in fact I began to feel the coolness after the first hour.

You ask after our frig now. Well, it's all repaired and working. In fact it was only out of action a day, and it only cost $1 – no that place in Hapthong Road didn't do the repairs, we know of a cheaper firm, a big one.

You speak of Mrs. Tubbs's suggestion, of trying from this end to get to the Cape, but I'm afraid nothing can be done about that. What perhaps I should have done was apply for my relief at the end of the three years and at the same time express my willingness to serve at any other non-tropical station, and then take a chance. That way there might be just a chance of getting South Africa, but I expect a bigger chance of going home. Jim Dawkins was hoping his application might land him at the Cape but it didn't – anyway, I've already said I'll stay here another year, so that's that, in any case for a year. You mention hearing that two were going to America, but I don't think it's coming off. They said they were willing to go to America <u>at once</u>, but if wanted at home couldn't leave until spring. However, home it is. Their wives are going to Singapore to pick them up, and should they (the wives) arrive in Singapore first then they have to keep themselves there until hubby arrives from Hong Kong, at their own expense. That's not good enough, you know, after being moved at the Government's insistence, but it's the ruling at the moment. Well dear, that's about all I have to say again, although I won't close the envelope until the morning, in case I think of anything more. Goodnight, my dear.

Good Monday to you, dear, and in a few moments it will be goodbye for another week. No further mail has come in and I have no further news; what do you mean in your letter when you say you have heard things of Hong Kong folk?

Lovely weather here, now. It's much cooler, so I suppose I might be getting a bit of tennis directly, if the overtime packs up. Anyhow I'm going to get the racquet re-strung in case.
Goodbye then, dear
George

Edward (choirboy).
(Referenced in the letter of October 15th 1941)

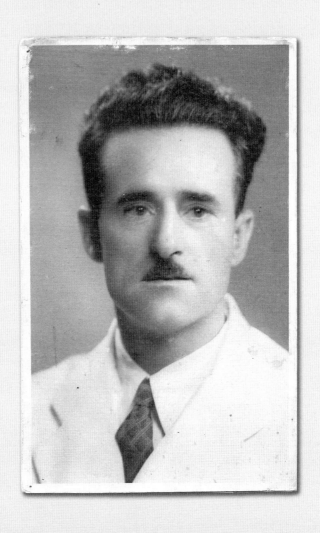

George, Hong Kong, October 1941.
(Referenced in the letter of October 11ᵗʰ 1941)

October - December 1941

...our flat seems more empty than ever tonight.
Perhaps too, it's the feeling that all those hopes we had,
however faint they were, were better than the present knowledge
that return is now hopeless.

Thursday October 2ⁿᵈ 1941
(Posted October 6ᵗʰ)
Hong Kong

Dear,
If we really had trouble in Hong Kong, at least I'd have something that would make an interesting letter – I think <u>that</u> nearly every week as I make a start on your letter, by reviewing what bits of news I have for you. This week's review didn't take long. Your letter of September 16th arrived yesterday, so at least I have <u>that</u> to help me, but that I'm afraid wasn't full of questions to which I could supply the answers. Sorry you hadn't received mine – you should have done, as I caught the post here all right.

Yes, I'm writing this from the office again, so it rather looks as though you wouldn't have seen much of me this summer even had you been in Hong Kong. From your point of view that wouldn't have been too good, always having a husband that's working – but from mine, well, it must be very nice to have a wife waiting for me at home, or <u>even</u> sometimes at the ferry. I very nearly didn't work late this week as we aren't nearly so busy as we have been, However, a job came along at the right time and so I had to carry on – you know, making hay, etc (quite considerable hay, too).

I haven't been out this week, much to Jim Dawkins' disgust, but I believe we are going to pictures, last house, tonight – I'm not too keen on midweek trips when I'm working late – I'm quite content to have chow and read a chapter or go to bed, whereas Jim, by the time I get home, is just about fed up to the teeth and wants to go out and moans like blazes when I don't go. Of course, not being able to sleep too well makes it worse for him and he often goes up the club for an hour, after I've gone to bed.

Well, Hilda, Saturday evening, now and another small contribution – just getting over a spot of tummy trouble through eating prawns for supper Thursday evening. I hadn't eaten a thing between tiffin and supper, went to the pictures and then directly I laid down in bed I wanted to be sick – and was I sick. Yesterday the old tummy was uneasy and I think it's better today so I'm hoping I've got rid of it. Looking back to last June I think, when we were both bad, I can remember we had prawns for supper then on Saturday night, but weren't bad until Sunday night. I really think the prawns was the cause then, and through the poison staying in the stomach so long, made us really bad – six weeks before I was really rid of it – and pretty bad for two. Anyway, no more prawns in Hong Kong for me.

On the "evacuation" front, I have something new to report. Our friend Duff Cooper has replied to the telegram stating that when the situation in the Pacific improves the position of the women will be considered again – that is something new isn't it! Or is it? There was a big turnout at the Peninsula last night for the Tin Hat Ball, in aid of the Bomber Funds, and today is Tin Hat Day with all the women selling emblems, but we're all on strike and won't buy one. What a difference if you'd been here – probably a very enjoyable evening, and oh, yes, I expect a fat head this morning.

I'm glad you've sent some parcels home and they might just get them for Xmas – have they limited the size you may send now? It's only a very small parcel allowed from here. Yes, they certainly are dear, but never mind about that, I expect they're glad enough to receive them at home.

Sunday evening now and the start of the last chapter – it's late on Sunday evening, too, as we've been to the pictures. I went out this morning instead of writing to you and then this afternoon we went along to the Kowloon Football Club to see the finals of the Colony Bowls Championship. It was nearly 7 o'clock when we left there, so we called in at the K.B.G.C. for some sandwiches and then on to the Alhambra to see the picture you recommended – "The Strawberry Blonde". Yes, a very nice picture – I think Olivia de Havilland is the best actress on the screen at the moment. That was pictures two nights running for me, as yesterday they had a "do" at the Club and Jim didn't put in an appearance at home for supper – I wasn't surprised and didn't wait for him, so pushed off to the pictures on my own. I saw "My Love Came Back", which turned out to be a musical picture and very nice indeed – the acting wasn't up to the standard of "The Strawberry Blonde", but the music made up for that.

A little while ago you asked after prices in Hong Kong and you were right about them rising – everything is going up fast; it wasn't too bad up to a couple of months back, but it's making up for it now. A decent suit now costs around about $100, I had a look in some shops this morning, and they don't bargain with you either, now; $100 and take it or leave it. Your "Night in Paris" stockings have been $2.40 for some time, and now they only have a few of the very dark shades left and won't be getting any more. The gas bill arrived yesterday; and with it a notice that there will be a 20% rise in price in the future; grub, I think goes up a few cents on each article each week. No, Hong Kong is certainly not the place it used to be, although I suppose it must be even worse at home. And I suppose it is just the same in Sydney too, isn't it? And it will get much worse yet.

Tummy is all right today, dear, so I think I got out of that lightly, and we have now made a start on Hong Kong's very nice winter weather, so everything should be O.K. now for a few months. We're still in whites so far, but it won't be many weeks more before we put them away again. Tell the boys that there won't be any more of the Centenary stamps, as when I went to the Post Office last week four out of the six were sold out, and they are not renewing them. Tell 'em to watch the letters from home, as there is a new issue – I think four of the lower priced stamps have been reissued. They're the same, but a slightly paler colour – and that was done to save dye – I ask you? And that I think is all again – pity in a way, for I have all this nice clean page – but unfortunately nothing to put on it. So goodnight and Goodbye again, Hilda, George

Saturday October 11th 1941
(Posted October 13th)
Hong Kong

My Dear,
I received your letter this week, on Thursday morning, but haven't had
a chance to answer it before, and even now this is only going to be
one of my short epistles, as it's nearly time to go home. I've been very
busy again this week, so once more I haven't very much except work to
write about – although I did have one interlude Wednesday evening.
Remember me telling you last October about meeting Tom Middler
– he had joined the Navy and his ship came out our way – well this
week they paid Hong Kong another visit, so who should walk in the
office last Tuesday, but Middler. They're only here for a few days, so on
Wednesday he came home with me when I knocked off at 8.15 and after
chow Jim Dawkins and I took him out to see the sights. We met one or
two others, also, presumably on the same lay, so it was a fairly amusing
evening if nothing else. Details, though, won't go in letters. They'll have
to wait for that "long yarn".

Well dear, Sunday evening at 10 pm now and at last I can make another
start. I've been out at the beach all day and returned about half past
eight to find Tom Middler waiting for me. He thinks they are pushing
off directly and had come to say Goodbye – anyhow we gave him
dinner and I then persuaded Jim and him to go to the pictures so that I
could get on with my letter.

Yesterday afternoon, by the way, I had almost reached the bottom of
the first page, and then was interrupted by an Indian policeman who
threatened to send in a report to the police if I didn't get a tap repaired
that was leaking very badly. Of course, being Saturday afternoon, you
wouldn't believe the fuss I had before I got the job done and it was too
late then to carry on my letter. Pamela called just after I reached home,
with the offer of a yachting trip to the beach and so promptly at 9.30
this morning saw me at the Star Ferry to meet Bob Pullen and her. We
had a very pleasant trip this time, a bit warm at times perhaps, but at
least we did get some wind, and so the trip was accomplished by 12.30.
We had a setback then as Vic, who was playing bowls in the morning,

hadn't arrived with the chow – it appeared afterwards that he had met one of the Wellow gals and a bloke, with their car broken down, so he stopped to lend them tools. It was 3 o'clock when he arrived, so you bet he got into trouble – and I don't mean from Pamela only – however, in the meanwhile, we had had a nice long bathe. Tonight I came back by car with Pamela, and Vic returned in the yacht – yes, your letter was on my mind; anyhow, a very nice day.

I liked the picture of the three of you very much – it's very good of you, but of the boys I think it's <u>extremely</u> good. Aren't they growing too; I compared it with that one you sent me from England Xmas 1938 – I know that's just over 2 ½ years ago, but they've grown immensely since then – it's a bit frightening you know, especially when we are wasting all this time. Yes, that's looking at you, that reminds me again of all I'm missing. Well dear, I have had a photo done, but they've come out bl---- awful – I don't know if I do look so grim as these make me out, although that is not their only fault. The first opportunity I'll have another try, but in the meantime I'll send one of these on – it will have to be next week as I haven't an envelope that will take it. I only got them just before the shop closed last night and through going to the beach today I still haven't one. By the way, I showed yours to Pamela today and she liked it very much – I also had to remember her to you.

Well Hilda, at last I've had <u>official</u> notice that our furniture has been destroyed, and also they enclosed a claim form that I have to fill in and return; so if you haven't already returned your estimates, will you do so, so that I can get the claim off. I'm getting two copies typewritten of that list, itemised as by Chaplins, and then against each item I'll put our estimate. I did have a go during the week but several of the items I had no idea of their value – I only made the total come to about £50, so I expect that will be considerably revised when I get your list, although I suppose with the exception of about three items, none of them will come to a very long figure. I'll let you know my final figures.

Well Hilda, that's about all my news again, although I still have one question to ask – in your letter this week you say, "I'll never forget last winter". Now, which winter exactly has been worse than the others? Only with you having different time to me for your winters I'm not quite sure which one you mean – I think you mean on the occasion of your arrival in Australia. Is that right? Ah well, the first seven winters are the worst, and on that optimistic note I'm going to finish – I can hear them playing the "King" over at the Star so our visitor will be in, in a few minutes.

Goodbye dear, and all my love to you.

George

P.S. Yes, I'll answer Edward's letter, and as a Birthday is coming, there might be something in it. Cheerio.

Have just discovered the picture <u>will</u> go in, but I'm not very glad as I don't like sending it.

Wednesday October 15th 1941
(Posted October 20th)
Hong Kong

Dear,
Thought I'd just have a short yarn with you, although I'm really too tired to write much, or should I say talk. It's 10 o'clock and I'm still in the office and it will probably be gone eleven before I get away. Actually this is my last night on overtime for a little while, but half way through the evening the Chief rang up about a job of Owen's – it had to be finished tomorrow night so must do so and so tonight; Owen had gone home, so I had to gather what hands I could and carry on for tonight – anyway, Bob will take over tomorrow.

Well dear, hardly had my letter been posted on Monday than yours arrived (dated September 28th) with Edward pictured as an angel, I mean choir boy, and then yesterday I had your sea-mail package with the other photos, all in good condition. Jolly fine pictures, all of them, and only last week I sent that scabby one of me. Yes that big one is good of David; pity they didn't choose a better background than a brick wall, but it's such a natural un-posed photo – very good indeed. Edward's, too, is fine – what a sturdy chap he is and it's just how he squares his shoulders when walking along – that cricket group of his is a very nice picture and how it reminds me of my old school photos. I haven't left off looking at last week's photo yet – the one of the three of you in the Botanical Gardens. I think I like that one the best of all, for the more I look at it, the better it gets – it has a very intimate air about it as though all three of you had it done just for me. You look at it again, dear, and see if you can see that. Anyway, Hilda, you see what all those pictures have done for me, but no, I don't think you can know all I've felt. Looking at them I am very proud of my family and glad they belong to me, and I to them.

What would you like me to do dear? Get two or three copies of David to send home, although you should have bought those from the news people – any paper sells their pictures fairly cheaply and the original would be better than copies. Do you think it worth trying? As regards Edward's (choir boy), shall I get that enlarged and also two or three copies for home, say, one for your mother and one for mine. Well, Hilda, I've had my say for tonight, and now I must go and see how the lads are getting on. Goodnight dear.

Sunday evening now and so once again I'm on the last lap of my homework – yes, I'm afraid it is our letters that are always referred to as "homework". Well, nothing exciting has happened since Wednesday except that, as no doubt you know, on Thursday they announced the lifting of the ban on women going to Singapore. We eagerly awaited Friday's papers to see what Hong Kong was going to do, but they were full up with the new "Pacific Crisis"[68] and the Colonial Sec: Mr. N. L. Smith (who has a wife and two daughters here), when interviewed, said that as far as he knew, "The position had not changed". Anyway, I'm afraid that if your hopes rose very high on receipt of the Singapore news, they're due for the usual drop back to zero again. Damn!!

---

68. Tension had continued to escalate. Germany and Italy had recognised the Japanese-backed puppet government in China, the Wang Jingwei regime, and Chiang Kai-shek had issued a statement to 'friendly nations' – Britain, the Soviet Union and the United States – describing the world as divided into two blocs. The failure of negotiations between the United States and Japan on the Far East situation, mainly concerning the question of Japan's continued occupation of areas of China and French Indochina, had led to the resignation of the Japanese Prime Minister, Prince Konoye (also Konoe). In his place, General Hideki Tojo was pro-German and a strong advocate of Japanese expansionism.

Have just reread your last letter – Edward seems to have done fairly well at that half-term exam. What are his chances of passing for Sydney High? Only that might help in getting him into a school in England. I don't quite know what to tell you to do about the cheques – perhaps you had better let them go, at least you won't then have to look after 'em – but you needn't worry about the rest of the money, that will be transferred to a bank in whatever place you go to (providing it is, as you say, in the Sterling bloc). I've transferred my bank account, from deposit to current account so I now have a cheque book – I did that as it's more convenient for paying bills, and also you are allowed only to put in $200 a month and I had rather a large sum I wanted to put in.

By the way, on the subject of money, we've had a rise of 1/6 to date from last May – also today is the official date of my completion of my three years, so tomorrow I get 1/- rise. All that on the credit side, but now I'll tell you something not (?) so good – I have been informed, unofficially at the moment, that my establishment has come through so that providing I'm O.K.'ed by the doctor, I will have the privilege of being one of the staff and also of paying income tax. I haven't worked it out how much that will be, but I should say roughly £1 a week on an ordinary week's money, but I'll let you know more about this later on, also about passing the doctor. Actually, I expect it will be January or February before I am really established, as it won't be dated until the Hong Kong report gets home.

Have you sent me your "furniture estimates" yet – and did the box of china include our Japanese tea service? The Tubbses certainly seem to have fallen on their feet in South Africa, although I should imagine they have to pay a good bit for that flat – it sounds expensive, but I expect he is getting good money. Pity about his furniture, but even then he's better off than us, as he did get some compensation and it's a bit doubtful if we will.

Well, Hilda, that's all my news again for this week, so it's time to say Goodbye. Thanks for the pictures, in fact thanks for <u>everything</u> dear. Cheerio then.
George

Friday October 24th 1941
(Posted October 27th)
Hong Kong

Dear,
Friday evening and once more I have an hour to spare, and so here goes for a start on your letter. That sounds as though I've been frightfully busy again, doesn't it? But it's not so as it happens, and this is the first night this week that I've worked overtime, and this will only be for a few days. Still, even so, I've had something to do each night, especially as Jim Dawkins has been home sick since Wednesday and as he's alone all day he expects me to entertain him a bit in the evening – but I'll tell you about him in a minute.

Monday I nearly finished a letter to Auntie. I hadn't written to her for two months, so thought I had better get one off for Xmas – yes, I have a few more Xmas ones to write yet. Tuesday we went to Mr. Harrington's Silver Wedding anniversary, which, of course, unfortunately had to be celebrated in the absence of his spouse – about 40 people there I should think, you know, just sitting around yarning, plenty of snacks and drinks, interspersed of course with complimentary speeches. I left about one, but I heard afterwards that "the few" finally left about 4 o'clock in the morning. I guessed the Smiths would be there, so I took along the postcard size pictures to show them – they thought they were very good indeed and Eve was particularly struck with that one of you. It was during this evening at the Harringtons that Jim D had to go home as his knee, which had been troubling him for the last week, came up very big and he could hardly walk – he's had a doctor in and it's housemaid's knee, and when I got home he was sitting on the bed with an ice-bag round his knee, and the Doc says it will probably be 10 to 12 days before he can go to work. Well, Wednesday was a blackout and as Jim had some visitors to keep him company in the dark, I went across to the "Star", and then last night I finished off Auntie's letter and played chess with Jim. Oh, while I'm on the week's doings, I might as well tell you that Tuesday evening early, I went and got measured for half a dozen evening shirts, long sleeved for the winter.

Well, so far on Friday, and now it's Sunday evening again and I haven't long returned from the beach. We got back just before 8 o'clock as at eight the wives were going to broadcast from Australia, but apparently something must have gone wrong, as they never did, or at least if they did it never reached us.

Went to the Peninsula last night to a dinner given by the Club – you see as they haven't given other functions like the Children's Party, Xmas concerts, etc, the funds accumulated a bit, so they decided to give all members a dinner. It was purely a Stag Party, about 130 were there and of course all the officers of the Yard – dress optional, but about 75% dressed. I wasn't one of them, I just couldn't be bothered. Dinner wasn't too bad and the entertainment afterwards very good – Stanley Smith, Foster and Owen formed our table and I got home about 1.30. It was there that I heard the Smiths were going to the beach today, so I joined them and we went out by taxi – yes, I woke up with a bit of a head, but it didn't last long and we had quite a nice day – overcast all day and a wee bit cool out of the water, but I thought nice in, although judging by the length of time the others stayed in, I was the only one that thought so. I took Mrs. Tubbs's letter that you'd forwarded on to me for them to read and they seemed quite interested – and I had to remember them to you again.

Glad to hear the big cheque had arrived and no, you hadn't told me before – did you get a thrill when you saw it? I never even had that pleasure.

Yes Hilda, as you say, we certainly have both been very discreet in our letters as far as other people are concerned, but this week I'm going to break that rule and tell you something. He's become "public news" now and no doubt it will all be published, so I don't think in this case I'm doing any harm. Remember that chap who was sued by the Hong Kong Hotel? Well, he's in trouble again. The trouble this time started two weeks ago – you know he's working outside the Yard and apparently not always on the job when he should be. Well he did it once too often and was picked up and of course found himself on the carpet in front of the Chief – threatened with the sack, etc, next time, and was told he would hear the punishment for this time later. He then goes sick for four days, comes in last Wednesday and gets two days' suspension on Thursday and Friday and now, what took place Friday evening is not quite clear and is gathered mostly from Chinese newspapers, but a little bit appeared in our papers. He had a row with what the Chinese papers call his "Chinese wife" and tried to shoot her – the gun didn't go off so he hit her and rumour (lying jade) says fractured her jaw, and he then tried drinking Lysol himself. I don't think he could have tried very hard, as after both were rushed to hospital, he was only detained two hours. Now it is possible he will be charged with attempted murder and suicide – the electrical department are doing well, eh! Well dear, what do you think of that for my big scandal? I think we've got all you in Australia beaten now, as I'm sure none of the wives have got that far yet. No doubt there will be more news of him to follow later, but I should think it must end with him going home sooner or later.

Well my dear, I haven't very much more to tell you this time, except that I've accepted the offer of establishment and during the week passed the doctor O.K. Jim Dawkins' leg is much better now, but it will be at least another week before he goes out – he's stuck it fairly well so far.

Well, this is Jim's pen I'm using, mine was left in the Yard, and he has to finish his letter yet, so I think I'll call it a day. Goodbye dear – I still think of you in connection with nearly everything I do, and that's been quite a lot lately.
Cheerio then
George

Wednesday November 5th 1941
(Posted November 10th)
Hong Kong

My Dear,
See the date, November 5th – and no fireworks! I suppose if you had all been home, I would have been dashing off presently, in order to be in time to "superintend" our little display. Instead of that I have peace and quietness, damn it, to go home to – how true it is to say that one can get too much of a good thing. Yes, I'm still working late, for yet another

week, although each one threatens to be the last – and tonight will not be a very long contribution as I really have very little to write about and the Australian mail is not in. Every day we hear, "It's coming tomorrow," and so far all we get is a disappointment, a fortnight tomorrow our last one arrived and I haven't had your letter of October 12th yet – still it's coming tomorrow – Oh Yeah!

Well Jim Dawkins has heard something concrete at last and is now arranging his final programme. His relief leaves England about the middle of November, so should get here, say middle of January (rather optimistic) to middle of February. No approval for him to go via Australia, and his wife and son have approval to return to Hong Kong to rejoin him. He immediately applied to Commodore for them to be brought back as soon as possible, but they wouldn't have that and have approved that arrangements be made, so that they get here "about the end of January". That at least gives me the date that I shall be left up in the air again – still something may turn up – why they might even bring you all back by then. Jim is still home, but his leg is mending rapidly now, although I shouldn't be surprised if it's not the middle of next week before he returns to work.

Our poor old Kim is the latest invalid. Yesterday morning he took French leave and when he returned in the afternoon could hardly walk. You know how the ends of a dog's toes end in quite thick pads on which he walks, well on both hind legs there's one or two torn, or worn, right off, so what he's been up to I don't know. (I could guess perhaps, but if my guess is right – well it's not worth it – or is it!) I don't see anything can be done but wait for the skin to harden again, in the meanwhile poor Kim walks about like the proverbial cat on the hot bricks.

Bought a pair of blankets this week – yes, same shop; got one of the fellows to pick them up for me. Not quite full size – will cover a full size bed, but a bit doubtful about the tucking in. Anyway, they were a good deal cheaper than we'll be able to get at home, so I thought them worth getting – 35/4 the pair. Well, Cheerio for tonight, as I'm now going to shave, and then – go home to that peace and quietness.
Good night dear.

The week's very nearly gone again for this is Friday evening – I was going to do such a lot of letter writing tonight, only Mr. Ellis took it in his mind to talk in the office at 5 o'clock and there he stayed until gone half past six, so time I'd shaved, my plan for letter writing was a thing of the past. Well, dear, since writing as I did on Wednesday evening, I've been showered with letters – first of all two from you, October 12th and 19th, I received the same evening, just as I was leaving to go home, and then yesterday I had three from home; Mum, Winnie and Auntie, and today one from your mother. It must be nearly two months since I heard from them last, but everybody is O.K., although Auntie speaks of Mum having lumbago. Auntie's main topic in this letter is Income Tax. Jack Bearman has to pay £30 for the year, Uncle Will £14 and Kathleen £3, etc, so I shall have to tell her that mine after next January will be £200. Mum's only real piece of news was that Eddie had packed up his job on the buses and gone back to boat building, "on the river at Twickenham". There! That's just as she wrote, so what made him do that, I don't know – although of course it's no good judging him by anybody else's standard. Still it is a pity, as you suggest, that they don't move right out of the district. Winnie and your mother had nothing startling, but I'll send them all on to you. Before I leave them, though, Auntie says you've never told her all about her stepsister in Sydney, so if you haven't already done so, you'd better spin her a yarn or two about them, or else you'll be in Auntie's bad books for ever – you know what she is where "family" is concerned.

Saturday p.m.

Well, there is, I'm told, a signal going around the Yard to the effect that the ban has again been put on women going to Singapore – that's a bit rough on anyone in Australia, though, who might be just making arrangements to rejoin their husbands there. As for this place, it seems to me to be hopeless for some time to come – Ah, me – and even when they do lift the ban, I expect they will make you pay your own fare back and that will probably be round about £150 as I think David counts as an adult now, with the steamship companies – still we won't worry about that… yet.

Our A.R.P. enquiry is finished and will be quite missed as a source of amusement, although they are now going to start another one into the prevalence of bribery – so if that is held in public we shall still be entertained. Mr Steele-Perkins[69] was cleared of all suspicion and will now carry on to India – his trouble, I expect, will start when he meets his wife, for he wasn't cleared of suspicion where Mimi Lau[70] was concerned, although that of course had nothing to do with his A.R.P. conduct.

Yes, October 22nd was the date I left England, and November 24th my arrival in Hong Kong – of course, you know, your trip from England has been far more "hectic" than mine; the evacuation weekend, Manila, Australia with its various moves, will always stand out in your memory, while here, I'm afraid monotony has been the keynote in general, once the evacuation had taken place.

So, you're now getting the child endowment for Edward – 5/- a week isn't it? He's something to us at last (tell him I said that) – or is he claiming it for pocket money, but don't tell him that bit, or it might put ideas in his head. The Cashier this week has been distributing demands on those husbands whose wives incurred doctors' bills and gave them to the Australian authorities to pay – apparently the Australian people pay them, and then forward them to Hong Kong for the money to be recovered from the husbands.

What do you think of our money, now that it's all ruddy notes? It's going to be a darned nuisance fishing for a 10c note to buy a paper or pay the rickshaw boy. Japan is short of nickel and so there is a ready sale of Hong Kong coins at a profit, I believe a 10c piece can be sold for 13 cents as metal, and so all our coins have been disappearing out of the Colony and we now have notes for 1c, 5c and 10c, as well as the usual ones. I enclose specimens of the 5 and 10 cents for the boys (if I remember to put them in). That's all then, dear, for today, and I will just add a note tomorrow. Cheerio.

---

69. The Director of Air Raid Precautions in Hong Kong.
70. Working for one of the companies supplying the A.R.P. Department, and rumoured to be Mr Steele-Perkins' girlfriend.

Sunday evening and this is the "tailpiece", and as I have nothing much to add, it won't be a long one. I played cricket, for the Yard, against Craigenower Cricket Club at Happy Valley – had my usual duck, but I quite enjoyed playing nevertheless – we beat them, too, 103 to 91, which was rather a surprise as they had a strong team. One of the store-housemen, gave us victory, by knocking up a very nice 48, just when we thought it was hopeless.

And now as the last item, let me tell you that on Thursday I had the dubious pleasure of writing the telegram that I've been waiting to write all these months, only I had to sign it "Dawkins". Yes, I sent his telegram for him – "Return H.K., sail end December, love Dawkins." I told him it was rubbing it in to ask me to send it. I wonder when I shall send my own? For at the moment that represents the apex of all my hopes in life.

My love to you dear, and Goodbye again.
George.

Sunday November 16th 1941
Hong Kong

Dear
Sunday evening, and this time I'm only just starting your letter, which is rather unusual, as I mostly have a couple of goes at it during the week and then just finish it with a short bit on Sunday night. That plan was upset this week as our busy time came in the wrong place – Monday and Tuesday were easy days, I was going to play my first game of tennis on Tuesday but it had to rain that night. Wednesday and Thursday we were really busy and I had to work over, but unfortunately I had to work and not letter write, and then Friday we had a blackout which we spent yarning and listening to the wireless in the dark – so you can see it hasn't been a very exciting week.

However, yesterday I had my first tennis, and judging by how I feel now I think I'm going to have a job to move for the next two or three days. We played a match against the Royal Engineers at Happy Valley and won 5 ½ to 3 ½ and then Warren and I accepted a challenge from their best pair and beat them 2 to 1, which meant that I played six sets – it was a lovely afternoon though and I thoroughly enjoyed it. Today we had another match against the wireless station at Stonecutters Island and won 9 sets to 0, but it wasn't anything like the walkover the score suggests. Now you can see why I shall be stiff tomorrow.

Well dear, I received your letter this week, way back on Monday but unfortunately I had just posted mine or else I would have put another list of the furniture in that. I'll send one with this, and you return it as quickly as you can as I want to get that claim off – I've already had some typewritten sheets done, and only have to fill in the various amounts.

I suppose all the women were greatly heartened by the home Government's announcement this week, that you would not be allowed back to Hong Kong yet – well, they tempered the blow to us, for the Local Government thought it advisable that a committee be formed to facilitate the return of the wives, once permission had been granted. Of course, even they say it won't be yet, but surely if they think a committee is necessary for that reason now, that corner can't be so very far away, so keep your pecker up dear. No doubt you've seen about the Canadian troops arriving in Hong Kong[71] – so perhaps now that they've decided to defend the place in earnest, they might let you all return.

Jim Dawkins is still at home with his leg and the doctor says it will be another week yet – he can hobble about now though and perhaps will

---

71. The British government's policy towards the defence of Hong Kong was that it would be impossible to defend the colony effectively against a Japanese force with Japan already in occupation in parts of China – including the area bordering Hong Kong's New Territories. Unsuited to serve as an advanced naval base, strategy-wise Hong Kong was also deemed expendable. With only a small garrison force of four battalions – the 5/7th Rajputs, the 2/14th Punjabis, the 1st Middlesex and the 2nd Royal Scots – plus volunteer units, sending reinforcements to the colony had previously been ruled out and at one stage reducing the size of the garrison had even been considered, to avoid unnecessary waste of manpower in what was perceived as being a lost cause should Japan attack. However, there had never been any question on the British government's part of implementing an open city policy such as the one that allowed German troops to march into the Channel Islands unopposed in 1940 – and in September 1941 the British Prime Minister, Winston Churchill, re-assessed the garrison situation. It was decided that deployment of even a limited number of additional troops to the colony would help delay the advance of any Japanese attack and crucially gain time for other British held territories in the Far East to organise and strengthen their defences. Two Canadian infantry battalions arrived on November 16th 1941, the Royal Rifles of Canada and the Winnipeg Grenadiers.

have his first trip out towards the end of the week. That's a month home now and he's fast reaching the point when chains will be needed to keep him in – I'm afraid there will be a reaction when he does get about. It certainly came the wrong time for him, as there is a fair bit of getting about necessary in connection with his going home – I suppose <u>she</u> is all hot and bothered now and it shouldn't be many weeks before she sails by the time you read this.

Well dear, I've reached the scratching about stage and I'm tired tonight, so you'll have to forgive a short letter this time – I'm going to write out the furniture list and then it's me for bed. Good night dear, and my love to you all.
George

Wednesday November 19th 1941
(Posted November 24th)
Hong Kong

My Dear,
Wednesday evening and all is still quiet on the Hong Kong front, in spite of the doleful suggestions in the various papers; they try and lead you to believe that every day is a deadline and if you took any notice of them you'd be a nervous wreck in a week – I suppose it's just the same down your end, but if so don't let it worry you. The situation at the moment doesn't make our prospects very rosy though, does it?, although it's just as likely to improve as quickly as it worsened. Sometimes I think that anything would be better than this stagnation, although in my saner moments I know I would soon alter that tune if it did come to war – actually, as I see it, I think the present "scare" position will continue for a long while yet – (still, who am I?)

Well dear, I almost had this week working ordinary hours, as on Monday I looked ahead to a very quiet week – and then of course today, Wednesday, along came the inevitable panic job, and so it's working late I am again tonight – only for a few days, though, perhaps till about next Tuesday. Anyway, I've arranged for Saturday afternoon off as we have another tennis match, this time against the Yard Officers on our courts.

I don't know all the Officers' team yet, senior officers by the way, but our Chief won't be playing as he is apparently the victim at the moment of Hong Kong, or athlete's, foot.

Sunday morning now, dear, and having read through my letter up to this point, I realise how much one can write without "saying" anything, if you see what I mean – for all I told you on Wednesday was that we were going to play a tennis match. Well anyway, said match is now over, as I know this morning by a few more aches and pains, and resulted in a severe defeat for us. We lost 7 sets to 2 and then since we had a fair amount of time, played them again, and still lost 6-3; they were very good, though, and we had the hardest games we've had in any of our matches.

Well dear, I received your letter, this week on Thursday. It's just as eagerly awaited as ever – it's rather funny at times as sometimes the mail arrives in two parts and then only some get letters and of course the remainder instantly ring up the main office demanding their letters to be sent down. In our office are Mr. Wellow and Amies, both of whom have their wives here and they are always being charged with not troubling about our letters – it's probably not true but we've got to moan at somebody.

Congratulations to Edward for getting his place in the cricket team – that will surely bring joy to his Grandad's heart; 20 runs too, very good, and certainly better than his father did in his match.

Went to another "husbands" meeting last Monday in the Peninsula, but it was disappointing – actually I don't think it can be anything else – yet – for they're just banging against a closed door. They ridicule and draw attention to each and every additional woman that arrives but it apparently doesn't do much good, although if this goes on, we shall arrive at the point where only service people remain in Australia – considerably reduced numbers of those too. Do you know it must be getting on for nearly half of our people have gone home, or to other stations – you just think of all the people you've heard about – so there won't be so many to come back.

My invalid is out now and returns to work tomorrow. He still limps a bit and will have to go carefully for some weeks – he is sitting across the table from me, also letter writing and has just been pointing out the fact that he only has two more weeks of letter writing to do – what a glorious feeling that must be. Did you see in the papers of the arrival of the Canadian troops in Hong Kong? I don't know if that is a good augury or not, but it does look as though now they mean to make a <u>serious</u> effort to defend Hong Kong – if it's necessary. One drawback, though, is that with so many new arrivals, the prices have gone up – yes, everybody profiteers these days.

Rather a dull and cold day today, for which we are very glad, as last week it was exceedingly warm and muggy, the sort of weather when everything feels damp, which is unusual for this time of the year – the cold weather is much more acceptable although it could be brighter. Your weather is just warming up, I suppose.

Well dear, tomorrow is the 24th November: my arrival date in Hong Kong; what a mixture that three years is made of, certainly not what we had planned. But if fate is kind it can still be made up to us, so here's hoping. My love to you, dear, and once again, Goodbye
George

Sunday November 23rd 1941[72]
Australia

My Dear George,
Another month, and another Christmas will be here – it seems a lifetime since the old days, those jolly London ones, with the piece of "real English sirloin" and all the good things your mother used to get. Winnie's letter made me smile, where she says she has no intentions of queuing up but Mum does – that is so typical of both of them – your mother would think a day well lost if she could triumphantly bring

---

72. Letter from Hilda - returned, "service suspended".

home something nice for tea – if it was only a kipper. Which of them is right, I wonder.

Now my dear, to answer your letter. You began by a reminiscence – and so have I – perhaps that's a sign of old age – still though, I secretly hated November 5th. I always got frozen to death and I am always really afraid of fireworks.

I would cheerfully manage to stick home a month if we could have back the old days.

I wonder why the mail was so late for you – there are no typhoons to cause delay here – and we pay ninepence a letter. I'm glad Mr. Dawkins has news at last. I met Mrs. Dawkins at Mrs. Field's last Thursday – and she is going to visit me before she leaves. She read me one of his letters in which he speaks of how comfortable he has been at 16 Hankow Road, and how he has nothing but praise for Amah. They have apparently never struck one half as good. So I hope, for both your sake and hers that you can carry on when he leaves. You say, "Why they might bring you all back by then," – oh, my dear! I read and read, and read that though I know it was blarney. I met someone the other day, ex of Hong Kong police, who has retired here. He says Hong Kong is a dreadful place, no grub, and stinking with Chinese. He can't think what we want to go back for – so I said, "Ho! You wouldn't know –" that sort of cackle makes me sick. He was in an almighty hurry to get here – what for!

Hope Kim is better, poor chap. He must be a heart-breaking sight.

Glad about the blankets, dear – that was remarkably cheap for normal times – and those I have with me are not too good. It would be an idea to invest in another pair if possible. They are, by the way, quite unprocurable here – that sounds tripe – but the thing is, while this is a wool-raising country – they send it all home to be woven and made up – then buy it back!!! And there aren't any coming now.

I did write and tell Auntie all about her relations – all there is to tell, but I supposes that's another letter gone west, but I don't visit 'em much – I don't like them and they won't give me any information about the side of the family who were really the people who were decent to your father. They are a mysterious crowd – seem afraid you're going to discover something. They sent me a message that the old lady was dying – which, as I've told you wouldn't cause them many tears, so I called round. But they made me feel so uncomfortable I didn't stay long. The old lady is dead – did I tell you and between you and me she had outlived her usefulness and certainly their affections.

I haven't heard that the ban is on Singapore again, but three left from here about a week ago. Yes: I suppose when I'm back home I shall enjoy telling of my life in the Philippines and Australia, but it won't be a phase of my life that I shall dwell on to myself – I'm damn well fed up with this life.

I was out some place every day last week, and tonight I feel very irritable – and bored. I hear Mr. Field beat Warren in a singles and a doubles game – so perhaps you had better get your game over quick while he is off form.

Funny, what you say about sending the telegram – because when she showed us, I insisted on holding it up to the light – turning it upside down and generally acting the fool.

To go back to family news, Edward started his cello lessons on Friday. I believe he got a bit of chaff on the tram, but it doesn't worry him – I had them practising together this afternoon.

Well, I started this page forgetting that Edward has a letter to enclose[73] – quite a well put together letter – but disgracefully written. He really writes better than that, but he was anxious to go surfing so I didn't make him rewrite. Well goodbye now dear – a pretty ghastly week as far as the news is concerned.[74] On Tuesday we were sure there would be a

73. Letter has not survived.
74. Relations between the United States and Japan had continued to deteriorate, and Winston Churchill had pledged to declare war on Japan should Japan go to war with the United States.

clash – and I still fear it today, unless that gesture in Libya[75] has pulled them up again – what a life. Latest forecast I've heard is for ten years' wait. Anyhow if that's so – it will be time for you to irritate some of the Hong Kong folk and get sent some place. Goodbye dear.

I'm a misery tonight.

Hilda

Monday November 24th 1941
(Posted December 1st)
Hong Kong

My Dear,

Yes, it's Monday evening, and I only posted your letter this morning on my way to the ferry, but the P.O. elected to give us a pleasant surprise this week, by bringing along the Australian mail extra early, and so your letter of the 9th November was waiting on my desk for me when I arrived back in the office at 11.30. Tonight I'm staying on in Bob Owen's place, who decided this morning he had a cold that warranted him going back home for the rest of the day – bit of a fuss box, our Bob, as talking to him you wouldn't know he had a cold – anyway, I'm here and your letter's here, and so I'm making good use of both facts.

So you didn't altogether enjoy the wives' broadcast – no, neither did I, but there you know what I think of that business. There's another one from here for Xmas, but I'm afraid I shall not be one of 'em quite apart from the fact that it's rather doubtful whether I'd get the chance. You see, they draw from the hat to see who shall broadcast, and you know what that means in Hong Kong, especially where Naval Yard people are concerned – but I think you know as much as I do about Z.B.W.'s[76] method of selection.

---

75. The Allies had continued on into Libya following the 'good' news from Egypt commented on in George's letter of December 16th 1940, and the Allies' recapture of Sidi Barrani, and took Tobruk from the Italians in January 1941. Intent on its recapture, the Germans had Tobruk under siege from April 1941, and on November 18th 1941 the Allies launched an attack to relieve the port.
76. The Hong Kong Broadcasting Committee operated Station ZBW on behalf of the Hong Kong Government.

Now dear, as regards the shopping you mention, I wrote a long time ago, just after my misfits with the shoes, that I wouldn't get any more without measurements, if you wanted any clothing let me know details. You say you would like shirts and pyjamas for the boys, well let me know all the details of material and a few measurements and I'll see what I can do.

Suggestions for Shirt Measurements: Size of collar band, width of shoulders, length of sleeves, length of chest measurements.

Suggestions for Details: White or coloured? Collars attached or separate, and anything else you can think of. For pyjamas include length of leg and whether silk or not, and from those measurements I should be able to get other underclothes. Things have gone up tremendously here now, and are still going up, but no doubt that's the same in Australia, but of the two I expect Hong Kong is the cheaper still – I paid $2.50 (about 3/11 Australian) for those shirts of mine, with two separate collars to each. Suits, good ones, are well over $100 now, and shoes for me about $14 are two examples, while silk stockings, I think, are something over $4 a pair.

Sunday morning at home now, just a leisurely one, but this afternoon we have another tennis match over at Happy Valley, against the Royal Army Ordnance Corps. It's been a fairly busy week for me at work, in fact the Monday evening that I commenced this letter turned out to be the only slack time in the week, and then I went shooting instead of carrying on with writing. You see, to encourage the blokes to keep up their efficiency with the rifle they've established a miniature rifle range, at which anybody can "have a go" at a cost of 10 cents for 10 shots. Of course, it's supposed to be in our own time, but who is going to come all the way back for 10 shots, so you can guess who are the customers. The range is next door to our office, so we often pop in of an evening and as a matter of fact, "said he modestly", I am one of three (so far) to have scored 10 bulls with 10 shots – and that's including the Marine instructors too. Anyway, after Monday I didn't have time for any shooting and such nonsense and yesterday, Saturday, I had to cry off a tennis match against the R.A.F. Warren is secretary of the tennis and I must admit he has certainly been enterprising as far as matches are concerned – very nice turnouts they have been. This afternoon will very likely be another defeat especially as there's eight in a team and we have a job to get eight good ones now.

Yes, I see your point re Edward and his school – if he were staying in Australia, to continue where he is for a year, and then straight into Sydney High would definitely be his plan, but as it is even I am hoping there <u>won't</u> be another year, and so perhaps as you say, a year or part of a year at Randwick will start him in Secondary school work.

No dear, I'm afraid the question of leaving them at school in Sydney wouldn't be of much use <u>unless</u> we intended to stay here a few more years, even if the war ended, and that might even lead to them getting jobs and staying in Australia – mind, I believe from their point of view it might be a good thing, but I can't see myself staying in Hong Kong long enough for that to come off – this eighteen months has taken the sparkle from this place for me. By the way, you are jumping ahead too, aren't you, with the bungalow out of town somewhere? Don't think I'm against the idea, but it will want more consideration – where the boys are working, etc, for we don't want to be too isolated. Did you forget the car?

You ask about our house – didn't I tell you, the site has now been cleared I understand from Auntie, so our neighbourhood must look a bit bare. Mrs. Fenwick's house was in ruins mixed up with bits of her furniture for months I believe, but they got the furniture out of ours – anyway five houses our side have been cleared and five opposite. No, they won't rebuild until after the war and then I expect we shall have to wait a long while as they won't be able to rebuild thousands of houses at once.

Well dear, I don't know when this letter will reach you, but it should be near enough to Xmas to make you feel a bit Xmasy and so, Hilda, a Happy Xmas to all of you and may the New Year see our reunion. I have remitted £5 (sterling) to you, that should reach you soon after this letter; £1 to each of the boys and the rest to you, to be spent solely on yourselves. Goodbye dear, I love you all and how nice for Xmas if – but what's the good.
Goodbye
George

P.S. Jim Dawkins has only two more letters to write as Mrs. D leaves about 1st week of January – how I envy him, but our turn will come!! One day?
Goodbye dear.

Sunday November 30th 1941[77]
Australia

My dear George,
I've just finished the inventory and having wiped the sweat from my brow, I'm making a start on your letter. I really mean that about the wiping, as it is a gruelling day, hardly a breath of air. And you know money matters always make me sweat. I think you said you only estimate at about £50 – so I've beaten you this time, but I'll just go through my estimate.

No. 1 – Mangle: it was old fashioned, it is true, but we had two new rollers just before we left which cost around 35/- – still if you think that is too high cut it as it is silly to overestimate. The lino was quite good from our bedroom. The hallstand – I quite forget its price – but also I'm keeping in mind the probable cost, when we have to restock. Now as regards the carpet, I think that is in Hong Kong so the mistake is theirs, but if it isn't that was new. The chest of linen contained two sets of curtains for all over the house, so it will cost all of £4.00 to replace that. Now the pictures were, I think, my three diplomas in very good oak panes but my Royal Academy of Music – that is here. The flower bowl was one of your prizes. Then the two little front room chairs <u>were</u> good ones and I loved them, so I've valued them at <u>my</u> value. The box of china <u>did</u> contain the Japanese tea-set and all the Crown Devon was there, and my two busts of Bach and Beethoven and while I don't know what the table cost, again I valued it very much. However – if you think this is over-estimated, alter it to what you think. Also, I've allowed for the inevitable reduction when it reaches the – well! whoever it has to reach. I shall anxiously wait for your reply as to what you eventually

---

77. Letter returned - "service suspended".

claimed. As I think I told you, the sideboard piano, thick plush curtains, your cello and the Indian vases are at Mum's, and so up to the present they are safe.

But now I'll leave this worrying business and say how are you? I hope the stiffness has all gone now, but I was glad to know you had started tennis again, but I see you are still the same. Six sets on your first day! I guess next week you'll tell me you have a cold.

The rest of the husbands do not seem very sanguine re the proposed committee for our eventual return. They think it is a sop to the husbands. But what concerns me more this week is the fact that a showdown with Japan seems certain – and I still wonder what of Hong Kong – they are sure to drop a few bombs I suppose – and what of our home there. No, I suppose in any case you will be billeted in the Yard. Anyway, take care of yourself dear, as I must have you back.

Mrs. Dawkins is coming to lunch with me on Tuesday, to say goodbye before leaving. I met Miss Hurren in the city and she says they have had word from Melbourne that, as the situation is so serious again they will not be able to go to Singapore – what a game. At least we haven't had that bitterness.

David has finished his exams so I've just got to sit tight until the report arrives. He is, however, doing quite well with his fiddle, much better than I had hoped and the small bloke is tackling the cello in his usual brisk and lively style. Mrs. Field and I have decided to pool our resources and have Christmas together. As she says, we'll have a real English one – although we shall picnic all day – but with nuts and crackers – and all the lovely mess, and as we are going to her place that suits me! Well dear, that's about all, so goodbye for the once more. All my love to you <u>dear</u>.
Hilda

Tuesday December 2nd 1941
(Posted Friday December 5th)
Hong Kong

My Dear,
I worked late last night again, but today has been fairly slack, so after calling in the library I arrived home about 5.30 – just before leaving the office your letter arrived, and somehow after reading that, our flat seems more empty than ever tonight. Perhaps too, it's the feeling that all those hopes we had, however faint they were, were better than the present knowledge that return is <u>now</u> hopeless. Just before I started this letter I listened to the 7.30 wireless news and it started with the announcement that there were still vacancies aboard the evacuee ship from Hong Kong – at midday today, over a hundred had registered, not that that is many, of course, but it will be interesting to see who the "rats" are amongst those "brave" souls that remained when evacuation wasn't necessary. We don't know, of course, that it's going to be necessary now, but certainly things look a bit black at the moment and precautions are being taken here that have never been done before.[78] Still, once more, I expect that by the time you read this, another crisis will be a thing of the past, and we shall be grumbling for your return again. So, the Sydney "wives" meeting wasn't a very exciting affair. Still it doesn't do any harm to let them know from your end that you want to get back – if only things looked better I'd say a few suffragette methods wouldn't hurt – you know a procession of women with banners, "Lift the Ban", and "We are the dear deported", etc, but there I almost forgot, I didn't feel like joking when I started writing. You see what effect even writing to you has.

What great news that was of Edward! I'm proud of him. Surely they won't stop him from going to the "High" now on account of his age. Well done Edward. A thought has just struck me, that it is possible that his age, combined with the fact that he probably won't remain long at

---

78. The Japanese had rejected American proposals for improving relations between the two countries and from December 1st 1941 increased naval and aerial activity around Hong Kong. This led to the military in Hong Kong to work on strengthening the defences within the colony.

the school and would be keeping some other permanent scholar away, might be the reason why they want to bar him – anyway, I do hope he is accepted and will anxiously await further news of that. Bit of luck that his birthday letter arrived on the day – with yours, too, in spite of the fact that it was posted four days after yours. So they both have their instruments now. What a band we will be able to have – if I haven't forgotten mine – I've been expecting you to say that David had formed his first dance band or some such thing.

By the way, I forgot to tell you just now, that this afternoon, after Bob and I had read our letters, Bob says that his wife had told him all about the wives meeting and went on to say that they had a collection for Funds but <u>she</u> wouldn't give anything as <u>she</u> wasn't going to pay for Mrs. Warren to fly about the country and put up at first class hotels. I passed the remark that there was always the few who were willing to let other people do the paying and that although you didn't say what you had done that I would be disappointed if you hadn't given something – he looked as though he was going to start something, and then changed his mind and said nothing at all – but that is Owen all over.

Well dear, this is the next evening, Wednesday now. I got so far and then Jim D arrived with some pals and I had to finish abruptly. Anyway, I have something to say, that I've been thinking of doing something and made up my mind today. With regard to the money, you know that I thought it "safer" in Australia, in your care, not that I thought it unsafe here, but it was a sort of insurance. At the same time I told you I had been making hay while the sun shone, and I had collected quite a decent sum here that I hadn't told you about, meaning to give you a pleasant surprise on the "happy day". I haven't got the wind up, don't think that – still looking at it from the insurance point of view, I just think that as the position has worsened, it's time I transferred a bigger proportion down to you. So today, round to the bank I went and arranged for a Bank Draft which I have to call in for tomorrow – I shall now post this letter on Friday together with the Bank Draft, so you'll be getting it a bit earlier this week – I hope. The Draft is for £160 Australian, that is £128 Sterling, and even than I have some left, but I'll keep that in case it should be needed. I don't know how the Draft works, so whether you can just pay it into your account or whether

you'll have to go to a certain bank and get the cash I don't know –
anyway that won't be hard to find out. Well dear, I have no other news
tonight, so I'll leave a bit to add tomorrow after my visit to the Bank.
Good night my dear.

Well here I am again, and as the ruddy thing is considerably bigger
and heavier than I anticipated, I had better go easy on the paper so I
won't start another page. I see they tell you what Bank to cash it at so it
should be easy enough. Let me know if you received it O.K. as I have a
duplicate that I keep until I know the original is safely in your hands.

Well dear, no further news. All quiet in Hong Kong, but of course
everybody standing by just in case – I still think it will die down again.
Anyway I hope so. By the way, the evacuee ship has been cancelled as
they didn't get enough application to warrant chartering a ship – the
Government cried "wolf" too loud and long last time, I think, to get
anybody to bite. Perhaps things are just at their worst now and will
improve from now on and this will be the last Xmas we'll spend apart –
I hope so. Goodbye for this week and then dear, All the best for Xmas
and my dear, all my love to you. Goodbye,
George

Sunday December 14th 1941[79]
Australia

My dear George,
Weeks and weeks of waiting and hoping – and then on Monday
morning last my landlady knocked on my door and told me the
dreaded thing had happened and immediately the phone went and
Mrs. Field was saying – "Have you heard?!!"[80] And somehow we have
gone on doing things. Mrs. Little and I even did our stuff at a concert
on Thursday – in fact I played out on Thursday afternoon and evening
and Friday afternoon – but oh!! what a week! The watching of the clock

---

79. Letter returned to Hilda.
80. On December 8th 1941, the Japanese crossed the border into Hong Kong's New Territories.

for news time, the nerve-racking blather that they put in to fill up time and then just the barest mention of Hong Kong. The chief reaction of all of us was anger – and still is – that with all these months and months of waiting the Japs could have caught us napping so. The "damn fool Englishman" sums our people absolutely, always late, always the perfect gentleman, even if it does mean men's lives and ships. Oh! We are a nation of hypocrites and fools if there ever lived one, and Churchill and Roosevelt make speeches that make me want to hurl something at the wireless. Still, all this gets us nowhere, so we will just keep smiling and praying and oh, God send it is not for too long. Will you have been under fire now, dear? I guess you are used to it now – have you had to move into the yard permanently? Poor Amah – after such good service – what is she doing? Oh, the things we want to know – but I guess we won't get letters for a long time. I received your letter on Thursday and it was so cheerful with its Christmas messages, and thank you, my dear, for the "presents" – they haven't come yet but I'll let you know as soon as they arrive.

One bright spot this week, my dear. Edward has definitely passed for Sydney High – although in view of the evacuation plans[81] I doubt if he will ever see the place. But I'm not leaving here unless I'm made to. David holds true to form by coming 41st out of 44 – but I'm not worrying about that – he'll do all right. No dear, in my rosy picture of a bungalow when we get home I did not forget the car – I think I said the railway line should be electrified by that time – which would solve our problem – but yes! I did say away from everyone – well! Although I know this isn't really practicable – but dreams like that keep one's mind off this blasted business.

Poor Jim D – another disappointment – gosh, I'm sorry for them. She was apparently very upset.

I'm writing this letter in my little sunroom. The time is 6.45 Sunday morning – I wake up very early these days – and today I have the little

---

81. Japanese threats towards Australia had led to evacuation plans being drawn up for civilians living on the coast.

person who lived with me at Double Bay coming to tea as when she was with me she said in the event of our having to evacuate we could have one of her cottages in the country and on Wednesday she rang me to say the offer still held. Pretty decent of her, eh! But I shan't go, as I said earlier, unless I have to. We are so happy and comfortable here and I'm definitely going to try and get a job. I don't care what, or how hard I work, etc, I would be glad to be doing something to help – and the money will be useful when we have to start another home and that time <u>must</u> come, dear. On your theory of compensation, or is it the law of averages, we have that due to us, and we shall make a good job of it – as I'm being drastically cured of my tendency to worry, you won't call me "worry guts" any more. I'm going to live and enjoy each day and think no more of the future.

Yesterday was Mrs. Green's birthday and while she had some glorious flowers from her husband she has had no mail this week and also the card enclosed with the flowers was not as is usually the case in his writing – so she was a bit disappointed, so I made her come to pictures with Mrs. Little and me. We saw Judy Canova in "Scatterbrain" – very good – and "Convoy" – which in spite of its war character was really excellent. And now I'll say goodbye for the moment and listen to the news.

Another day gone, dear. Miss Summer came – and Mrs. Green came in so we had another tea party. She said again about going to the country and also said she had heard there was a possibility of our not getting our money, so if I was in any bother she hoped I would call on her, as she would be glad to help me. Pretty decent, don't you think? But I hope we shan't have to go anyway. I'm tired of moving around.

We are still in the dark as to the real situation in Hong Kong, but no doubt those that live longest will see most. And now it is post time – so goodbye, my dear. No need to say I'm thinking of you all day and every day, but I'm keeping smiling and little Mrs. Green and Mrs. Little are splendid – but Mrs. Field to the surprise of all of us is taking things very badly. Oh, God, send these anxious days don't last long. We can only hope and pray. Goodnight dear.
Hilda

Hilda and Amah, Hong Kong.

Hong Kong - December 1941

*I was sorry to tell you that your house all the furniture
and clothes was take out by the Indian of next door
now all the things was chip by them...*

At the beginning of December 1941, the military in Hong Kong had decided that, even with the addition of the Canadian reinforcements, the garrison was too small to mount an effective defence at the border. A defensive line stretching across mainland Hong Kong from Tide Cove to Gin Drinkers' Bay (famous for its parties, and hence its name) was made first line of defence[82].

The overall military strategy for Hong Kong was that a long-term defence of the mainland wasn't practical as once inside the New Territories Japan would soon have the densely-populated Kowloon within shelling range. The plan was to eventually abandon the colony's territory on the mainland to concentrate on defending Hong Kong Island.

The colony had six battalions of troops, plus members of the auxiliary units, the Hong Kong Volunteer Defence Force and other volunteer units, such as the Dockyard Defence Corps stood ready in defence – 14,500 personnel in all. In addition, China's Nationalist leader Chiang Kai-shek had promised to send troops to help against any attack.

British forces were told to defend the colony for as long as possible – but for at least six months – and to hold the Gin Drinkers' Line for no less than three weeks.

---

82. Work had begun in 1936 on the Gin Drinkers' Line – a network of paths and trenches linking a series of bunkers, machine gun posts and artillery batteries – but halted in 1938 when government view was that a defence of the colony would not be practical. Work on its construction resumed in November 1941, with the arrival of the Canadian reinforcements, and a defence deemed feasible.

On Monday December 8th 1941, the Japanese attack began early morning, Japan having also launched attacks on the Americans at Pearl Harbor, against the Philippines, Singapore, and Malaya. In Hong Kong, the Japanese crossed the border from China and marched into the New Territories.

By 10.00am their planes had destroyed the aerodrome at Kai Tak, close to Kowloon, and all but two of the colony's planes.

The Japanese infantry continued its advance through the New Territories, and by December 9th the Japanese had reached – and by the 10th had breached – the Gin Drinkers' Line. The Line's defenders fell back to Kowloon[83].

By December 11th the Japanese were on the outskirts of Kowloon and the British began a withdrawal to Hong Kong Island.

At the onset of fighting George had been mobilised along with fellow members of the Hong Kong Dockyard Defence Corps. The Corps' main purpose was to defend the dockyard, although in the days that followed many members also saw fierce infantry fighting in areas outside the dockyard as reinforcements attached to other units.

At some point in December Amah was able to get a letter through to George.

Dear Mr Bearman,
I was sorry to tell you that your house all the furniture and clothes was take out by the Indian of next door now all the things was chip by them, till now I was very poor and no money to buy food to eat and the other ahmah have thief much things ran away now I hope that you not worry every times and happy from
Amah
Lan San Chun

---

83. Despite the addition of the reinforcements to the colony's garrison, the numbers defending the Line had proved just too few, vastly outnumbered more than two to one by the Japanese force, and were under-equipped and in most cases untrained for fighting in the terrain and environment of Hong Kong's New Territories.

On the 13th the last of the colony's forces defending from Kowloon reached Hong Kong Island. On the 13th, and again on the 17th of December the Japanese demanded the British surrender. Governor Sir Mark Young refused on both occasions.

On the night of December 18th–19th the first of the Japanese landings on the Island took place, and the colony's defenders fought on as the Japanese continued to land troops and advance across the Island.

There were instances of great bravery, but the British garrison was growing short of food, ammunition and increasingly of men, with most of those left still fighting having been in action continually since December 8th. And Chiang Kai-shek's troops were still too far away to provide the promised support.

So, on December 25th – Christmas Day – on the advice of the naval and military commanders who could see the situation was by then hopeless, the Governor surrendered to the Japanese forces. The surrender took place at The Peninsula, the hotel in Kowloon which had hosted so many of the colony's parties and dances.

British, American, Canadian and Dutch civilians were interned, and military personnel taken prisoner of war. Some reports estimated the civilian casualties for the three-week period December 8th-25th at 4,000 with 1,000 dead, while some put the number of civilian dead at 4,000. The true figure would never be known. Of the 4,500 colony military casualties reported killed, missing or wounded, more than 1,000 were dead, including members of the volunteer forces.

News was slow to leave the colony and it was months before lists of internees, prisoners of war, and casualties were released. The evacuees in Australia, and family and friends back home and located in other towns, cities and countries across the world, could only wait.

WAR ORGANISATION
OF THE
BRITISH RED CROSS SOCIETY and ORDER OF ST. JOHN OF JERUSALEM

FOREIGN RELATIONS DEPARTMENT
Directors:
THE RT. HON. THE EARL OF CLARENDON, K.G., G.C.M.G., G.C.V.C
MAJ.-GENERAL SIR JOHN KENNEDY, K.B.E., C.B., C.M.G., D.S.O.
Deputy Director:
MISS S. J. WARNER, O.B.E.
Assistant Deputy Director:
MISS M. G. CAMPION, O.B.E.

TELEPHONE No.:
ABBEY 2511/5

Allied Prisoners of War Packing Centre
Head of Packing Centre:
MISS M. M. MONKHOUSE, O.B.E.

WARWICK HOUSE,
ST. JAMES'S, LONDON, S.W.1

PLEASE QUOTE REF.

MI/A.12/CBI.

17th July, 1942.

Dear Madam,

The following official information has been received through the International Red Cross :-

"BEARMAN, G.H. 26/12/00., Private Hong Kong Dockyard Defence Corps.
IS PRISONER OF WAR IN HONG KONG."

This information may already have reached you from another source, but we are glad to be able to confirm it.

We do not think that you need be unduly anxious about conditions in Hong Kong. With the consent of the Japanese authorities, a Delegate of the International Red Cross Committee has been appointed to the City, and the International Red Cross Committee Delegate at Shanghai is also visiting the City. No reports have yet been received, but attempts are being made to get relief locally, and also to send out large consignments of Drugs, Food and clothing.

P.T.O./

Captivity

...so at least I know he is still alive,
and can look forward again to the day when this wretched
business will be over.

17th July, 1942 (Sent to George's sister Mrs. Winnie Haslen)
War organisation of the
British Bed Cross Society and order of St. John of Jerusalem
Foreign Relations Department
nt/a.12/cbr.

Dear Madam,
The following official information has been received through the
International Red Cross:-
"Bearman, G.H. 26/12/00., Private Hong Kong Dockyard Defence
Corps. IS PRISONER OF WAR IN HONG KONG."

This information may already have reached you from another source,
but we are glad to be able to confirm it. We do not think that you need
be unduly anxious about conditions in Hong Kong. With the consent
of the Japanese authorities, a Delegate of the International Red Cross
Committee has been appointed to the City, and the International Red
Cross Committee Delegate at Shanghai is also visiting the City. No
reports have yet been received, but attempts are being made to get relief
locally, and also to send out large consignments of Drugs, Food and
clothing.

For the present, individual food parcels cannot be sent, but letters can
be sent by Prisoners of War Post; (for instructions apply to your local
Post Office). Should any more news reach us, we will let you know
immediately.
Yours sincerely, N. Tollenaar

Tuesday August 8th 1942

Flat 5. 1030 Old South Hd Rd
Rose Bay N
Sydney N.S.W.
Australia

My dear Mum, Dad and John,
How very different I do feel this week, after having received news of
George. I feel like a reprieved prisoner must do. My friend had news
nearly three weeks ago – and I waited day after day, until at last, in
desperation, I cabled Winnie. I thought she may be more likely to have
news than you, as they would regard her as nearest of kin, the name
being the same and after five more days, imagine my relief to get her
cable, "George prisoner of war". And within an hour of receiving that I
had a letter from the Red Cross saying the same, so at least I know he
is still alive, and can look forward again to the day when this wretched
business will be over.

Did you get news from Admiralty? I haven't received it from them,
even yet. Still, I suppose they think, what's a few more weeks, after eight
dreary months – ye gods! What a year! However, things look better
now. I have sent George two letters through the Red Cross and am
hoping to get one from him <u>one</u> day.

On Sunday I had some friends to tea (to celebrate) and one was a
fiddler, and another a cellist, and also a vocalist, so we had a real old
time "do", and on Saturday I went to a party and met some celebrities of
Sydney's literary world, although I didn't know they were until the party
was over, when my hostess gave me some facts concerning them while I
was putting on my hat and coat. And people have written, and rung me
up with such nice messages about my good news – so you see I'm not
by any means lonely here, although I still get very homesick at times.

Have I told you we are rationed for clothes now? Fifty-six coupons
each, to last until next November and David takes twelve for a pair
of shoes. It will take some wangling to keep decently covered. Our
concern these days is not, "Is it worth the money?" but "Is it worth the

coupons?" But our tea ration has been increased, and nothing else has been rationed, although some things are difficult to get. However, we keep smiling.

I am still teaching music at the school – and they tell me I just must not speak of going home to England as I can't be spared. I really do like being there, although it makes it hard going at times with all the home duties – still it keeps me out of mischief! David is now fourteen (in every way) – as tall as me and filling out – he wants "longs" now and he is quite the man of the house, and "junior" still makes a determined effort to be as big. They are very funny and my friends and I get some laughs out of them. They are really doing quite well with their music too. Edward's choir had a test for head boy – and the winner got 46 ½ out of 50, Edward getting 46. But he does sing very nicely. Wish you could hear him.

They were delighted with Granddad's letters, as was I, and I've promised faithfully to answer them, so be prepared. I was glad to hear John has a nice girlfriend. Is she dark or fair, tall or short, musical? Tell me about her when you write. Anyhow, I'm glad to think he is happier now, and oh! I do hope he doesn't have to join up, but as he is on important work, I guess they will not take him.

Well Dad, I've just read this through, and you will be saying – that girl's writing gets worse and worse – but for one thing I'm writing on my knee, in front of the fire; and another I have so many letters to write in such a short while, so you must forgive me. But thanks very much for yours, Dad – it was great to get a letter from you – you don't know the feeling I have when I open the mailbox and see the old familiar writing. Goodbye now, and God bless you all.
Your loving
Dinah[84] and Boys

---

84. Hilda's nickname in the family.

Monday August 31st 1942

Flat 5. Victory Courts
1030 Old South Head Rd
Rose Bay. N. Sydney N.S.W.
Australia

Mr. G. H. Bearman
C/o S.E.E.D., H. M. Naval Yard, Hong Kong

My dear,
Once again I write to you but with a much better heart than last time, as I told you in that letter, several of the women had heard news of their men from England. But the weeks went by and still I heard nothing, until the two days after sending your last letter I received a cable from Winnie – and later, letters from Melbourne and the Red Cross, to the effect that you were a prisoner and so hope returned. We can still look forward, still hope, however bad things seem just now. Do you like the snap, dear? The young gent is our David. Do you recall a picture we had, of a young man in Auntie Hillie's garden in his first long suit? Can you see any likeness? He is very like you.

I am writing this on my verandah in the warm sun, as I am on three weeks' holiday from school, and you can be sure it is welcome. I'll do all my "just" jobs, and believe me there are some, especially arrears of correspondence, etc, but I'm still very happy at school, and the weeks go by so quickly. I often wonder what you are doing – even after all this time. I still have a feeling of "unreality", this thing couldn't have happened to you, and a year ago we were grumbling because we couldn't get back!

We had an official list of civilians, but I could see no mention of Pamela and Vic, or Eve and Stanley, but I don't suppose you know either. Mrs. Green and I sit so often wondering and wondering. She is a really nice woman and I'm very glad to have her with me.

Everyone is well at home. John has become engaged again. By the snaps she is no beauty, but looks a fine healthy girl –and Mum says she is very nice, and something like me. So there's hope, eh!

Now what else can I say? So many things I want to talk about but only one page allowed, and so many things I am afraid to put, in case they are indiscreet, and if we could only get one from you.

Mrs. Dawkins and about ten other wives went home last week. Sometimes I wonder if I should have done, but I funk a sea journey now, and the boys are doing so well, and we are really leading a pleasant healthy life here, with plenty of good food – and a lovely climate. I don't like to change for what might prove worse. Goodbye now, dear, and keep hoping, and looking forward – remember your "law of compensation".
Hilda

Flat 5. Victory Court
686 Old South Hd Rd
Rose Bay. N, N.S.W.
Australia

My dear Mum and Dad,
Once again I start my letter to you, although I really don't know what to say to you. Life jogs on in the same old way – work, sleep, and eat – and still no word from George. I really do feel disappointed over that. So many of the women have heard, but mostly civilians whose husbands are "internees", while our poor men are "prisoners", which is a very different matter. They are under much more strict guard, and have very few privileges. So far, I have only heard of two Naval Yard wives who have received letters from their husbands. Oh dear! Will this horrible business never end? Almost a year now since we had any word – or they any of us. Still – "keep on hoping" a bit longer.

I was so glad to hear how happy and comfortable John and his wife are. We are all just longing to meet her and she is still working – well, I can appreciate all that means, as I'm still at school, but in two weeks I go on six weeks' holiday and I shall indeed be glad of the time off to catch up on my jobs and correspondence, etc.

Well Mum, so far on Sunday and I got tired of trying to write with a broken nib. I have broken my pen, so I borrowed David's and goodness knows how he ever manages to write with it. However, here is Thursday – and on coming in from school, tired and bad tempered, what should I find in the box but a letter from HOME and oh! my dears, you have to be in "exile" to know what that means. So I just put the kettle on, made myself a cup of tea and read your letter. Oh, it was good to hear from you again. You speak of sending the wedding groups. I would love to see them, but I wouldn't risk sending a big one, as they are so expensive and might get lost. What about a postcard one and keep me a bigger one for my new home in England. So, her name is "Peggy", I've asked in two letters what we had to call our new auntie. She must be a good and energetic girl to do all she does, but oh! I love to hear of your games of Bagatelle and the old Ludo. It is so great to think of you as so happy together and isn't it splendid that John has not had to join up. Please God he never will have to – and also that there will never be any need for the Home Guard to go into action.

You make me smile, Mum, about the ladies in trousers. Yes! Quite a lot wear them here – and with painted toe nails, and they brown their legs when they wear no stockings, but as I am employed in a convent school where the girls have to wear regulation uniform and go to school in gloves – I leave it to your imagination as to what the nuns would say if I turned up in trousers and red toe nails. I couldn't even go stockingless. We can still get plenty of clothes at a price, a suit for David (the one in the snap) cost me £3.5.0 ready made – his shoes about 25/- and repairs 7/6, and of course we have to give coupons. However, they are now granting 40 extra coupons to school children who have to have adult size clothes, so as D is over 5' 3" (Yes! Grandad, he has beaten you) he will be better off for coupons. Unfortunately, they don't supply the cash: ha, ha!

David has attained a job for the Christmas at the Post Office, so he is feeling very bucked with himself. I expect he'll come home with a flea in his ear – he is sure to invent some new gadget for them, or something. While on the subject of David, I am very glad to say Mum, that he really does seem to be outgrowing his trouble, so I count that one of my blessings.

So Dad says they won't have you for fire-watcher – the idea – at least you wouldn't fall asleep on the job like some people I know. Never mind Dad, you are sure doing a grand job and I'm really proud of both of you. Don't I spout to some of these Aussies how my Dad is still working – and Mum running a shop and nearly seventy.

Well my dear, I must finish as I'm nearly asleep – and I've got the cramp not in my leg as you had, Mum, but in my hand. So good night and God bless and keep you all safely and may we soon be shaking the old dice again.
Your loving
Dinah and Boys

May 30th [85]
GEORGE HENRY BEARMAN
No. 3642
HONG KONG
PRISONER OF WAR CAMP
"S"[86]

DEAR HILDA.
AT LAST I CAN WRITE A FEW LINES TO ENGLAND, AND I ONLY HOPE IT WILL REACH YOU ONE DAY, SO THAT AT LEAST YOU WILL KNOW I AM STILL IN THE LAND OF THE LIVING./33[87] ACTUALLY I AM QUITE FIT AND EVERBODY HERE STILL MANAGES TO KEEP A SPIRIT OF OPTIMISM GOING, AND IF WE CAN, I'M SURE YOU CAN. 56/

WE ARE NOT BADLY TREATED BY THE JAPANESE AND THE ONLY WORK WE ARE DOING UP TO NOW, IS ALL THE NECESSARY CAMP WORK. PLENTY OF TIME ON OUR HANDS BUT EVERY DAY THERE IS CRICKET AND HOCKEY TO WATCH. WE HAVE A VERY KEEN CHESS CLUB AND MOST OF MY TIME

---

85. 1942, but received by Hilda many months later.
86. Sham Shui Po prisoner of war camp, Kowloon.
87. Word-count – although not accurate.

IS SPENT IN THAT WAY. WE ALSO HAVE A WEEKLY CONCERT, A BAND, AND CHURCH ON SUNDAYS./88

I SENT A BANKERS DRAFT TO YOU JUST PRIOR TO THE WAR; IF YOU DID NOT GET IT, THE MONEY WILL STILL BE CREDITED TO ME IN THE BANK HERE; A LITTLE OTHER MONEY IS ALSO THERE./122 WELL, I HOPE YOU AND THE BOYS AND MUM AND ALL OUR OTHER FOLK ARE KEEPING WELL, AND I SURE SPEND SOME HOURS THINKING OF YOU ALL./144 I MANAGED TO SAVE THAT LAST PHOTO OF THE THREE OF YOU AND I SAY AGAIN NOW AS THEN, THAT I AM PROUD OF MY FAMILY./164 MY LOVE TO YOU DEAR AND REMEMBER I AM STILL QUITE FIT AND LOOKING FORWARD TO BEING WITH YOU ALL AGAIN.

I BELIEVE I CAN WRITE ONCE A MONTH. GOODBYE. GEORGE.

Sunday May 2nd 1943
686 Old South Head Rd
Rose Bay. N, Sydney N.S.W.
Australia

Mr G. H. Bearman
C/o S.E.E.D., H. M. Naval Yard,
Hong Kong

My dear,
Sunday evening – the boys are at church so I have been practising – and always then I think of you. "Music, it makes me remember, it makes me forget." – it certainly does both. Last Sunday, listening to gramophone records at a friend's house – they put on the Jonny Heiken Serenade – and nearly did for me – just a little too exclusively "ours", eh? But I'm tough these days so no one guessed. Silly way to begin your letter when I'm only allowed one page, and yet is it? I usually feel that you will read my letter and think – how and where did I meet that person. But I am still very conscious that our correspondence is public property

these days and of course anything of a news character is definitely not allowed and our doings are so much the same every week that if you have received all my letters – and I have been writing once a month for eleven months, you must find them very "sameish".

I had a greetings cable from Mother and Dad for my birthday and everyone is well and happy. John has seemingly found a very nice wife and is very happy. Eddie is still as he was and Winnie teaching more than ever and with no domestic help at all. Your mother says, can I imagine it – but the Bearmans can rise to the occasion, eh? Our two particular Bearmans are still doing well. David 5' 6" and will soon start shaving – he has definitely discarded shorts now, and regards himself as man of the house. Has a few pimples which he doctors with peroxide. Edward has just taken Junior Division Trinity College for cello and is one of the leading choir boys – oh, I wish you could hear him sing, but I wish that so many times.

I heard of one lady who received another letter from her husband in Hong Kong last week, so our hopes have gone soaring again – just perfect if I could get one on my birthday.

Well my dear, space is used up – so again goodbye. Always we are thinking, talking, wondering about you and living for the day when this will be something to smile about.
All our love to you
Hilda and the Boys

GEORGE HENRY BEARMAN
HONG KONG
PRISONER OF WAR CAMP "S"

DEAR HILDA.
THIS IS MY THIRD LETTER[88], AND I'M WRITING IT ON EDWARD'S BIRTHDAY[89], SO OF COURSE I WISH HIM MANY

---

88. Second letter did not get through.
89. November 12th 1942, but not received for many months.

HAPPY RETURNS OF THE DAY. BOTH HIM AND DAVID MUST
BE GETTING BIG BOYS NOW, I'M AFRAID I WON'T KNOW
THEM.

I AM STILL ALL RIGHT AND STILL HOPING, BUT IT'S A LONG
DREARY WAIT. I SOMETIMES GO OUT FOR A DAYS WORK, FOR
WHICH I GET A SMALL SUM OF MONEY, WHICH OF COURSE
GOES TO BUY A FEW CIGARETTES, FOR AS YOU KNOW I CAN
** 90

I TRUST THE BOYS ARE STILL DOING THEIR BEST AT SCHOOL
AND STILL HAVE AN OCCASIONAL THOUGHT FOR THEIR OLD
DAD. AND YOU DEAR – WELL I CAN ONLY SAY, DON'T WORRY
TOO MUCH AND STILL KEEP HOPING. I HAVEN'T HEARD
FROM YOU YET AND SHOULD YOU GET THIS, REMEMBER ME
TO ALL THE HOME FOLK. WELL, IT'S GOODBYE AGAIN HILDA,
WITH ALL MY LOVE.
GEORGE

January 16th 1944
686 Old South Head Rd
Rose Bay. N, Sydney N.S.W.
Australia

Dear Mum and Dad,
So glad to get your letter dated 5.10.43 – but postmarked 6.11.43.
Anyhow it has been a long time coming – you know, Mum, the Air
Mails do sometimes take longer than sea, it is hardly worth sending
them. I received your air graph and the nice one from John – so glad to
have it especially as he took precious moments of his leave to write to
me, and he sounds so happy with his Peggy. You can guess how glad I
am about that and I do pray that they will soon be able to resume their
happy life for years and years. I am so longing to meet her, I feel I know

---

90. Censored – line cut from the page.

and love her already, especially as she is so nice to you. Anyone who likes my Mum and Dad is my friend for life, eh! But what I really mean is, that with us both away, I feel so glad that you have someone nice and understanding still with you.

Did you get my cable telling you that I had heard from George again? I received the letter at teatime on the Tuesday before Christmas, and my friend also had one. We phoned the Post Office to ask if you could get a cable by Christmas so they said yes, if we sent the "special rate" they thought so. This is also a "special price" but we decided that if you could get it on Christmas Day it would indeed be worth it. I do hope you did.

George's letter was only a few words to say he was working, is well – and telling me to keep smiling, but he had received no word from us and I have written every month. It's heart-breaking – but we can send photos again – (and hope they receive them). So I'm sending him that nice one of the three of us in the park. Did you receive the one I sent you? David is even bigger than that now, as he has grown.

We are all very well and thoroughly enjoying our long vacation. Edward is away in the mountains, but returns tomorrow. David decided to have a lazy holiday with me at home, and we have. He is a nice kid and loves to take me places, and is delighted that I have been swimming with him this holiday. We are waiting the results of his Intermediate school exam. If he has passed he wants to leave school and go to sea as a navigation cadet – I think the life would suit his roving out-of-doors disposition, but I am not keen on his going to sea just now. However, he has now suggested that he would like to go to the Marconi School, and then go as wireless operator, so tomorrow we are going to see about this. I do miss George when I have to decide these things – but I can only do what seems the right thing at the moment – looking back over the last five years, I can think of a lot of things I would have done differently, but there! Life is like that, eh!

Anyhow, we have been spared the horrors through which you have passed – and for the boys' sakes I'm glad of that. But when I get letters of this and that one in Scotland – I think, that could have been us. Still things look a little nearer a clean up now, so I'll stick the chin up a bit higher – never say die, what, however sick we feel.

I was very sorry to hear from Winnie that Auntie Hillie has been so ill. I do hope she is better now. Delighted to know that Peggy is taking piano lessons, wish I was around to help her.

My love and best wishes to all Aunties, Uncles and cousins, and kindest regards to all friends and many thanks for all their kind messages. Cheerio my dears. God bless and keep you.

Now really goodbye my dears, and may this new year bring all your wishes true – because if they come true, so will mine, as I've a hunch we are wishing the same things.
Your loving
Dinah and Boys.

FROM
Name. G. H. Bearman
Nationality. British
Rank. Private
Camp. Osaka P.O.W. Camp,
Sakurajima Sub Camp.

To:
Mrs. H. G. Bearman
2, Banksia Road,
Bellvue Hill, Sydney,
Australia

IMPERIAL NIPPONESE ARMY.

I am interned in Osaka Prisoner of War Camp,
Sakurajima Sub Camp.

My health is usual.

I am working for pay.

Please see that yourself and Boys are taken care of.

My love to you: <u>GEORGE</u>

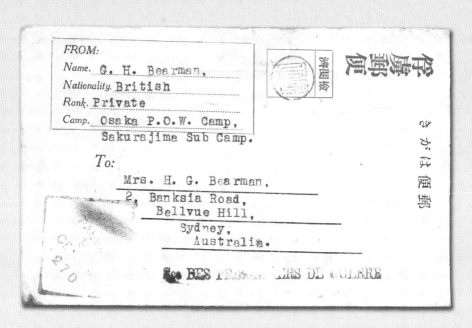

IMPERIAL NIPPONESE ARMY.

I am interned in Osaka Prisoner of War Camp,
Sakurajima Sub Camp.

My health is usual.

I am working for pay.

Please see that yourself and Boys are taken care of.

My love to you. GEORGE

George sent this brief note after his arrival in Japan sometime in 1943.

Transport to Japan

My health is usual.
I am working for pay.
Please see that yourself and Boys are taken care of.

In 1942, the Japanese began sending prisoners of war to Japan to provide labour for their factories, mines and dockyards.

The ships used to transport the prisoners of war became known as 'hell ships' due to the conditions on board – insanitary, with overcrowding, and lack of food.

Many prisoners died during the voyage as a result of the conditions, while thousands were lost due to attack from Allied ships, as the Japanese ships were armed, carried troops, and bore no identification indicating that prisoners of war were on board.

Many from the Sham Shui Po camp were among the 1,816 prisoners of war on the *Lisbon Maru*, torpedoed on 1 October 1942, with 828 losing their lives.

George sailed on the *Tatsuta Maru*, arriving in Japan in January 1943. He, and many of his colleagues from Hong Kong, were set to work for the Hitachi Dockyard Company at the dockyard in Osaka, two miles from their camp.

George's postcard was sent at some time following his arrival in Japan, but not received for many months.

Conditions in the prisoner of war camps were harsh, and food was scarce, illness rife, and medicine in short supply – and George's undated, short message was to be his last.

239

15 OCT 1945

<table>
<tr><td>Communications should be
addressed to :—
THE UNDER-SECRETARY OF
STATE.</td></tr>
</table>

COLONIAL OFFICE,
(ENQUIRIES AND
    CASUALTIES DEPT.),
2, PARK STREET,
W.1.
(Tel. : MAYfair 8166).

Your reference..............................

C.O. reference....10001/45..
   (G.H.Bearman)

30ᵗʰ January 1945.

Madam,

     I am directed by the Secretary
of State for the Colonies to inform
you that a telegram has been received
from the Japanese authorities in
Tokyo, through the International Red
Cross Committee at Geneva, giving a
list of members of the Regular Army
and the Local Volunteer Defence
Forces who have died in Osaka Camp,
and to express his deep regret that
included in the list is the entry
"Pte.BEARMAN, George Henry,
Dockyard Defence Corps. Cause of
death acute pneumonia." The date of
death is given as the 28th of March
1944.

    2. The Secretary of State desires
me to express his very deep sympathy
with you in your bereavement.

       I am, Madam,
        Your obedient servant,

          S.J.Cole

MRS.W.HASLEM.

Colonial Office notification - January 1945.

The End of the Story

I retained his wallet and case of shaving gear because the Japanese were destroying most of the personal belongings of deceased prisoners – we managed to save very little of Mr. Dawkins' kit.

30ᵗʰ January 1945
COLONIAL OFFICE,
(Enquiries and Casualties Dept.),
2, PARK STREET, W.1.

C.O. reference 10001/45
(G. H. Bearman)

Madam,
I am directed by the Secretary of State for the Colonies to inform you that a telegram has been received from the Japanese authorities in Tokyo, through the International Red Cross Committee at Geneva, giving a list of members of the Regular Army and the Local Volunteer Defence Forces who have died in Osaka Camp, and to express his deep regret that included in the list is the entry "Pte. BEARMAN, George Henry, Dockyard Defence Corps. Cause of death acute pneumonia." The date of death is given as the 28th of March 1944.

2. The Secretary of State desires me to express his very deep sympathy with you in your bereavement.

I am, Madam,
Your obedient servant,
S. J. Cole

19th February, 1945

WAR ORGANISATION OF THE BRITISH RED CROSS SOCIETY
and ORDER OF ST. JOHN OF JERUSALEM
FOREIGN RELATIONS DEPARTMENT
Clarence House
St. James's, London, SW1

Please quote reference CF/MDB/FBr.

Dear Mrs. Haslem,

We have just heard from the Colonial Office of the death of your brother, Private George Henry Bearman, of acute pneumonia, on the 28th March, 1944, in Osaka Camp, Japan.

May I say how extremely sorry we are to hear of your great loss, and I hope you will allow me to express our very deep sympathy with you at this time.

No details have been received of his illness or death, but if we should ever hear anything from the International Red Cross Committee's delegate in Japan, we will, of course, inform you at once.

Yours sincerely

B. Simmonds
For S. J. Warner

11th December 1945
Labour Branch,
Admiralty,
BATH.

This is to certify that according to
information received from the Colonial Office,
George Henry Bearman, Chargeman of Electrical
Fitters, H. M. Dockyard, Hong Kong, who served as
a Private in the Hong Kong Dockyard Defence Corps,
died of Acute Pneumonia at Osaka Camp on
28th March 1944.

N. Abercrombie
HEAD OF LABOUR BRANCH

Hilda had always said that she would wait until the war was over before returning home from Australia, but on receiving the news of George's death, she decided that she'd 'had enough' and booked passage for home, sailing with the boys on the *Stirling Castle*. They were docked in Bermuda when they heard the news that the war in Europe was over, May 8th 1945.

The war in the Far East continued until August. After the United States dropped an atomic bomb on Hiroshima on August 6th and on Nagasaki on August 9th, the Japanese finally surrendered on August 15th. The following day the Japanese forces in Hong Kong were told the news.

The Governor, Sir Mark Young, had originally been held as a prisoner in Hong Kong, but by the summer of 1945 was being held in Manchuria, China. In his absence the Colonial Secretary, who was still an internee in Hong Kong, arranged to be sworn in as Acting Governor and on August 28th announced that Hong Kong was again under British rule. On August 30th British ships returned to Hong Kong Harbour.

Throughout Japan the prisoner of war camps were liberated. Sakurajima Branch Camp (Osaka 4-D) had closed on May 18th 1945. Thirty-eight prisoners of war had died in the camp.

The civilian internees (less the Americans who had already been released on an exchange programme) and those prisoners of war who had remained in Hong Kong and who had survived were released.

Of George and Hilda's Hong Kong friends, those who died included Eve and Stanley Smith, Inspector Kettle, Powell, Bob Owen, Field, Sully and perhaps most tragically of all with their family reunion so close, Jim Dawkins.

Their names, and the names of all George and Hilda's friends and colleagues have been altered, because while they played a vital part in the lives of George and Hilda and the boys – and their story could not be told without mentioning their friends and colleagues – with so much tragedy in many of their stories, these friends and colleagues may just not have wanted them told. But they were real people and everything about them that is related in this book – as with George and Hilda, David and Edward – is true.

No one knows what happened to Amah, or to Kim the dog. With the Japanese unwilling to accept responsibility for the welfare of the Chinese in the colony, and food and employment in short supply, over 1 million Chinese had fled. With the food situation so dire, it's unlikely Kim survived.

At his death, aged 44, George was cremated and his ashes kept at the Jugan Temple in Osaka-city until taken to be buried at Yokohama War Cemetery at the end of the war.

In December 1946, Hilda received a letter from one of George's colleagues.

December 2nd 1946
Dockyards Department,
Pulteney Hotel, Bath.

Dear Mrs. Bearman,
I had better introduce myself – my name is Harry Grieves and I was in the Electrical Department in Hong Kong. In January 1943 I was drafted to Japan as prisoner of war and on arriving in Osaka I was fortunate enough to have my bed space next to your husband. In fact, except for a few days when one of us was ill, I slept and lived next to him until a few days before his death on the 28th March 1944. George was a real man throughout and never once did I hear him complain although like the rest of us, he was continually looking forward to the day when he would be free.

In those dark winter days, many men were lost because of the cold. Poor George caught a chill while working in the shipyard and in a few days, pneumonia set in. Notwithstanding the efforts of the R.A.M.C. staff and the doctor who, I am sorry to say, were not too well equipped with the necessary drugs, George passed peacefully away at about 8.30 a.m. on a day when we were all at rest from work.

I retained his wallet and case of shaving gear because the Japanese were destroying most of the personal belongings of deceased prisoners – we managed to save very little of Mr. Dawkins' kit.

Yesterday I was in the Dockyard and managed to find Mrs. Powell's address. Visiting her last evening, I was pleased to be able to get your address.

At long last, I am able to forward George's kit. If there is any way in which I may be of assistance to you or if there is anything that you may wish to know, please write to me at the above address where I shall be after the 14th January. Until then, I am afraid that my exact whereabouts will not be fixed for as you will realise I am on holiday and doing a lot of visiting.

Please accept my best wishes for a Brighter New Year.
Yours sincerely
Harry Grieves

Once back home in England, Hilda had set up home with the boys in Southampton. In 1964 she moved to share a house with David and his family, in Datchet – where Winnie and Sid had stopped for a drink during that day on the river in June 1941, and the village to which George refers in his letter of September 4th 1941, asking if Hilda fancied a summer on the river with the boys.

Hilda never remarried. A photo she'd taken of George at the top of Lion Rock, a mountain in Hong Kong, sat on the sideboard in her sitting room. She had a busy and fulfilled life, full of music, and interest in and love for her family. She would often say how lucky she was and had been throughout her life, but that, "God did just let me down over George."

In 1987, Hilda died, and she and George finally had their reunion.

Top: George on top of the Lion Rock Hong Kong 1939.
Bottom: Hilda, David and Edward on the family hike, Hong Kong.

Hilda, David and Edward, May 1944.